"Students will be the ultimate and major beneficiaries of this timely and profoundly thoughtful study."
—Robert M. O'Neil, president,
University of Virginia

"Fascinating and, quite simply, full of valuable insights and opinions."
—Frances D. Fergusson, president,
Vassar College

"Packed with information, insights, and uncommonly good sense. . . . It can be read with profit by those associated with any category of post-secondary institution."
—Howard R. Swearer, president,
Brown University

"Boyer has an eye for the overlooked facts. . . . The Carnegie report is unsettling but not ungenerous. It finds much to celebrate on the nation's 2100 campuses."
—Colman McCarthy, *Washington Post*

"A landmark book. All of us in the academy should read this book and learn from it."
—Arthur S. Link, professor and editor,
The Papers of Woodrow Wilson, Princeton University

"[*College* is] more than an examination of the undergraduate experience; it's also a statement about what is good and important in academia today." —Sheldon Rothblatt, chairman,
Department of History, University of California, Berkeley

"A wonderful study."
—Rev. Theodore M. Hesburgh, president,
University of Notre Dame

"An important and eminently readable study, sure to be of interest and value to educators as well as students and their parents."
—*Kirkus Reviews*

"It's a thoughtful analysis of the undergraduate experience that will highlight issues and provoke discussion for years to come."
—Christopher C. Fordham III, chancellor,
University of North Carolina at Chapel Hill

"The report is terrific, timely, and powerful. I hope it foreshadows a new era in undergraduate education—and, in fact, we may already be entering one if the presidents I talk to are typical."
    —Robert L. Hardesty, president,
       Southwest Texas State University

"*College* has many ideas about how a diverse campus such as this one can achieve a greater measure of unity . . . and through a greater common purpose provide a broader and better education to the students." —Thomas E. Everhart, chancellor,
       University of Illinois at Urbana-Champaign

"[*College*] will be a major contribution to the quality and sanity of the recurring debate on undergraduate education. The chapters on assessment, evaluation, university governance are particularly valuable."
    —Wesley W. Posvar, president,
       University of Pittsburgh

"I am making it required reading for all my senior people."
    —Frank E. Vandiver, president,
       Texas A & M University

"We have given a copy of *College* to every Earlham trustee, and on campus to every member of Administrative Council. This spring we will spend the first part of each weekly session of Administrative Council in discussion of one chapter."
    —Richard Wood, president,
       Earlham College

"I have found the important questions raised in *College* extremely helpful in my work for Wellesley College and in the work of our Board of Trustees."
    —Luella G. Goldberg,
       chairman of the Board of Trustees,
       Wellesley College

"[*College*] is in fact something of a student's bill of rights: the right to greater honesty in a college's appeal to them; the right to know a college's goals; the right to better guidance in selecting the right college; and, once admitted, the right to more attention from the faculty."
    —Fred Hechinger, *New York Times*

COLLEGE

THE UNDERGRADUATE
EXPERIENCE IN AMERICA

THE CARNEGIE FOUNDATION
FOR THE ADVANCEMENT
OF TEACHING

Ernest L. Boyer

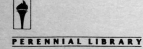

PERENNIAL LIBRARY

Harper & Row, Publishers, New York
Cambridge, Philadelphia, San Francisco, Washington
London, Mexico City, São Paulo, Singapore, Sydney

A hardcover edition of *College* is published by Harper & Row.

COLLEGE. Copyright © 1987 by The Carnegie Foundation for the Advancement of Teaching. All rights reserved. Printed in the United States of America. No part of this book may be used or reproduced in any manner whatsoever without written permission except in the case of brief quotations embodied in critical articles and reviews. For information address Harper & Row, Publishers, Inc., 10 East 53rd Street, New York, N.Y. 10022. Published simultaneously in Canada by Fitzhenry & Whiteside Limited, Toronto.

First PERENNIAL LIBRARY edition published 1988.

Designer: Sidney Feinberg

Copy editor: Bitite Vinklers

Library of Congress Cataloging-in-Publication Data

Boyer, Ernest L.
    College : the undergraduate experience in America.
"Perennial Library"
    Includes index.
    1. Universities and colleges—United States.
2. College students—United States. I. Title.
LA227.3.B678 1988   378.78   85-45182
ISBN 0-06-091458-0 (pbk)

88 89 90 91 92 MPC 10 9 8 7 6 5 4 3 2 1

CONTENTS

PART IV: A TIME TO LEARN

PART V: CAMPUS LIFE

PART VI: PATTERNS TO PURPOSES

PART VII: GRADUATION AND BEYOND

ACKNOWLEDGMENTS

This book involved the work of many people. The research, crafting the text, and shaping conclusions all were accomplished with the help of friends and colleagues.

The Trustees of The Carnegie Foundation for the Advancement of Teaching must be acknowledged first. They enthusiastically endorsed the project from the first and have been continually supportive. While the author must assume responsibility for the book as published, it is the trustees who were generous and constructive with their encouragement, time, and ideas. Without their interest and support, this book could not have been written.

We have also benefited from the active interest of several colleagues who served as senior consultants, advisers, and critics throughout the project. They included Arthur Chickering, director, Center for the Study of Higher Education, Memphis State University; Marilyn Cohn, director of teacher education at Washington University, Saint Louis, Missouri; J. Eugene Haas, president, Human Ecology Research Services; Timothy Healy, S. J., president, Georgetown University; Irving J. Spitzberg, Jr., executive director, Council for the Improvement of Liberal Learning; Sheldon Rothblatt, chairman, Department of History, University of California at Berkeley; Joseph Katz, director, Research for Human Development and Educational Policy, State University of New York at Stony Brook; Martin Trow, Director of Studies in Higher

Education, University of California, Berkeley; Russell Edgerton, of the American Association for Higher Education; and James A. Perkins, chairman, International Council for Educational Development.

The names of the observer-reporters who spent several weeks on campus of the twenty-nine institutions included in our college site visits appear in Appendix A. In all, these colleagues spent at least ten thousand hours attending classes; interviewing students, professors, and administrators; and absorbing campus life. The information they provided has been invaluable in helping us understand the undergraduate experience and in enriching the statistical data and printed reports. Unnamed, only for reasons of confidentiality, are the presidents and site visit coordinators at colleges and institutions included in the project. They have our deep gratitude for graciously making available their campuses and extending to our visitors complete courtesy and cooperation. We also were richly served by the hundreds of administrators, teachers, and students who helped with the site visit arrangements and gave us candid interviews.

Verne Stadtman, vice-president–general services of the Foundation, and Jacqueline Crawford provided day-by-day direction for the research phase of the study. Mr. Stadtman coordinated the site visits and edited the final manuscript. Ms. Crawford organized an extensive search for information in the recent relevant literature on American colleges. She was assisted by Hilary Dingle, Gertrude Dubrovsky, Anthony Gambino, Alexander Marshall, Laurel McFarland, and Jack Osander. Ms. Crawford provided an excellent service in critiquing research reports and guiding special investigations.

Robert Wright and Lane Mann, assisted by Mary Jean Whitelaw, worked weekly miracles producing statistical information needed for the report.

Anne Groom edited the site visit reports and systematically extracted from them information that was relevant to our major themes. Ingrid Canright, assisted by Hinda Greenberg, Bret Birdsong, Patricia Morrissey, and David Twenhafel assumed responsibility for checking citations in the final stages of manuscript preparation.

As the project entered the final drafting stage, we were fortunate to have the very special help of three experienced writers who had participated in our site visits. Laurie Evans, Denise Graveline, and David McElwain each spent several months organizing raw research data into important, beneficial papers. Ingrid Canright, Gertrude Dubrovsky, and Dennis Stout also assumed important responsibilities as a part of this activity.

Marissa Endicott led the word-processing team that converted all of the raw manuscript into a long succession of drafts that seemed, at times, almost never ending. Many nights and weekends were sacrificed by her, Mary Jeanne Buckley, and Nancy Mihalik to produce the final manuscript. At the peak of the final drafting process, they were joined by Arlene Hobson and Carol Lasala. Their contributions were crucial and I'm deeply grateful.

Were it not for the sharp memory and organizational skills of Louise Underwood, the usefulness of all of this enormous productivity might, on more than one occasion, have been hopelessly buried in the mountains of drafts and printouts. Marla Ucelli provided invaluable administrative support, managing with great skill the endless flow of assignments in my office. And Rita Long is to be thanked for providing nourishment and attentive service.

In the final drafting, Verne Stadtman, Gene I. Maeroff, and J. P. O'Neill were enormously helpful in editing and reacting to chapters as they were completed and helping to make difficult decisions about the flow of ideas and the adequacy of substance.

Robert Hochstein and Warren Bryan Martin deserve very special recognition. They gave countless hours to the task of editing and critiquing and remained productive, creative, and good-spirited throughout. I am deeply in their debt.

Vito Perrone, who recently joined the Foundation as vice-president, participated actively in the planning of this project and served as an unusually valuable editor and adviser. And I am especially grateful to John E. Sawyer, President of the Andrew W. Mellon Foundation, for helpful suggestions on parts of the final manuscript.

Ernest Boyer, Jr., contributed many outstandingly useful ideas from the time this project was first planned to the moment of its completion, and a special critique by JB Hefferlin was of great value. S. Paul Boyer was very helpful in shaping the section on transition.

Sallie Coolidge, editor at Harper & Row, was an insightful critic and patient associate throughout the project. Working with her once again was a special joy.

To family, and especially to Kay, my love, I pledge a long vacation.

—ERNEST L. BOYER

FOREWORD

BY ERNEST L. BOYER, *President,*
The Carnegie Foundation for the Advancement of Teaching

Four years ago, The Carnegie Foundation produced *High School: A Report on Secondary Education in America.* We launched that study with the conviction that the quality of education in the public high school was imperiled. To strengthen secondary education, we called for, among other things, a clear and vital mission, a thoughtful examination of the curriculum, the reform of testing and evaluation, and, above all, the recognition of the teacher.

Now we have undertaken a study of college as a companion piece to the earlier work. We proceeded with the conviction that the confusion in the nation's schools reflects, at least in part, confusion at the collegiate level and that it is inappropriate for college educators to criticize the ineffectiveness in schools if they themselves are unwilling to engage in self-examination and are unable to reach consensus about their goals.

All educational levels are related, and there is, we believe, an urgent need to bring colleges and universities more directly into the national debate about the purposes and goals of American education. If the push for educational excellence is to yield results, the nation's colleges and universities must ask hard questions about the quality of their own work.

In this report, then, we consider the undergraduate experience in America, and we pay particular attention to the way the structures and procedures of colleges affect the lives of students. The specific goal of this report, as with all policy studies of our foundation, is to describe as carefully as we can what the current situation is, identify both the strengths and the problem areas, and suggest ways in which institutions might be strengthened and students better served.

We have intentionally limited the scope of our investigation to the baccalaureate sector of higher education. Graduate and professional schools and the two-year college sector are not within the purview of this report. This decision was made not because the other sectors are less important, but rather because the uniqueness of American higher education is rooted in preparation for the baccalaureate degree. The vitality of undergraduate education affects, we believe, all the others. Our intention is to examine the other levels of higher education in subsequent studies.

It should be noted, however, that much of what we say about the undergraduate experience at four-year colleges will be recognized as relevant to two-year institutions as well.

In the conduct of this study, we followed the same site visit procedures that were so helpful in our study of secondary education. Sixteen experienced observer-reporters were sent to twenty-nine colleges and universities during the fall of 1984 to get a first-hand view of campus life. (They are listed in Appendix A.) Campuses visited were carefully selected to represent the full spectrum in institutional types—liberal arts colleges, comprehensive colleges, doctorate-granting institutions, and research universities. Public and private institutions were included in the sample in the same proportion in which they are found among all American colleges and universities. Further, all areas of the country were represented.

At one end of the continuum was a church-related college in a sparsely settled area of the Northwest. Most students at this institution come from rural communities. They think of the medium-sized city where the college is located as a busy place. The campus is small, with a dozen buildings constructed more than fifty years ago. Faculty salaries are low, and the college struggles to attract students.

Yet, as the only college within miles, it is a cultural center for the region and commands loyalty and support both on and off the campus. With deep church roots, like so many other colleges that dot the American landscape, this institution reminded us that beyond academic achievement, issues of values and religion have been central to the tradition of higher education in America.

At the other extreme, we visited a sprawling campus in New England, part of a state university system. In the past twenty years, this institution has been transformed from a teachers college to a comprehensive university. Here, students who are state residents pay an average of $4,700 a year to attend and, because dormitory space is limited, most commute. Many students come from lower-income families. Because they have to work, many also spend little time on campus. At this "commuter college," as we call it, new programs have been added to attract adult learners and a flexible class schedule has been established to accommodate their needs. Public universities such as this have opened doors to nontraditional students. They have shown that the limits of a student's background need not fix the limits of his or her future.

We also included in our study a highly selective private college in the East, whose nearly two thousand students pursue higher learning on an ivy-covered campus with twelve academic buildings, an art center and museum, a chapel, and a student center. Nearly half of the students here come from private secondary schools. Tuition and other expenses exceed $16,000 a year. Students are academically talented and highly motivated. The library is almost always full. Faculty members, who are well paid, consider this college a good place to teach, yet one where a commitment to scholarly research is also well respected. Prestigious private colleges, such as this one, have maintained outstanding academic standards and provide a yardstick of excellence for the nation and the world.

Finally, we looked at a large public university in the West with nearly 140 buildings, more than twenty thousand students, two thousand faculty members, and ten thousand nonacademic staff members. This institution, with its national reputation as a research university, has several world-class scholars on its faculty. Tuition is just over $1,000 a year for in-state students. A football team of national standing and an award-winning student newspaper also enhance the reputation of the institution. This university, a part of the great land-grant tradition that applies new knowledge to old problems, demonstrates how research benefits higher education and how knowledge can be applied to human problems in useful and creative ways.

Our observers spent approximately two weeks at each institution, visiting classrooms, laboratories, student unions, and residence halls. They interviewed college officials and faculty members. They spent time with students during both day and evening hours. They immersed themselves in each of the institutions they visited. Their reports constitute a rich, vivid record of life in American colleges and universities. (Because institutions that cooperated in the site visits were promised anonymity, their real names are not used in the text of this report.)

A word about how these findings have been used. All of the reports were read and analyzed with great care in order to discover common problems and successes as well as unifying themes. Specific examples and quotations from the reports are used throughout the text. We have tried carefully to use their examples only as they illustrate, with accuracy, a larger point.

In the preparation of this report, we conducted through contract with Opinion Research Corporation, Princeton, New Jersey, national surveys of 5,000 faculty members and 4,500 undergraduates in a random sample drawn to represent the various institutional types in the 1976 Carnegie Classification of Institutions of Higher Education. Survey questionnaires yielded important information about faculty and students: their age, sex, ethnicity, and school academic achievement. They told us how they feel about teaching and learning experiences, about the goals of higher education, and how their attitudes compare with earlier foundation surveys.

One of the reasons our data base proved to be such a rich resource for this study is that it provided comparative information. A similar survey of students and faculty, albeit with even larger samples, had been carried out in 1974–75 by Martin Trow of the University of California, Berkeley, for the Carnegie Council on Policy Studies in Higher Education. That research had, in turn, built on data reported in 1969—again, involving many of the same questions raised with similar student and faculty samples. Thus, our study, reported in this book, has benefited from comparative analyses of data gathered in two prior studies. Longitudinal research is a luxury few of us can afford. We were especially fortunate to be able to make connections to this existing and relevant data base.

To learn about a student's transition from school to college, we commissioned Human Ecology Research Services to conduct a special survey of twelfth-grade students and their parents. Printed questionnaires were completed by a random sample of 1,187 students in 196 high schools. Additional information was obtained in telephone interviews with 232 randomly selected high school counselors and with admissions officers at our twenty-nine site visit colleges and universities. Throughout this book we refer frequently to the findings from one or another of these studies.

In preparing this report, we reviewed the extensive literature on higher education, including relevant reports of The Carnegie Commission on Higher Education and the Carnegie Council for Policy Studies in Higher Education.

Because of the importance of general education in the student's undergraduate experience, we arranged for Opinion Research Corporation to carry out a survey of 1,310 chief academic officers in American colleges and universities on the status of general education in their institutions. An uncommonly high response rate, 74 percent, involving deans who obviously cared about the subject and were willing to take the time to provide information, meant that we had indispensable data on current conditions as well as future prospects for general education in undergraduate colleges.

We also commissioned several special studies to supplement information gathered by our own staff. Robert T. Blackburn and Ruth B. Freeman at The University of Michigan investigated the extent to which there have been changes in the time required to earn a bachelor's degree since the Carnegie Commission on Higher Education advocated undergraduate education with *Less Time, More Options*, in 1971. Evan Ira Farber, librarian at Earlham College, provided a provocative report on changes in store for the undergraduate libraries on the nation's campuses. Gerald Gurin, Rosalie Meiland, and Peter Rush at The University of Michigan focused attention on part-time students and how their college experiences differ from those of their full-time counterparts.

From Gregory Jackson, at the Harvard University Graduate School of Education, we received the report "Who Doesn't Go to College." Jack Osander's professional experience with admissions and testing processes gave him useful perspectives for preparing a report on school-to-college transition.

William Toombs, director of the Center for the Study of Higher Education at The Pennsylvania State University, provided a special report on intercollege relationships and undergraduate study in large universities. John Williams, at Harvard University's Graduate School of Education, prepared a study of problems involved in identifying and measuring the consequences of a college education. And Arthur Chickering at Memphis State University prepared a splendid background paper on college outcomes and assessment.

Finally, we interviewed college and university presidents, students, and faculty members from institutions not included in our site visits. We used attendance at meetings of educators throughout the country as opportunities to learn about their current concerns and hear about new proposals for improving undergraduate education.

One additional point. This report is subtitled "The Undergraduate Experience in America," suggesting that we are looking at the college largely from the perspective of the students, especially those who go to college right after high school. We are mindful, however, of the growing number of older and part-time students. Their concerns are also reflected in this report. But the major focus is on the 18-to-22-year-old students who still constitute a majority of the college-going population at our nation's four-year institutions.

From all of this effort, we identify eight tension points in the undergraduate college that urgently need to be examined. If these problem areas can be better understood and at least partially resolved, the American college will be a better institution, students will be better served, and the nation's future will, we believe, be immeasurably more secure.

WILLIAM J. SULLIVAN
President
Seattle University

ALEXANDER TOMLINSON
Director
Center for Privatization

BARBARA UEHLING
Chancellor
University of Missouri-Columbia

PROLOGUE:
A HOUSE DIVIDED

The undergraduate college in America, with its long and venerable tradition, has a unique mission to fulfill, one that will enrich and, at its best, transform. Why else make it the prerequisite to professional study? Why else provide college for those who otherwise could be trained on the job or in a corporate classroom? It can only be because of the conviction that something in the undergraduate experience will lead to a more competent, more concerned, more complete human being.

This is the hope. It is one of the most enlightened visions any society has ever collectively endorsed. And the institution established to bring it about is one of the most vital and enduring in our culture. The undergraduate college is the place where higher education in America began, and the universities, which grew out of and around the college, have produced knowledge that has transformed the nation and the world. In the United States today, we have approximately 2,100 baccalaureate-granting colleges and universities,[1] each with its own unique history, traditions, and special sense of worth. This rich array of institutions has opened doors to citizens of all ages and all backgrounds. More than twelve million students are now enrolled in some form of postsecondary education,[2] a remarkable achievement unmatched by any other nation.

America's enduring belief in education has sometimes been inflated. Formal schooling has not always been the ladder to success.

Still, throughout our history, each new generation has been expected to do better than its elders, to set new goals, and even strike out in new directions. As a result, a growing portion of children from poor and working-class families have completed high school, entered college, and moved on to careers unimagined by their parents.

We have created the world's first system of universal access to higher education. It provides entrance somewhere to virtually all who wish to enroll and offers an almost unlimited choice of subjects to be studied. This system of higher education, with its openness, diversity, and scholarly achievement, is the envy of the world. Unencumbered by suffocating ideology, the vitality and integrity of the American college and university are unmatched.

And yet, while preparing this report we found that the undergraduate college, the very heart of higher learning, is a troubled institution. In a society that makes different and contrary demands upon higher education, many of the nation's colleges are more successful in credentialing than in providing a quality education for their students. It is not that the failure of the undergraduate college is so large but that institutional expectations often are too small.

During our study we found divisions on the campus, conflicting priorities and competing interests that diminish the intellectual and social quality of the undergraduate experience and restrict the capacity of the college effectively to serve its students. At most colleges and universities we visited, these special points of tension appeared with such regularity and seemed so consistently to sap the vitality of the baccalaureate experience that we have made them the focus of this report.

The first problem we encountered is the discontinuity between schools and higher education. Today, educators from the separate levels, with few exceptions, carry on their work in isolation. The curriculum is disjointed and guidance is inadequate. Students find the transition from school to college haphazard and confusing. They are, we found, dissatisfied with recruitment procedures, unclear about requirements for admission, and troubled by the costs. Part-time and older students, a rapidly growing part of American higher education, also face disturbing problems of transition.

The separation we found between school and college has led to a mismatch, a disturbing one, between faculty expectations and the academic preparation of entering students. Many young people who go to college lack basic skills in reading, writing, and computation —essential prerequisites for success. Faculty are not prepared, nor do they desire, to teach remediation courses.

We begin this report with the conviction that the nation's education structure should be a seamless web. And we ask: Is it possible for educators from the separate levels to work together to define a basic education and strengthen the proficiency of students in language and computation? How can the procedures for college recruitment, selection, and orientation be improved? And can the nation's colleges expand educational opportunities for the growing number of adults and historically bypassed students?

The second issue is confusion over goals. Scrambling for students and driven by marketplace demands, many undergraduate colleges have lost their sense of purpose. They are confused about their mission and how to impart shared values on which the vitality of both higher education and society depends. The disciplines have fragmented themselves into smaller and smaller pieces, and undergraduates find it difficult to see patterns in their courses and to relate what they learn to life. Archibald MacLeish observed in 1920, "There can be no educational postulates so long as there are no generally accepted postulates of life itself."[3] And colleges appear to be searching for meaning in a world where diversity, not commonality, is the guiding vision.

Closely related is the conflict between careerism and the liberal arts. Today's students worry about jobs. Narrow vocationalism, with its emphasis on skills training, dominates the campus. Several institutions we visited are virtually torn apart as new majors battle old. A department chairman at a Midwest college told us, "They're trying to turn this college into a supermarket where we're willing to put anything in the catalog so long as it will sell." But the president observed, "It's all right to talk about liberal arts goals but we have to face up to what students want today."[4]

These conflicts prompt fundamental questions: Is it possible for administrators, faculty, and students, with their separate interests, to agree on a vital mission for undergraduate education? Can the curriculum serve individual interests while providing a coherent view of the human condition? Is the academic major simply a means to prepare specialists with narrow technical skills? Above all, can the liberal and useful arts be blended during college, as they must inevitably be blended during life?

The third problem we encountered is divided loyalties and competing career concerns within the faculty. Professors are, quite appropriately, expected to function as scholars, conduct research, and communicate results to colleagues. Promotion and tenure hang on research and publication. But undergraduate education also calls for a commitment to students and effective teaching. Frequently, faculty are torn between these competing obligations.

There is the related matter of faculty renewal. In recent years, career prospects for young professionals have diminished. Opportunities for mobility are limited and options for professional growth restricted. At the same time the number of part-time faculty is increasing. These developments threaten the unity and vitality of the professoriate.

The challenge faced by the faculty is suggested by these questions: What is the balance that should be struck between teaching and research? Is it appropriate for different types of higher learning institutions to have different criteria for faculty evaluation? How can faculty be professionally renewed?

Fourth, we discovered tensions between conformity and creativity in the classroom. Time and again we heard faculty complain about the passivity of students whose interests, they said, are stirred only when reminded that the material being presented will be covered on a test. In all too many classrooms, we found an absence of vigorous intellectual exchange, a condition for which faculty as often as students bear responsibility.

Still, there remains a vision of the undergraduate college as a place where teachers care about their students, where, in the classroom, traditions can be challenged and new ideas tested. We consider, therefore, the following questions: Is it possible for students, during this era of mass education, to become independent, self-directed learners? How can faculty improve their teaching so as to encourage creativity and critique? And how can all resources for learning, on and off the campus, be connected?

Fifth, we found a great separation, sometimes to the point of isolation, between academic and social life on campus. Colleges like to speak of the campus as *community*, and yet what is being learned in most residence halls today has little connection to the classrooms; indeed, it may undermine the educational purposes of the college. The idea that a college stands in for parents, *in loco parentis*, is today a faded memory. But on many campuses there is great uncertainty about what should replace it. Further, we found that residential and commuter students live in two separate worlds.

We were especially impressed that many faculty and academic administrators distance themselves from student life and appear to be confused about their obligations in nonacademic matters. How can life outside the classroom support the educational mission of the college? How should tension between student freedom and institutional authority be resolved? And how can the college leave space for privacy while also providing activities that sustain community and encourage service?

The sixth problem is the disagreement we found over how the college should be governed. As the complexity of higher education has increased, confidence in the decision-making process appears to have declined. Presidents are caught in the crossfire of conflicting pressures. Faculty often feel more loyalty to their discipline than to the institutions where they teach. And when students are asked to participate in campus governance, their involvement is sporadic. Can students, faculty, and administrators build community through improved communication?

The next issue is how the outcome of a college education should be measured. Today, the academic progress of students is assessed by each professor, course by course. Class grades are dutifully recorded. The final mark of achievement is the diploma, which presumably signifies an educated person. But good teachers are not necessarily good evaluators and there is legitimate concern about quantifying a complex learning process. The college has few ways to assess the quality of education overall.

During our study we heard calls for a new approach to evaluation. Increasingly, state and national education officials, lawmakers, parents, and students are wondering just how much is being learned. How can college goals and the evaluation of student achievement be more closely linked? Should there be assessment beyond course grades? Are the testing procedures now used adequate to the task?

This brings us to the final concern. Though listed last, it touches all the rest. We found a disturbing gap between the college and the larger world. There is, we sensed, a parochialism that seems to penetrate many higher learning institutions, an intellectual and social isolation that reduces the effectiveness of the college and limits the vision of the student. We feel compelled to ask: How can the undergraduate college help students gain perspective and prepare them to meet their civic and social obligations in the neighborhood, the nation, and the world?

Here, then, are the eight points of tension: the transition from school to college, the goals and curriculum of education, the priorities of the faculty, the condition of teaching and learning, the quality of campus life, the governing of the college, assessing the outcome, and the connection between the campus and the world.

These problems are not new. They have, in one way or another, troubled higher education for generations. But the points of tension are today also points of unusual opportunity. On campuses all across the country we found renewed interest in general education, in the quality of teaching, and in the evaluation of the undergraduate experience. Above all, we found integrity and a wellspring of tradition and talent waiting to be tapped.

What we urgently need today is a constructive debate about the meaning of the undergraduate college and a willingness to make this part of the educational enterprise more vital and enriching. At the same time, the diversity of our system must be acknowledged and protected. The responses to the challenge of enriching the baccalaureate experience will surely differ from one institution to another and, in the end, the quality of the effort must be measured not by the certainty of the outcome, but by the quality of the quest.

The American college is, we believe, ready for renewal, and there is an urgency to the task. The nation's colleges have been successful in responding to diversity and in meeting the needs of individual students. They have been much less attentive to the larger, more transcendent issues that give meaning to existence and help students put their own lives in perspective.

This nation and the world need well-informed, inquisitive, open-minded young people who are both productive and reflective, seeking answers to life's most important questions. Above all, we need educated men and women who not only pursue their own personal interests but are also prepared to fulfill their social and civic obligations. And it is during the undergraduate experience, perhaps more than at any other time, that these essential qualities of mind and character are refined.

A ringing call for the renewal of the American college may, at first blush, seem quixotic. Not only has cultural coherence faded, but the very notion of commonalities seems strikingly inapplicable to the vigorous diversity of contemporary life. Within the academy itself, the fragmentation of knowledge, narrow departmentalism, and an intense vocationalism are, as we have acknowledged, the strongest characteristics of collegiate education.

Still, we believe the undergraduate experience can, by bringing together the separate parts, create something greater than the sum, and offer the prospect that the channels of our common life will be deepened and renewed. The college—set apart from graduate and professional education—remains, as Sheldon Rothblatt of the University of California, Berkeley, put it, the "natural home of liberal education, the primary form of higher education, where the well-being of the self and the problem of self and society are central."[5]

To accomplish this essential mission, connections must be made. All parts of campus life—recruitment, orientation, curriculum, teaching, residence hall living, and the rest—must relate to one another and contribute to a sense of wholeness. We emphasize this commitment to community not out of a sentimental attachment to tradition, but because our democratic way of life and perhaps our survival as a people rest on whether we can move beyond self-interest and begin to understand better the realities of our dependence on each other.

This vision of community is appropriate for campuses of all sizes. At small colleges there are often shared traditions that unify and enrich the full range of campus life. Large universities, on the other hand, often have a special climate of intellectual and social vitality sparked by their many communities of learning. During our study we observed outstanding examples of good practices at institutions both large and small. Therefore, while educators have common concerns about the undergraduate experience, there cannot be a single, prescribed response. Strategies for excellence will vary from campus to campus and be shaped by the unique mission and traditions of the institution.

We proceed, then, with the conviction that if a balance can be struck between individual interests and shared concerns, a strong learning community will result. And perhaps it is not too much to hope that the college, as a vital community of learning, can be a model for society at large—a society where private and public purposes also must be joined.

PART

I

FROM SCHOOL
TO COLLEGE

1

WHERE COLLEGE DREAMS BEGIN

Students go to college expecting something special. Their parents share this hope. Only in America is the decal from almost any college displayed proudly on the rear window of the family car. The message: Here's a family on the move. One high school student reflected this nation's almost touching faith in higher education when she said: "I think my main concern is that without a college education I'll have slim chances in today's world. I want a better life for myself. That means college."

Another student described her vision this way:

> I always had this big dream for myself. I always knew it was my responsibility to go to college. I want a family, and I want kids, but I want to have them later on—about the end of my twenties. I also want to have something to fall back on if anything should ever happen to my family. It helps out if both people can have jobs. But to get a good job you need education.

This student belief in the utility of higher education is shared overwhelmingly by students nationwide. When we asked one thousand college-bound high school seniors about their reasons for wanting to go to college, 90 percent said "to have a more satisfying career." Almost equal percentages said that college would prepare them "for a specific occupation" and help them "get a better job."

In this regard, one student told our interviewer: "I want to go to college to become a doctor, basically so I can make money and then take it easy." Another student told us: "I'd like to learn a skill so I can earn enough money and really have a good life."

Our survey revealed that priorities of parents differ from those of their children. We found that parents of college-going seniors consider "becoming an authority in a specialized field" a less important goal than do the students. Parents are more inclined to value college because it will help the student "become a well-rounded, more interesting person," and because it will offer "an opportunity to clarify values and beliefs" (Table 1).

Table 1 "Very Important" Reasons for Going to College As Ranked by College-Bound High School Students and Their Parents (percent agreeing)

	Parents	High School Seniors
To have a more satisfying career	88	90
To prepare for a specific occupation in which I am interested	84	89
To get a better job	82	85
To develop talents and abilities to the fullest	87	83
To learn more about things of interest	81	82
To gain a well-rounded education	89	80
To become an authority in a specialized field	42	64
To become a well-rounded, more interesting person	70	50
To become a more thoughtful, more responsible citizen	28	27
To have an opportunity to clarify values and beliefs	57	37
To have a few more years of fun	NA	12
To meet and marry a successful person	NA	9
To continue to be with friends	NA	8
To become a well-known and respected person	18	27

NA: Not available.

Source: The Carnegie Foundation for the Advancement of Teaching, Survey of the Transition from High School to College, 1984–85.

High school students believe that if a college has a good academic reputation this will lead to a better job. And, apparently impressed by "The Game of the Week," about one third say that an outstanding athletic team means that a college will have an "above-average" academic program. On the other hand, college-going seniors do not feel that a college with high tuition offers a better education. As one student said: "It's the teachers, not the high tuition, that make a college really good."[1] While they firmly believe that public colleges provide as good an education as private ones, students are about evenly divided over whether instruction is better at a small college or a large one.

Once again, the opinions of parents differ somewhat from those held by their children. For example, the parents we surveyed were less inclined to see a connection between a college's athletic record and the academic quality of the institution. We also found that parents, even more than students, feel that the level of tuition is not a reflection of academic quality (Table 2).

Table 2 How College-Bound Twelfth-Graders and Their Parents Judge Colleges (percent agreeing)

	Parents	High School Seniors
If a college has a good reputation, its graduates usually get better jobs.	83	85
Generally, public colleges provide as good an education as the private colleges.	74	72
The best size for a college is one that is between 1,500 and 3,000 students.	38	47
Colleges with students from many states and foreign countries tend to provide a better education.	44	46
The quality of instruction at small colleges is no better than at large colleges.	48	46
Older colleges with tradition usually offer a better education.	35	37
Colleges with outstanding athletic teams usually have above-average academic programs.	17	31
A college located in a big city is not a very safe place for a young student.	NA	23
On the whole, the higher the tuition cost of a college, the better the quality of education a student will get.	8	12

NA: Not available.

Source: The Carnegie Foundation for the Advancement of Teaching, Survey of the Transition from High School to College, 1984–85.

High school students and their parents may have strong feelings about college, but *choosing* one is a different matter. Indeed, one of the most disturbing findings of our study is that the path from school to higher education is poorly marked. Almost half the prospective college students we surveyed (47 percent) said that "trying to select a college is confusing because there is no sound basis for making a decision." Without adequate information, many students choose a college almost blindly. Then, once enrolled, they often are not satisfied with their decision and far too many, for the wrong reasons, transfer or drop out.

For most students the college search gets serious when, as juniors, they start receiving letters, booklets, and brochures. Colleges and universities, in launching their recruit-by-mail campaigns, purchase the names and addresses of prospective students from the Student Search Service, a program of The College Board. The names are drawn from a pool of about 1.6 million people, who, each year, take a form of the Scholastic Aptitude Test.[2] Once a student's name is picked—because of high test scores or some other characteristic of interest to a college—he or she will hear from an average of about twenty institutions.[3] Last year, the Student Search Service was responsible for millions of student contacts, and our national survey revealed that nine out of ten college-bound seniors receive at least one recruitment mailing and one half received ten or more.[4]

During our study we examined the viewbooks used by colleges during the recruitment of prospective students. The publicity material is, we found, attractive and well written. Still, promotional booklets and brochures are more visually appealing than informative and, if we judge from the pictures, it would be easy to conclude that about half of all college classes in America are held outside, on a sunny day, by a tree, often close to water. One admissions officer told us: "Market strategists have figured out that students want to be near water. So brochures appear with oceans, lakes, and rivers. I know one college that shows an oceanfront even though they are miles from the shore."[5]

But students are cautious consumers. They do not accept at face value the information they receive. For example, 40 percent of the college-going seniors we surveyed, when asked about college publications, said they felt the material does not "tell you what is really important about college." More troubling is the fact that about 40 percent even doubted the accuracy of the publications.[6] One high school student who had gotten lots of college letters told us, "I came to realize it was mostly form letters." Another said, "Colleges never tell you about the bad things." One student went further: "Brochures are dishonest."

We found that students, during their college search, put more faith in face-to-face encounters. Typical of many was a student who, on one October night in her senior year, went to a college night sponsored by the high school Parent-Teacher Association. She and her best friend signed up for three thirty-minute sessions featuring representatives from colleges she "had heard something nice about." In one session, the director of admissions from a small private college said classes at his school "never have more than thirty students," that "professors know the names of every student," and that the teachers are "willing to stay after class and give you help and attention if you need it."

The student was impressed. She decided on the spot that the "personal touch" was exactly what she wanted, and told us she "felt fortunate to have stumbled across this college by accident." Several of her friends, however, were even more determined than before to attend the state university, which, they said, offered "more programs and more fun."

College nights and fairs are popular with both colleges and prospective students. Huge fairs are held each year in major cities across the country, often with more than one thousand colleges in attendance. In addition, there are hundreds of smaller fairs in shopping centers, community colleges, and high school gymnasiums. Fifty-five percent of the high school students in our survey said they had attended at least one college night or fair and gave them high ratings both in terms of their usefulness and the believability of the information they received.[7]

Another student we talked with said he had filled out many

request cards at a college fair and soon began getting personal letters from one college "addressing me by my first name." He responded by asking for more information. More letters and phone calls that followed urged him to make a quick decision. "Knowing where you will be going to school will bring peace of mind," he was told. He admitted to liking all the attention. "In a school like that, I'll be an individual, not just a number. They don't even want my test scores. I guess they are satisfied with my transcript."[8]

The majority of college-going students check out their decisions by visiting a college of their choice. Our research revealed that 57 percent of all prospective students, in their college search, visit at least one campus and almost one in four visit three or more.[9] Any doubts students may have about their choices usually are dispelled when they see the attractive buildings and, as one student put it, "meet the friendly people." He said, "Students just came up to me and asked my name and asked if I was coming next year. That really excited me. I didn't feel as if I'm going into a strange place—and I really like the campus, too."

In general, what do prospective students learn on campus visits? While preparing this report, members of our staff went on several campus tours. At one university, the trip, which lasted an hour and a half, included a quick walk *past* the library and classroom buildings. The first stop was a lengthy exploration of the student union building—a self-contained mini-mall stuffed with things to eat, buy, and do, where visitors viewed the bagel bar, the carry-out sandwich bar, and the outdoor dining terrace. Tour members learned about its variety of services—from photocopying and check-cashing to swimming, billiards, first-run movies, and continuous videos shown on a large-screen television set.[10]

Again outside, the student guide told the group: "Each year on the mall, the campus has a student-run carnival with lots of booths where students push their projects and sell their wares." After passing the administration building ("This is where you get financial aid"), the group moved to the gymnasium. "A higher percentage of students participate in intramurals here than at any other college in the state," the group was told. The tour ended with a visit to a residence hall and a pep talk about the ins and outs of "dorm life."[11]

During this tour, prospective students and their parents learned about festive occasions, but not who teaches undergraduate classes. They visited the student union and the dorms, not the library. The winning football record was discussed, but no mention was made of academic honors. Visitors heard about "keg parties," not about concerts and lectures. One had the distinct impression that the campus was a place with abundant social life. Education was ignored.

Little wonder that when we asked students what influenced them most during their visit to a campus, about half mentioned "the friendliness of students we met."[12] But it was the buildings, the trees, the walkways, the well-kept lawns—that overwhelmingly won out. The appearance of the campus is, by far, the most influential characteristic during campus visits, and we gained the distinct impression that when it comes to recruiting students, the director of buildings and grounds may be more important than the academic dean.

Prospective students and their parents, looking for still more objective information, often turn to commercial college guides. Dozens of such books are now on the shelves, and yet, according to our survey, only *The College Handbook*, published by The College Board, is read by more than half the seniors who plan to attend college.[13] One parent told us he studied "every college guide I could get my hands on because they have the most objective information. I especially like the ones that tell you what college is really like."[14]

But trying to pick a good guide—one that provides important information—can be as complicated as trying to pick a college. In addition to *The College Handbook* and other standard works, such as *Peterson's Guide to Four-Year Colleges* and *The Selective Guide to Colleges*, there are dozens of others, such as *Everywoman's Guide to Colleges and Universities*, *A Guide to Post-Secondary Educational Op-*

portunities for the Learning Disabled, The Black Student's Guide to College, Guide to Christian Colleges, Where the Girls Are Today: The College Man's Roadtripper Guide to All Women's Colleges, and *America's Lowest Cost Colleges.*

Some commercial guidebooks report on such items as average freshman Student Aptitude Test (SAT) scores, college costs, and library holdings. Most of this information, though, is a year or more out of date. Others provide gossipy tidbits about food, sex, drugs, and alcohol. The problem is that each publication uses its own yardstick to measure excellence or decadence. Each tells the story it thinks students want to hear, and guidebooks, ranging from the serious to the raunchy, are placed side by side on the bookstore shelf.

So then, how to rate the raters? In 1984, fifty Carleton College students reviewed three guides: Edward B. Fiske's *The Selective Guide to Colleges,* Yale's *The Insider's Guide to Colleges,* and Lisa Birnbach's *College Book.* Measuring them on their overall accuracy of each description of Carleton, thirty-eight students thought *The Selective Guide to Colleges* was the most accurate, eleven chose the Yale guide, and one student chose *College Book.* [15] This is only one isolated sample, to be sure. But perhaps other colleges should ask their students to evaluate what guidebooks say about their institution in order to clarify how the portraits relate to the reality of campus life.

In their search for good college information, almost all prospective college students also seek help from parents, who are, we found, overwhelmingly the most influential source of information about colleges, followed by high school friends (see Chart 1).

Parents who did not, themselves, graduate from college appear to exert the most influence on their children in making the choice to go to college. Of students reporting much influence from their parents in making this decision, 54 percent were from families where neither the mother nor the father were college graduates, 26 percent were from families where only one parent had earned a college degree, and 20 percent from homes where both parents were

Individuals Offering the Most Influence
in Selecting a College as Reported
by High School Seniors: 1985

CHART 1

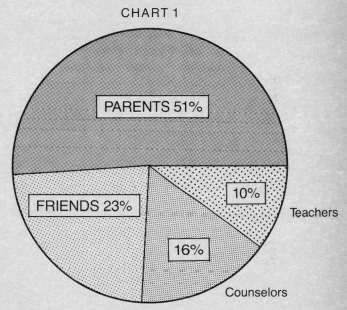

Carnegie Foundation Survey of the Transition from High School to College, 1985.

college educated.[16] In families where both parents held a degree, pressures may be less because going to college may just be assumed.

Eighty-eight percent of the parents we polled wanted their child to attend college the next year, while eighty-two percent of the college-bound seniors reported that their parents influenced the decision to continue education after high school graduation.[17]

High school counselors are also consulted, but their advice is rated far less influential by students—not because counselors are uncaring, but because they are overworked and not sufficiently informed. The typical high school counselor, for example, claims to have personal information on only about fifteen to twenty-five four-year colleges and universities, a generous estimate we suspect. And counselors say they have very little knowledge about institutions more than five hundred miles away.[18]

It is somewhat encouraging, then, that only 57 percent of the high school students we surveyed said, without qualification, that the information they received from counselors was "relevant" to their college search and only 10 percent said counselors were the "most important influence" in their selection.[19] One counselor told us, "We don't have that large a staff, and we have all the other problems to take care of. We see the kids for college guidance when they make an appointment. We don't do it automatically."[20]

Even with the flood of information—brochures, college guides, campus visits, and the like—the process of college recruitment and selection does not seem to be working very well. When we surveyed prospective students in December of their senior year, half of them said they still did not have "enough facts to make an informed decision about where to apply for admission."[21] About 80 percent wanted additional facts about costs and financial aid. Over two thirds wanted more information about academic programs, student activities, faculty strengths and weaknesses, and living accommodations on the campus. Parents, even more than students, expressed a strong need to be better informed, especially in matters related to tuition and financial aid (Table 3).

Table 3   What High School Students and Parents Want to Know About College (percent responding)

	Students	Parents
Costs of tuition, fees, books	81	85
Financial aid to students (scholarships, loans, jobs)	79	89
Academic programs being offered	72	76
Student activities and campus life	71	73
Strengths and weaknesses of faculty	68	75
Places to live and living costs	67	79

Source: The Carnegie Foundation for the Advancement of Teaching, Survey of the Transition from High School to College, 1984–85.

In the end, money, for most families, is the crucial issue. Indeed, the growing gap between tuition and family resources is one of the most urgent challenges colleges and universities confront. Our survey revealed that over two thirds of college-bound students consider college costs "outrageous" and fewer than 30 percent of prospective college students feel they can attend the college of their choice without some financial aid from outside their family. Further, 61 percent said they would need scholarships, loans, or part-time work to attend *any* institutions on their preferred list.

Little wonder. For the past five years, tuition at private colleges and universities has been going up at roughly double the rate of inflation, and double the rate of increases in family income.[22] Today, the average annual cost of going to a public college or university in America is about $5,200. At private institutions the cost is more than double—$10,500.[23] The student's family (or someone) must invest, on average, from about $20,800 to $42,000 in a four-year undergraduate degree. For students attending the most prestigious private institutions, the price is up to $60,000 or more.

Rising college costs take on special significance when compared with family income. We found, for example, that more than 40 percent of all undergraduates in our college survey come from families with an annual income, before taxes, of under $30,000. Sixteen percent are from families with an annual income under $15,000.[24] Therefore, it is not surprising that most of the high school students remain confused about how to close the gap between college costs and their ability to pay and say that they will need financial help to cover college costs.

We completed our inquiry into college recruitment with the firm conviction that the transition from school to higher education must be smoothed. To be helpful to prospective students, colleges should provide needed information and, above all, tell their stories with integrity and good taste. Most institutions are, we found, ethical in their procedures of recruitment. But we are concerned that increasing marketing may become the means that drive the end.

As the competitive pressure for students grows, abuses are likely to increase while the quality of the information may decline. A small advertisement in the classified section of *The New York Times* reflects the temper of the times. "Wanted: an exp'd person for ADMISSIONS OFFICE. Must have good speaking voice, telephone skills and ability to close."

During our study we found a few disturbing examples where colleges appeared to be more interested in filling slots than in serving students. An admissions officer, staffing a booth at a national college fair, said she is very uneasy about the way they go about recruiting. "The sad fact is that there are schools that will have to close, and we don't want to be one of them. But I'm concerned with the ethics of our marketing. We cheapen and tarnish the field when we misrepresent."[25]

Some years ago, the late Stephen Bailey warned that demography may destroy integrity and the predominant effect of a shrinking college market may well lead to a decline in the relative innocence of the past. Even if only a few colleges are careless about facts and make exaggerated claims, parents and students will begin to hold all colleges in low regard.

We conclude, then, that the path from school to college should be better marked. Students and their parents urgently need to be better informed about the full range of colleges in America and they should be given better advice about how to pick a college. Such information is essential if the undergraduate experience is to be strengthened.

As a first step, we urge public schools to take far more seriously their responsibilities for assisting students in the transition from school to college, as they should also for the transition to work. In this, they could learn a great deal from the best of our private schools, where transition to higher education is a matter of priority. In meeting this important responsibility, schools should be aided by the national testing organizations—the Educational Testing Service, The College Board, and the American College Testing Program. Specifically, we recommend that these organizations establish regional advisement centers throughout the country. Such centers would be places where high school counselors could learn about colleges in their own area, and nationwide. We also urge these national testing organizations to give grants to high schools, especially those with low college-going rates, to strengthen counseling services. We suggest, too, that travel grants be made available to high school counselors so they can visit college campuses—and the proposed regional advisement centers—to become better informed about higher education.

Further, we recommend that the Committee on Self-Regulation of the American Council on Education draw up an updated and strengthened code of conduct for college recruitment based on the work already done by the nation's registrars and admissions officers.[26] To assure compliance, we urge that the nation's six regional accrediting associations carefully review recruitment procedures as a part of their evaluation of every college and university.

As for students, we urge that they look beyond brochures, viewbooks, and the well-kept lawns. When preparing for campus visits, they should list specific questions—things they want to know about the college—focusing especially on teaching and learning and on the quality of campus life. During tours, prospective students should press for candid answers. And if what they hear is not sufficiently informative, they should arrange for an extended tour, asking for separate interviews with faculty and conversations with students.

More than one guidebook should be read, and we caution against colorful anecdotes about the college that may be fascinating but tell little about the educational quality of the institution. Again, the opinions of students and alumni should be sought.

Going deeper, students, in considering a college, should look carefully at *who* teaches lower-division courses. Are top faculty members assigned to freshman courses and are such teachers accessible to students? Is good teaching considered important for promotion and tenure on the campus?

How many of the learning resources, such as computers, described in college promotional literature are easily available to undergraduates? Students should always be asking "What's in it for me?"

Another issue: Prospective students should check into how the college treats new students. Nearly every college has an orientation program but the quality varies widely from campus to campus. At one major state university we visited, an optional two-day session for freshmen and transfer students is provided at a cost of $40, but only a handful of students show up, and the ones who do say it is only marginally helpful.

Prospective students should also look at provisions for academic guidance. Who advises? Colleges that have a low ratio of students to advisers and insist that faculty reserve a certain number of hours a week for students demonstrate a determination to provide support outside the classroom.

Numbers, too, are worth examining. The number of volumes in a library is often given, for example, but circulation numbers can offer better information about how academically challenging the college is. Having a large number of books on library shelves has little relevance to students who don't use them. And how does the library budget compare with other college expenditures—intercollegiate athletics, for example?

The average scores on national entrance exams are often used as a sign of an institution's selectivity. But here, too, numbers can be deceptive. Saying that the mean SAT score is 1,000 actually explains very little. Knowing the *full range* of scores accepted by a college is a more useful measure. And why not ask the college about the average SAT score of its *graduates?*

Prospective students should find out about the dropout rate. What percentage of the students return for their sophomore year? The fact that a high number of students do not graduate is not necessarily reason to take a college off the list, but it should make a prospective student more cautious.

At the heart of the college is the academic program. Does the college have a well-defined general education curriculum that is something more than a grab bag of distribution courses? Is the major a narrow or broadening experience? And what about life outside the classroom? Does the spirit of community vitalize the campus?

Does the college have a placement program that is useful, not only to business graduates but to those in liberal arts as well? What professional and graduate schools do the graduates attend? And does the college also give priority to public service?

These are a few of the conditions a student should consider when examining a college, issues and information that go beyond the lawns and lakes.

Above all, we urge that prospective students and their parents not be intimidated by the process. It is wrong to believe that there is one type of college that is right for all. A handful of colleges are highly selective, and if attending one of these institutions is the goal, some degree of competition must be accepted as a fact of life. But many lesser-known colleges offer a solid, challenging undergraduate experience. The key for prospective students is to keep options open; for colleges, the challenge is to give helpful guidance so students can fulfill, with confidence, their hopes and aspirations.

2

MAKING THE MATCH

While students worry about getting into college, colleges worry about how to get them in. The admissions officer at one institution in our study candidly confessed, "We're hurting, and while a few applicants obviously will be rejected, the truth is that if you have a high school diploma with passing grades you'll probably be admitted."[1]

There is a facade to American higher education. Prospective students believe that admittance to a college is a victory hard to win. The reality is quite different. Today a score of "hot" colleges is receiving record applications and, according to Edward B. Fiske in his *Selective Guide to Colleges,* competition at these institutions is intense. Stanford, for example, is admitting only about 15 percent of all applicants. At Amherst it's 16 percent, Harvard 17 percent, Princeton 17 percent, Yale 19 percent, Dartmouth 22 percent, Columbia 28 percent, MIT 30 percent, and Duke 32 percent.[2]

There are, however, probably fewer than 50 colleges and universities in the United States today that can be considered highly selective, admitting less than half the students who apply. At least one third are virtually open door.[3] During this study we interviewed each of the admissions directors at the twenty-nine site visit colleges in our study, asking them what proportion of the students who had applied to their college last year was accepted. We learned that the average rate of acceptance, overall, was three out of four, which is, we believe, a fairly good indication of the pattern of admission nationwide.[4]

Almost all colleges, regardless of their selectivity, ask prospective students to submit a high school transcript with grades and class rank as a part of their procedures for admission. In addition, they tell students to complete a list of required or "highly recommended" courses, but we found much confusion about which subjects should be studied. English and mathematics are widely accepted as a necessary foundation for collegiate study, but how many years of each should be required? A study of history also is acknowledged to be important, but which history, and how much? And what about science? Or foreign languages?

In 1636, when Harvard College admitted its first students, there was no confusion about the required preparation. The mandates for admission read as follows:

> When any Schollar is able to understand *Tully*, or such like classicall Latine Author *extempore*, and make and speake true Latine in Verse and Prose, *suo ut aiunt Marte;* And decline perfectly the Paridigm's of *Nounes* and *Verbes* in the Greek tongue: Let him then and not before be capable of admission into the Colledge.[5]

Knowledge of classical languages and cultures was judged the appropriate preparation for collegiate education among the first colonial colleges, and remained so for a century or more. But as knowledge grew, requirements were added. In 1807, Harvard announced that entering students must also know geography. In 1820, Princeton required English grammar. That same year, Harvard asked prospective students to study algebra, and in 1844, geometry was added. In 1847, Harvard and Michigan put ancient history on the list, and in 1860, Michigan began requiring modern history.[6]

The University of California, from its founding, in 1868, until 1900, required entrance examinations in six areas: higher arithmetic in all its branches, including extraction of squares and cube roots, and the metric system of weights and measures; algebra to quadratic equations; geometry—"first four books"; English grammar; geography; and United States history. For Letters (as opposed to agricultural or mechanical arts) the following were also required: Latin grammar; Caesar, four books; Virgil, six books of the *Aeneid;* Cicero, six Orations; Greek grammar; and Xenophon's *Anabasis,* seven books.[7]

In 1858, students applying to little Antioch College in Ohio were examined in English grammar, geography, history, Greek and Latin, and also in "Miss Peabody's Polish-American System of Chronology," Bojesen's "Roman Antiquities," and the Gospel of John.[8] Princeton University's catalog of that period declared that all prospective students would be expected to complete Caesar's *Commentaries,* Sallust, Virgil, Cicero's *Select Orations,* and the Gospels in the Greek Testament, just to name a few. In addition to the required readings, the catalog noted that: "In all cases testimonials of moral character are required. . . ." Princeton's "Terms of Admission" also contained a warning that "students imperfectly prepared for the classes which they enter, are embarrassed in their future progress and are seldom able to repair the want of solid preparatory instruction."[9]

Each college and university of that day drew up its own detailed checklist for admission and the pattern varied greatly from one institution to another. Nicholas Murray Butler, who, at the time, was a professor at Columbia University, said that colleges could agree among themselves "neither upon subjects to be offered for admission nor upon topics within these subjects." As an example, "If Cicero was prescribed, it meant in one place four orations and another six, and not always the same four or the same six."[10] Earlier, Dr. Cecil F. P. Bancroft, principal of Phillips Academy in Andover, had complained that "out of over forty boys preparing for college next year we have more than twenty Senior classes." Each class was getting students ready for a separate college.[11]

Frustrated by this crazy-quilt admissions pattern, secondary school leaders urged their colleagues in higher education to standardize procedures and, in 1900, the College Entrance Examination Board was born. The aim of this new school-college association was to define a college-preparatory curriculum that might be used by all institutions and to develop questions that would test the readiness of prospective students in key subject areas. The deeper aim was to bring more order and higher quality to the nation's secondary schools, which were now expanding at a rapid rate.

The battle for more orderly, commonly understood procedures was not won without a struggle. Some colleges worried about losing autonomy or being overshadowed by the prestigious "East Coast" institutions. The issue was joined by President Ethelhart D. Warfield of Lafayette College, who declared that his institution "does not intend to be told by any Board whom to admit and whom not to admit. If we wish to admit the son of a benefactor, or of a Trustee, or of a member of the Faculty, and such action will benefit the institution we are not going to be prevented. . . ."[12] Charles Eliot of Harvard, who supported the goals of standardized admissions, replied that Lafayette could, of course, continue to admit candidates on the strength of their character, "or on their promise of usefulness, or on their capacity to go on with the work of the college"—or "on their good looks."[13]

In the end, standardization carried the day. Led by The College Board, a new college-preparatory curriculum was defined with a core of nine academic subjects: English, history, chemistry, French, German, Greek, Latin, mathematics, and physics.[14] A standardized admissions test also was prepared and, according to Claude M. Fuess, in his history of The College Board, "[Teachers] spent hours going over the questions in each subject, making sure that they were of approximately the same difficulty and were genuine tests of proficiency and sound academic teaching."[15]

But the commitment to uniformity was short-lived. The twentieth century brought new students, new subjects, and new philosophies of education. The notion of a core of required courses would not hold. First, ancient languages lost favor. So, later, did modern languages. Chemistry and physics gave way to "physical science." History was folded into "social studies," and at some colleges the notion of preparatory courses was abandoned altogether.

By 1979, only 56 percent of the four-year public colleges nation-wide required English for admission. Only 51 percent required math. For the private institutions, it was 72 percent for English and 70 percent for math. Biological science, social studies, and physical science all were required by less than half of all public colleges and universities, and only 15 percent of the public colleges and 38 per-cent of the private ones required a foreign language (Table 4).

Table 4   High School Subjects Four-Year Colleges Require for Admission, 1979 and 1985 (percent of colleges requiring at least one year)

	Public		Private	
	1979	1985	1979	1985
English	56	71	72	72
Mathematics	51	61	70	68
Biological science	41	39	57	53
Social studies	45	52	63	64
Physical science	36	43	51	52
Foreign language	15	15	38	33

Source: Preliminary data from a study by the American Association of College Registrars and Admission Officers, The College Board, the American College Testing Program, Educational Testing Service, and the National Association of College Admissions Counselors.

Meanwhile, high schools lowered requirements for graduation and, in increasing numbers, students reached the nation's campuses inadequately prepared. But Scott Thomson, executive director of the National Association of Secondary School Principals, noted, quite properly, that the responsibility for the decline in academic quality is shared. "Colleges," he observed, "are genuine in their feelings that too many students are not adequately prepared for higher education. On the other hand, if the colleges had a modicum of conscience they must know that their own shift in standards and requirements had something to do with the situation that faces the schools today."[16]

By the early 1980s, efforts were under way, once again, to

tighten standards and let high school students know what would be expected of them. Admission requirements were being changed or reviewed for the public system of higher education in twenty-seven states, according to a survey in 1982 by the National Association of Secondary School Principals.[17] In Ohio, for example, the threat of legislative intervention forced Ohio educators to reexamine the relationship between secondary schools and higher education. The State Board of Education and the Ohio Board of Regents formed an advisory commission to study school-college transition.[18]

The commission quickly concluded that there was a need to strengthen the English and mathematics courses in high schools across the state. It recommended that the college-preparatory curriculum in every high school in Ohio include four years of English and at least three years of mathematics. Moreover, it recommended that every private and state-sponsored four-year college and university in Ohio require students to take these courses in order to gain unconditional admission.[19]

What was so stunning about all this was that, for the first time, the State of Ohio was telling students they no longer would be unconditionally admitted to a public college. The flexible policy of admissions was not abrogated, but suddenly students had an obligation to show that they had tried to prepare themselves adequately.

This story is typical of the pattern nationwide. From 1979 to 1985, the number of public colleges requiring at least one course in English increased from 56 to 71 percent; the number requiring a course in mathematics increased from 51 to 61 percent. Only biological science showed a slight decline during the same period. The foreign language requirement, already low, remained unchanged. Also, admission requirements at the nation's private colleges and universities, which have been, throughout the years, on average, higher than those of the public ones, held fairly steady during this period. (Table 4).

Clarifying standards for admission is a move in the right direction. But what we find troubling is that the focus is on credits, not on content; little attention is being paid to what is being learned. College-bound students are asked to take another course in English, or science, or mathematics, but educators are not asking what's behind the label. More English, yes, but which English? More history, but what is most worth knowing? What is it that colleges believe students need to know and understand as well as be able to do?

What we need today are forums that would, in the spirit of The College Board, assemble leaders from the separate levels to consider carefully the content of precollegiate education. As a first step we recommend that every state establish a blue-ribbon panel of school and college educators to consider what students need to know and be able to do in order to prepare effectively for college. In making such a suggestion, we are not seeking rigid prescriptions. Rather, we are hoping for thoughtful discussion and helpful guidance.

What might be the core of precollegiate preparations? As a starting point, we urge states to consider the important work done by The College Board in Project Equality. A series of booklets is now available from The College Board that spells out a proposed college-preparatory curriculum and suggests how the preparation of students might be assessed. It provides, we believe, good guidance to colleges and schools.[20]

Another suggestion: the Carnegie Foundation report *High School* recommended areas of precollegiate study. We suggested, for example, that all secondary school students become proficient in language, gain historical perspective, learn about social institutions, understand how science works, become familiar with a culture other than their own, and be introduced to the world of work. In that report, we also proposed that all high school seniors write an essay on a consequential topic. Clear and effective writing and critical thinking are, we said, the most essential skills both for further education and for work.

We now recommend that every college and university—in addition to the basic academic preparation—also ask prospective students to submit an essay as part of their application for admission. Such a requirement would underscore the importance of effective writing and also tell the college more about the language needs and strengths of incoming students. We recognize that reading such essays is time consuming and that evaluating them is hard, especially if balance and fairness are to be achieved. Yet, we believe the time and hard work involved in completing such an assignment are worthwhile, both for the applicant and the college.

Although a core of required courses, grade-point averages, and rank in class are the most important criteria for college admissions, the Scholastic Aptitude Test, commonly called the SAT, is the most widely known and, we found, the most feared. Today approximately 1.6 million SATs are administered to high school students every year.[21] The test is divided into two parts. The verbal portion consists of 85 questions that examine vocabulary and knowledge of language. The mathematics portion includes questions in arithmetic, algebra, and geometry. Answers on both sections are multiple choice.

The other major national examination is the ACT assessment, prepared by the American College Testing Program, administered to about one million high school students annually.[22] This test covers English, mathematics, social sciences, and natural sciences. The ACT examination, which seeks to measure student achievement, is related, at least indirectly, to the curriculum of the schools.

Students who take one or both of these examinations are anxious about results, believing that their college choice will be either significantly enhanced or restricted by the results. Many high school students are told that if they do badly on the test, regardless of their school record, "good colleges will reject them."[23] Feeding off this anxiety, books and computer programs, offering sample exams and test-taking hints, line bookstore shelves, and "cram" schools that coach students are flourishing. Even many of the high schools now offer SAT preparation courses. These programs promise to raise

SAT scores as high as 150 points on average and help students "build needed skills" and "reduce test anxiety."

The irony is that while students worry mightily about these national examinations, the results are often not taken seriously by the colleges. During in-depth interviews we asked each admissions officer at our twenty-nine site visit colleges to rank, in order of importance, the criteria used for admission at their institution. Only one administrator placed test scores at the top. At all other colleges, the student's academic performance—grade average or class rank— was reported to be the most important yardstick for admission.

We also asked these admissions directors how last year's freshman class would have differed if there had been *no* SAT or ACT scores available for consideration. Sixty-two percent said the absence of such scores would have made *little or no difference* in either the size or the composition of the class. One admissions officer said that at his school test scores were used only "when making borderline decisions, when the school record was particularly weak." Another stated: "We might use the scores to weed out a handful of the weakest applicants, but after that it doesn't mean much."[24]

There is, in short, a wide gap between the public view of the importance of test scores and their actual use. Indeed, Alexander W. Astin of the University of California, Los Angeles, suggests that standardized testing may be required not so much to help colleges choose students, but to perpetuate the folklore of institutional excellence.[25] This conclusion was reinforced by one admissions officer in our study who told our site visitor, "If we didn't ask for the scores, we would be regarded in the marketplace as having very low prestige. We can't afford that." Another put it this way: "It's like a dance where everyone continues to go through the motions after the music has stopped."[26]

To require students to submit scores because "that's the way it's always done," or merely to enhance the image of the college, is a disservice both to the student and the institution. We found, for example, that if a student, after completing a national examination, feels the test scores are "too low," as many of them do, he or she is inclined to "apply down." A student discouraged by test scores may decide *not* to go to a preferred college or he or she may give up on college altogether. Still others may decide not to take the SAT at all because they are convinced they will not do well.

Recently, the Dallas Independent School District received a $1.04 million grant aimed at improving student performance on college placement examinations and increasing the number of test takers, particularly among minority students. Only 18 percent of Dallas's minority twelfth-graders took the SAT last year. In justifying this cram approach to testing, a spokesman for the school district reported that some of the students who did not take the test are college material, but "they're scared off by these tests."[27]

To explore this matter further, we asked college-bound seniors to tell us whether their test scores would, in fact, influence their college choice. If so, how? Twenty-two percent of the respondents said that their scores were good enough for them to consider *any* college. On the other hand, nearly two thirds (62 percent) of these high school students concluded that their choice of a college would be restricted because of their scores.[28] They would not select their first-choice institution.

The science of assessment, if we may call it that, has become increasingly sophisticated. And we take pride in the fact that determining who should be admitted to college is decided on the basis of merit, not family rank or social status. Nonetheless, we must ask: What do our examinations really measure? And are we defining ability too narrowly? Do the so-called objective tests reinforce the values and habits of only one sector of our population? Does the "aptitude" test really tap human potential? And in the final analysis, who benefits from national admissions tests? Are we subjecting individuals to the expense and pressure of examinations from which they themselves may derive no substantial benefit?

We conclude that there is an urgent need for new and better ways to assess students as they move from school to higher education. Specifically, what we propose is a new assessment program, one that would evaluate not only the *academic* achievement of the student—linking it to the curriculum that has been studied—but would evaluate other areas of talent, too. The assessment program we need is not to screen students out of options, but help them move on with confidence to college and to jobs. In pursuit of this objective, we call for the formation of a national panel to study all aspects of the high school–college transition, looking especially for ways to achieve a more appropriate matching of the interests of individual students with future work and learning options.

Meanwhile, we urge colleges and universities to demystify the selection process. Each institution should describe in its literature the various criteria used for selection and give prospective students a profile of the student characteristics that seem most closely linked to the culture of the institution.

Further, test scores should be put in perspective. Standardized entrance examinations play an important role as the nation's most selective colleges are forced to choose candidates for the next year's freshman class from a large pool of highly qualified students. But we urge that if a college does not use the SAT or ACT scores as a yardstick for the selection of students, the tests should not be required. When scores are appropriately used, colleges should report not only the *average* scores, but also the scores of admitted students *by quartile*. Such minimal information would clarify further for students their prospects for admission.

Above all, the primary concern of every college should be not just filling the slots, but serving the interests of the students. And is it too much to ask that colleges explain to parents and students the characteristics of those who do *not* succeed at their institution as well as the characteristics of those who do?

This leads to the third dimension of admission, the personal and social characteristics of the applicants. We found that beyond academic "aptitude" and achievement, most colleges in our study also say they want "well-rounded" students. For example, the bulletin at one Ivy League institution reads as follows: The University "seeks to identify those applicants who seem best qualified to meet . . . academic requirements and who show promise of contributing to the life of the University and the world beyond it. These goals require selecting a diverse undergraduate student body with interests, backgrounds, and abilities that will generate a vital campus atmosphere."[29]

High school students, especially those with an eye on high-prestige institutions, do their best to appear well rounded. They join clubs, work on the school paper, and travel in the summer, all of which they hope will boost their chances for admission. A high school junior told us: "You hear a lot about how colleges are looking for good students who are well rounded. You get the idea that it's important to join activities in order to show colleges that you're interested in something besides grades." Another student candidly confessed: "Students don't join the French club to experience French culture but because Yale will be impressed."[30]

But once again the myths are not matched by the reality of the process. While a few highly selective colleges seriously consider the nonacademic activities of prospective students, most institutions give them slight attention. In fact, the personal characteristics of students and the out-of-classroom activities in which they have been engaged are hard to describe and even harder to assess. It is not surprising, therefore, that some admissions officers at our site colleges told us that "personal characteristics" and "extracurricular activities" are the least important factors in admission.[31]

And yet, there is growing evidence that such activities are, in fact, linked to college success. Researcher Warren Willingham, in a revealing report, identifies four factors—other than high school rank and test scores—that significantly relate to the performance of students during their collegiate years. Willingham says that "of a large number of measures examined, the best additions were high school honors, successful follow-through in extracurricular activities, a well-written personal statement, and a strong reference from the secondary school. These four measures improved prediction of which students would be most successful (in college) by 25 percent over school rank and test scores alone."[32]

Follow-through is, perhaps, the most intriguing. By follow-through, Willingham means accepting a responsible position in a club, student government, the school paper, and the like, and completing the assignment successfully. Such behavior reveals something about a student that grades cannot convey. This point has also been developed well by the work of Cliff Wing and Michael Wallach, who labeled such nonacademic factors as "accomplishment characteristics,"[33] and in studies conducted by John Holland and James Richards for the American College Testing Program. The latter wrote, "If a college wishes to find students who will do outstanding things outside the classroom and in later life, then more attention needs to be given to nonacademic accomplishment."[34] Therefore, we recommend that all colleges, in the admissions process, give enlarged consideration to the extracurricular activities of applicants. To do so would give colleges valuable information about the candidate and also send a powerful signal to the student.

During our earlier study, of the American high school, we found that many of today's teenagers are isolated and unconnected to the world around them. They have few, if any, deep commitments, no sense of being needed, and few opportunities to give meaning to their lives. In response to these findings, we proposed in that report that high school students be asked to complete a new "Carnegie unit"—a term of voluntary service that would involve them in day-care centers, youth clubs, libraries, retirement homes, or tutoring at the school. We now recommend that colleges make a term of voluntary service—the proposed new Carnegie unit—an important criterion in their admission process.

There is one remaining issue that must be urgently confronted. When all is said and done, the procedures colleges use in the selection of their students cannot be divorced from institutional goals, nor can they be separated from the social context in which colleges carry on their work. And it is distressing to note the decline in minority student enrollment in our colleges over the past four years. With this in mind, we strongly recommend that every higher learning institution reaffirm, as an essential objective, its commitment to educational opportunity, especially for historically bypassed students.

Colleges and universities that are highly selective have a special obligation to maintain diversity on the campus. This means working closely with the schools and providing mentoring and summer services for minority students, who should be given special encouragement and tutoring during the early years of formal education.

The face of young America is changing, and in the future, the school population will include more blacks and Hispanics. By the year 2000 about 30 percent or more of all students in the public schools will be from minority groups. And yet, while the number of such students graduating from high school is increasing, the percentage of those enrolling in higher education is going down.[35]

If our sense of nationhood is to be strengthened, if a generation of new citizens is to be brought into the mainstream of American life, colleges and universities must recommit themselves to the task of equality of opportunity for all. They must assure that their recruitment and admissions procedures bring them significant numbers of students from underrepresented populations. Perhaps more than any other institution in our society, it is the college that is crucially important to advancing prospects for black and Hispanic students. We strongly urge that colleges give priority to need-based awards. And at the federal level, we also strongly recommend that, to meet this need, the Pell Grant Program be expanded, not diminished.

Almost twenty years ago, the Carnegie Commission on Higher Education declared: "Our colleges and universities must maintain and strengthen academic quality if our intellectual resources are to prove equal to the challenge of contemporary society. At the same time, the nation's campuses must act energetically and even aggressively to open new channels to equality of educational opportunity."[36] These twin mandates—quality and equality—remain the urgent unfinished agenda for higher education.

Here, then, is our conclusion. During the past quarter century, almost all conditions surrounding the passage from school to college have changed. We urgently need creative, new approaches to match the new conditions.

Therefore, the first important step in improving the undergraduate college is to help students move from school to higher education. What is involved is not new marketing procedures. Rather, the goal must be to provide more helpful information and make it possible for students to begin with confidence an educational journey that will lead them to the right college and extend far beyond the college years.

PART

II

A CLEAR AND

VITAL MISSION

ORIENTATION:
AFFIRMING THE TRADITIONS

The first weeks on campus are critically important. This is the time when friendships are formed and attitudes about collegiate life take shape. And yet, we found during our study that new students have little sense of being inducted into a community whose structure, privileges, and responsibilities have been evolving for almost a millennium.

The term "matriculation,"* a word as old as the university itself, has largely disappeared from the vocabulary of the modern American college, and with it the sense of a student's formal installation into a learning community. An early-nineteenth-century college spelled out its requirements for matriculation as follows:

> Every person who may be accepted upon examination, and be permitted to join the University, shall be on probation, and shall not be admitted as a member of the Society in full standing, until after one term.[1]

Only after proving himself worthy of a company of scholars was a freshman of that day allowed full membership in a corporate body dedicated to learning. Whether a college of that day was any more successful in creating a community than colleges are today, we cannot say. But at least there was no question about the institution's goal.

*The matricula was a list, or register, of persons belonging to a society or order; to matriculate is to incorporate someone into a society or body of persons by insertion of his name in a register.

Today a feeling of anomie is not uncommon among freshmen, who come to campus with high hopes, then soon lower their expectations. The editorial in a student newspaper had this warning:

> You're all out in the wilderness now, away from your homes and your roots, wandering around trying to spot where you can settle down—you are trying to fit in. . . . The first thing you're going to have to learn about student life after orientation is that there isn't any. No, you are not going to die, but a lot of the time you're going to feel no one at this school would really care if you did.[2]

Many new undergraduates arrive on campus with an idealized view of college life. Eighty-five percent of the college-bound seniors we surveyed felt that it was possible to do well in college and still have "a lot of interesting social activities." About half believed that college students party every weekend. And 92 percent agreed that "half the fun of going to college is making new friends." On the academic side, most prospective students believe that college teaching is better than high school teaching and that, in college, they will have to work twice as hard as they did in school (Table 5).

Table 5   How College-Bound High School Students View College (percent responding)

	Agree	Disagree
Doing really well in college means you miss out on a lot of interesting social activities.	15	85
Most college students party every weekend.	51	49
Half the fun of going to college is making new friends.	92	8
The quality of teaching in college is usually no better than in high school.	17	83
College students have to study almost twice as hard as twelfth-grade students.	82	18
Being in college helps to clarify one's values and beliefs.	81	19

Source: The Carnegie Foundation for the Advancement of Teaching, Survey of the Transition from High School to College, 1985.

For whatever reasons, too many students, once they get to campus, do not make a satisfactory adjustment. Some, for the best of reasons, transfer or drop out, planning to return. Others drift away from campus because of an absence of "a feeling of belonging or fitting in at the institution." Here's what one young woman said: "For some reason, this college isn't exactly what I had pictured, so I'm not really happy here. When I go home on weekends, I'm not excited to come back. I'm not sure why, maybe it's just not as different as I had hoped. It seems like a glorified high school that just has a lot harder curriculum."[3]

Still other students, after the predictable bump that comes from any major move, soon settle in and become committed members of the college community. One freshman described to us her early tensions this way: "When I first got here, I was scared to death! I didn't know my way around. I wasn't rooming with anyone I knew. After my mom left, I was just plain scared. I sort of felt like crying. I thought, 'I'm here all by myself and I know I'm going to get lost.' But after a while I began to find my way around." Another said she had been to a party every single night since college began. "There's the prediction," she said, "that freshmen will just fall overboard, and I hate being in that category, but it happened. For the first two weeks, I averaged four hours of sleep every single night."[4]

New students have a strong urge to get acquainted and get along. They juggle the old and the new and improvise as best they can. The question for the college is: Should undergraduates be protected from their own mistakes or is self-discipline learned only by suffering the consequences of its absence? Some institutions we visited deliberately follow a sink-or-swim approach. Others try hard to acclimate students early to rituals and traditions of campus life. Some succeed, others fail.

A Pacific Coast institution with nearly 16,000 students has a popular seven-day program called "Welcome to Campus." Participation is optional, but about 60 percent of last year's 4,600 new students took part. The cost is $33 per student. A freshman on this campus told us, "Orientation is one of the best things they do at this college. They stick you in with twenty people you've never seen in your life, and you spend all your time with them for a week. It helps you get acquainted with the school, the community, and the campus. It's also a good way for freshmen to get to know a senior. Two of my roommates were counselors this fall, and they still have all their freshman friends come over and ask them for advice."[5]

An optional two-day orientation session during the last two weeks of June is featured by a major university in our study. But only a handful of students attend. Seminars include "How to avoid a hassle" and "Straight facts about the other side of campus life—information about drug laws, liquor on campus, ripoffs, parking problems, personal security, and alcohol awareness."[6] Looking over these topics one wonders if the student is being prepared for a college education or a weekend in Manhattan.

An older transfer student told us he had not received any information about orientation and added, "They didn't do anything for me when I arrived—I had to find my way around. I would have liked more help getting started. I didn't even know my way to the library." Administrators on this campus worry that students fail to attend orientation. The student body president, who went through the program and enjoyed it, made this point: "Orientation is good—it helped me. But you have to remember this: For the majority of students, we've done a real shoddy job of latching onto them once they get here and getting them excited about the university atmosphere. It's almost an individual effort. You're on your own around here and you have to find what's out there, with little help."[7]

There is no simple response to the challenge of orienting new students to the campus. Some are less secure and need to feel part of a group; others prefer to make it on their own. Still, we are convinced that colleges should be as committed and creative in helping students adjust to college life as they are in getting them to the campus in the first place. Such a view does not deny the maturity or the independence of students; it simply recognizes that each university or college has a culture of its own and that understanding that culture contributes immensely to the quality of learning—and to retention, too.

During this study we heard faculty and administrators complain repeatedly about students who, they said, were wholly uninformed about the traditions of college life and failed to appreciate the liberal arts. One professor told us, "My students have no idea what scholarship in my department is all about."[8] Probably true. And yet, where in the undergraduate experience are students told about such values? How are they to appreciate traditions about which they have not heard?

A college junior with whom we spoke had, during the summer months, been hired as a waitress by a major hotel in an eastern city. During her first day in an orientation session, the new recruit was shown a film on the corporation, its scope, and traditions. She toured, with an assistant manager, every department in the facility —from kitchen to housekeeping—and was told what it meant to be a part of the "hotel family." After telling this story the student said she had been given a more exciting and helpful introduction to the hotel than to the liberal arts college where she was enrolled.[9]

Research makes it clear that the greater a student's social and academic integration, the more intense his or her commitment to the college.[10] Orientation, when well accomplished, improves the student's day-to-day ability to cope and it has a positive impact on persistence.[11] Further, as new students learn about the college, the spirit of community grows, loyalties build, and the quality of the educational experience is strengthened. But where to begin?

As a first step we recommend a preterm session for all new undergraduates, one that may extend into the first semester. A southern college with 1,200 students has an orientation program appropriately called "The Bridge." It begins with a "preview weekend." There are seminars on the honor system, for example, and physical fitness sessions in which students plan an exercise program, undergo a physical evaluation, and discuss diet with a professional.

At the heart of "The Bridge" program are weekly seminars that extend through the first semester. Those freshmen meet in small groups to discuss literature, psychology, history, current events, or the arts. To prepare for this "mini-term," all incoming students are assigned summer readings. Faculty who guide the seminars become "mentors" to students, often meeting them for dinner or inviting them to their homes. This partnership is expected to persist through all four years. Mismatches occur but only about one fifth of the students change mentors.

The editor of the student newspaper said, "Orientation is what keeps the attrition rate from being higher than it is." Faculty speak fondly about watching freshmen mature during the four years of college. As one faculty member put it: "Well, there's all this talk here about 'close student-faculty relationships,' but I think it really does happen. We work very hard to get at what makes students tick and to become close to them."[12]

We next urge that all colleges schedule a special orientation convocation at the beginning of the academic year, one that would be as significant for matriculating freshmen as the commencement ceremony is for departing seniors. The purpose would be formally to receive the entering class into the community of learning, by participation in a shared, symbolic experience. At Gettysburg College in Pennsylvania, each freshman class is received into the institution through a beginning-of-the-year convocation. The student body officers lead the procession and the service. The faculty march in academic garb, and a faculty representative speaks to the freshmen about collegiate life. The upperclassmen and other guests sit in the sections around those reserved for the honored class to observe with pride this day of commitment and celebration.

We further propose that all colleges offer a short-term credit course for new students, perhaps entitled "The College: Its Values and Traditions." Such a seminar, while telling students about administrative procedures and extracurricular life on campus, should pay special attention to the academic traditions of the college and help students understand how scholars carry on their work. Topics that might be considered: How and why was the college founded? What are its traditions? Why do we have a general education program? Has the college been noted for any form of service? What significant events have shaped the college? What goals is the college seeking to accomplish?

The University of South Carolina has an orientation course called "University 101" that focuses on academic life. In this course students consider the purposes of higher education and are introduced to the university's traditions and procedures. Results are impressive. Students who enroll have higher retention rates and increased knowledge and use of university resources, and become more actively involved in campus activities.[13]

We especially urge the college president to be a leader in introducing students to the college. Typically, presidents follow with keen interest the career success of alumni. They often are conspicuously involved in homecoming events, and former students who come back to campus are smothered with attention, especially if they are celebrated and successful. We conclude that at a college of quality, incoming students should be placed equally high on the president's agenda.

We also recommend that colleges and universities give special priority to the difficult but essential task of orienting *part-time* students. Unless these students are taken seriously by the college and integrated into campus life, undergraduate education in America increasingly will become simply a process in which part-time students drift on and off the campus and credits and credentials are earned and appropriately recorded. The most essential values of a liberal education will be lost.

We found that nontraditional students—those who are older and part time—do, in fact, have an especially bumpy introduction to the campus life. Part-timers, who now constitute 29 percent of all those enrolled in four-year institutions,[14] have complicated schedules— they work and have family obligations—and yet, orientation activities and even college office hours often are not arranged conveniently for them. One older student told our site visitor, "Every place I turn around here, it's a Catch-22. I can't even find someone to take my money."[15]

Part-timers present a fascinating pattern. Two thirds are twenty-five years of age or older, and the majority return to college after having "stopped out." Slightly over one half are married, and almost 60 percent are employed full time. Academically, part-time students have a lower high school grade-point average than the others,[16] but their college grade-point average is slightly higher. Surprisingly, our research revealed that career success and material well-being are less important for these students. And we also found that part-timers are as inclined as full-time students to support more course requirements for graduation (Table 6).

Table 6   Characteristics of Part-Time and Full-Time Undergraduates at Four-Year Institutions

	Percent	
	Part-Time	Full-Time
Age: twenty-five years old or older	67	13
Dropped out for some period since entering college	58	16
Married, divorced, separated, or widowed	53	10
At present employed full time	59	4
Father's occupation: professional or managerial	54	65
skilled or semiskilled	42	32
Father's education: high school or less	55	36
College grade-point average of B or higher	61	55
These goals are "very important": career success	57	63
financial success	40	43
intellectual development	70	69
The chief benefit of a college education is that it increases one's earning power	38	44
College should require all undergraduates to take more courses in: literature	25	26
science	41	32
computer science	73	74
the arts	30	27

Source: The Carnegie Foundation for the Advancement of Teaching, National Survey of Undergraduates, 1984.

To better inform part-time students about campus services and activities, some institutions assume the cost of mailing information directly to their homes. Others run a special column for part-timers in the student newspaper; some institutions issue special newsletters for them. Still other colleges schedule orientation seminars for part-time students on weekends or during evening hours, when they are more likely to be free. And one institution put an orientation session on videocassette so it could be viewed not only by the parents of incoming young students, but also by part-time students who find it difficult to attend briefings on the campus. Regardless of the strategies used, we strongly urge that all colleges with nontraditional students find creative ways to help them become full partners in the community of learning.

Orientation, while essential, is only the beginning. After the flush of newness fades, all new students soon discover that there are term papers to be written, course requirements to be met, and conflicts between the academic and social life on campus. Students need to talk about these tensions. One freshman told us, "I call home a lot, especially when I have a big exam. The main thing my mom wants to know is whether I'm eating right and getting lots of sleep, which really doesn't help much, but at least I feel better just talking about my worries."[17]

The successful college offers a well-planned program of advising for all students, one that provides support throughout the entire freshman year. This is the goal, and yet we found advising to be one of the weakest links in the undergraduate experience. Emergency services, such as a health clinic and psychological counseling, are found on most campuses, but only about a third of the colleges in our study had a quality advisement program that helped students think carefully about their academic options. One student at a college with no formal advising structure said, "At registration time I couldn't get much help. I finally decided to talk things over with my roommate."[18]

When we asked students in our national survey how they feel about the quality of advising services on their campus, we learned that at least half the students had never sought advice on financial, vocational, or personal matters. And almost one in seven had never

LIBRARY

sought advice on academic matters (Table 7). But again, patterns varied widely from one type of institution to another. As one moves from the large research university to the small liberal arts college, the students rate the advising as more highly adequate, reflecting the fact that on small campuses the faculty are often more actively involved.

At one small liberal arts college in the Midwest, we found that members of the faculty do most of the academic advising. A student at this college told our site visitor, "I can see my faculty adviser almost any time, and we sometimes meet in the student union for coffee just to talk things over." At a medium-sized college in the South we found an advising program called "Safety Net." Members of the faculty meet freshmen individually and in groups and receive teaching credit for their advisement work. The main worry we heard expressed is that some students unburden themselves of emotional problems that faculty members feel ill equipped to handle.

A senior professor who plays a central role in the program told our researcher, "The idea is not that we are somehow *in loco parentis* — we're not trying to be surrogate parents. But in some cases we've been that. And if you get a student who really unloads, why, you have an awful lot to pick up on. That's why we back this thing up with a counseling center. We encourage faculty, when they're faced with a problem they can't handle, to get on the phone and refer the student to a professional counselor."[19]

Almost without exception, we found that faculty at large institutions are less actively involved in formal advising, although they still spend time informally with students, especially those who have selected their academic major. On these campuses, a professional counseling staff does most of the academic advising for the lower division students. At one such university, freshmen who need approval for their course load report to the dean's office, leave their names with the receptionist, and sit, waiting to be called. Long lines are common. When an adviser is free, he or she goes over the student's proposed program, checking to see that general education requirements will be met.[20]

Table 7 Undergraduates' Assessment of Institutional Advising Programs, 1976 and 1984 (percent responding)

| | All Institutions | | | | 1984: By Type of Institution | | | |
	1976	1984	Public	Private	Research University	Doctorate-Granting University	Comprehensive College	Liberal Arts College
Vocational advising								
Highly adequate	6	7	6	9	6	8	7	8
Adequate	21	23	22	27	24	21	21	32
Not very adequate	15	11	12	10	12	13	11	10
Never sought advising	58	59	60	54	58	58	61	50
Academic advising								
Highly adequate	15	17	15	23	15	14	17	27
Adequate	44	47	47	46	47	47	47	46
Not very adequate	22	18	20	12	21	20	19	12
Never sought advising	19	18	18	19	17	19	17	15
Financial aid advising								
Highly adequate	9	10	9	13	8	8	10	17
Adequate	22	25	25	26	23	23	26	30
Not very adequate	14	15	14	16	14	15	15	15
Never sought advising	55	50	52	45	55	54	49	38
Personal advising								
Highly adequate	8	9	8	12	6	7	9	15
Adequate	15	16	15	19	15	16	16	21
Not very adequate	8	7	7	6	7	7	6	8
Never sought advising	69	68	70	63	72	70	69	56

Source: The Carnegie Foundation for the Advancement of Teaching, National Survey of Undergraduates, 1976 and 1984.

Most of the advisers on this campus are doing their best under difficult conditions. A flood of students must be seen during the two-week preregistration period and advisers have little time to talk about academic goals. In the hurry-up sessions we observed, we found that deciding whether a student should take an anthropology course or one in the history of dance was determined more by schedule-juggling than by what would be in the best interest of the student. The problem was not an uncaring attitude. Rather, it reflected the press of too many students to advise and, to some extent, the ambivalence on this campus about the role faculty should assume.

To what extent should faculty members be personal as well as intellectual mentors to students? Is it the kindly, caring Mr. Chips or the stern, detached law professor characterized by John Houseman in *Paper Chase* who embodies the ideal relationship between faculty and students? We found in our surveys and interviews that the faculty "role" has no one definition but is determined by the culture of the institution. Mr. Chips is alive and well at many liberal arts colleges, and large research universities have their fair share of John Housemans.

When we asked students directly about faculty influence, about one in four said there is *not* even one professor on their campus who takes a personal interest in their *academic* progress. On the other hand, about the same number said they were able to identify a member of the faculty who had greatly influenced their academic careers. As to nonacademic matters, 39 percent of the students said there are professors at their college whom they feel free to consult on *personal* concerns. However, this was down from 53 percent in 1976.

Especially revealing, and perhaps most disturbing, is the fact that almost half the undergraduates (48 percent) in our survey said they felt that students at their colleges are treated like numbers in a book. But here again we found a sharp difference between the public and private institutions and also between the liberal arts colleges, where only 9 percent agreed, and the research universities, where 62 percent of the respondents said students at their school are treated like numbers in a book (Table 8).

Table 8 Student Attitudes Toward Their College: 1976 and 1984 (percent responding "yes")

	All Institutions		1984: By Type of Institution					
	1976	1984	Public	Private	Research University	Doctorate-Granting University	Comprehensive College	Liberal Arts College
Are there professors at your college who take a special interest in your academic progress?	63	59	57	68	52	56	61	73
Are there any professors at your college who have had a great influence on your academic careers?	46	44	42	50	38	43	46	53
Are there professors at your college whom you feel free to turn to for advice on personal matters?	53	39	36	49	30	37	41	54
Most students at my college are treated like numbers in a book.	45	48	55	23	62	57	45	9

Source: The Carnegie Foundation for the Advancement of Teaching, National Survey of Undergraduates, 1976 and 1984.

There are trade-offs in American higher education. Small colleges, because of size alone, find it easier to stay in touch with students, and larger institutions, although more impersonal perhaps, provide diversity and a richness of programs, and frequently set standards for scholarship and research in higher education. We need variety, and while advising undergraduates may pose a special problem for large institutions, the difficulties are, we believe, not insurmountable. They should be viewed, in fact, as an important challenge.

Several years ago, the University of Maryland opened an Undergraduate Advising Center after the campus senate became concerned that many students were selecting majors too hastily. The Center, staffed by several full-time advisers, helps students clarify their goals and make academic choices. The Maryland program also has a "resident aide" who is available to students after regular hours. On this campus an outstanding faculty adviser is selected every year from each of the five major academic areas.[21]

Wichita State University has a comprehensive advising program for all incoming students that has dramatically reduced attrition, and Miami University in Ohio has a successful program called "The Freshman Year." Entering freshmen at Miami attend a summer orientation program at which faculty members from each of the academic divisions advise and register incoming students. A freshman adviser lives in each residence hall. Since it is not necessary for students to make an appointment or wait for "office hours," their questions can be addressed as they occur. Miami, by staying in close touch with students and by taking advising into residence halls—which are small communities—has an impressive retention rate, one well above the national average.[22]

We strongly urge that all institutions, large and small, plan a comprehensive program of counseling and advising throughout the freshman year. Full-time professionals, who report to the chief academic officer of the college, should coordinate the program. On some campuses part of the load of each full-time faculty member may be assigned to advising; on others faculty may come in only occasionally to lend support but it is crucial, we believe, for advising and the academic priorities of the campus to be closely linked. On several campuses we visited, special forums brought faculty into residence halls to talk with students and to help them consider their academic options.

Graduate students and upper division students also may be effective as aides, especially in advising freshmen. And members of the faculty who are at or near retirement may be helpful, too. Senior faculty are well acquainted with the realities of life, just as they know a lot about the college. Their relationship with undergraduate students can be mutually rewarding, generating friendships that span generations. Above all, we urge that advisers be carefully selected. Seminars to improve their advising skills should be scheduled, and colleges should show, by rewards and sanctions, that advising is a high priority on the campus.

Can the modern college find its own meaning for matriculation? Is it possible for today's students to feel both the excitement and the responsibility that come from joining a community of learning?

We conclude that a successful freshman-year program will convince students that they are part of an intellectually vital, caring community. In such a setting counseling will occur in scheduled sessions and also in hallways, over a cup of coffee, or on a stroll from one building to another. The spirit of community will be sustained by a climate on the campus where personal relationships are prized, where integrity is the hallmark of discourse, and where people speak and listen carefully to each other.

Above all, incoming students should understand the purposes and traditions of the institution and be reminded of both the opportunities and obligations that guide a collegiate education.

4

TWO ESSENTIAL GOALS

An effective college has a clear and vital mission. Administrators, faculty, and students share a vision of what the institution is seeking to accomplish. The goals at such an institution flow from the needs of society and also from the needs of the persons seeking education.

But can the modern college, with all its separations and divisions, be guided by a common vision? And can the search for goals be something more than a diversion?

Writing thirty years ago, James B. Conant said:

> When someone writes or says that what we need today in the United States is to decide first what we mean by the word "education," a sense of distasteful weariness overtakes me. I feel as though I were starting to see a badly scratched film of a poor movie for the second or third time.[1]

Educators who have braved service on a curriculum committee or endured interminable meetings of an academic senate will appreciate Dr. Conant's "sense of distasteful weariness." Faculty, caught up in endless discussion of aims, will agree with the late Charles Frankel that "there is less than meets the eye in much of the educational theory, which, for our sins, is visited upon us week by week."[2]

Still, the matter of objectives cannot be so easily dismissed. The undergraduate college must be something more than "a skillfully coordinated department store," to use the vivid description of Gerald Grant and David Riesman.[3] And yet we found at most colleges in our study great difficulty, sometimes to the point of paralysis, in defining essential purposes and goals. Colleges, searching for students, are adding programs that they think will sell. The curriculum is controlled by academic departments. Teaching is organized around single courses that are only loosely related, if at all. Common goals are blurred.

A prestigious eastern college we visited, with about two thousand students and more than a century of tradition behind it, has no statement of objectives. The registrar told us: "We've had a half-a-dozen committees at different points in the past looking at what our goals are, were, and should be. Then, sometimes, they get as far as making a statement, which doesn't provide for any action, and of course is lost or forgotten by the time someone else decides in a year or two that we really need a committee to set goals."[4]

At a large public university, we asked an associate dean about institutional goals. She pointed to the front flyleaf of the university catalog and read a statement that emphasized vaguely worded references to "usable skills," "the expansion of knowledge," and "improvement of the quality of life."[5]

A faculty member at the same institution said the university's goals are meaningless to faculty and students: "I'll bet you a thousand dollars if you asked students, 'Do you know what the University's goals are for you?' they would give you blank looks." We asked and they did. Even the student body president, who might be expected to have a better idea of such things, said: "If there are any goals around here, they haven't been expressed to me."[6]

In contrast, several institutions we visited seem confident of their objectives. One middle-sized college defines its mission as follows:

> The college stands for an education that will give each student the skills of communication, the ideas and principles underlying the

major areas of modern knowledge, the understanding that learning is a continuous lifetime process, and the courage and enthusiasm to participate in the creation of a better world.[7]

At an urban, church-related university in the West with nearly six thousand students, the statement of purpose stresses the following convictions: "To pursue truth, to strive for excellence in teaching and learning and in scholarly endeavors, and to improve and enrich the community which the University serves and from which it draws its support."[8]

An administrator at the institution said, "I think the distinctive dimension of our university is the religious emphasis. I think there's something distinctive about the people who come here. A graduate of our university will bring certain moral and religious values with him."[9] What we found impressive was not the printed statement but the way the goals were talked about during day-to-day decision-making. This university had a clear idea of what it was trying to accomplish.

America's first colleges were guided by a vision of coherence. The goal was to train not only the clergy, but a new civic leadership as well. These struggling institutions sought "to develop a sense of unity where, in a society created from many of the nations of Europe, there might otherwise be aimlessness and uncontrolled diversity."[10]

The confidence of professors and their students in this era "owed much to their membership in an established middle class, a commitment to European learning, and a Christian conception of character and culture."[11] Within that framework, bitter disputes sometimes did rage, but from today's perspective the colonial college seems stiflingly monolithic.

The first students at tiny Harvard College advanced in lockstep fashion, studied a common curriculum, one subject a day, from 8:00 A.M. until 5:00 P.M., Monday through Friday, and a half day on

Saturday. In the first year, there was logic, Greek and Hebrew, rhetoric, divinity catechetical, history, and the nature of plants. The second year included ethics and politics, Aramaic, and further studies in rhetoric and divinity catechetical. The final year of college was capped by arithmetic, astronomy, Syriac, more Greek, rhetoric, and, of course, divinity catechetical.[12]

This academic core was considered absolute and immutable, to be accepted, not criticized or questioned. The goal was to discipline the mind and, through such training, graduates were to move comfortably into prestigious professions—the clergy, business, medicine, law, and civic leadership.[13]

As more colonial colleges were founded—William and Mary in 1693, Yale in 1701, and Princeton in 1747[14]—they, too, were designed to train the clergy and a new civic leadership; combat the restlessness of youth; instill piety, loyalty, and responsible citizenship in their students; and transmit knowledge that would be useful, not merely in the classical sense of preparing gentlemen, but for the practical demands of a changing world.

Following the Revolution, minds were on the future. The patriot leader Dr. Benjamin Rush wrote: "The business of education has acquired a new complexion by the independence of the country. . . ." The nation's colleges, he predicted, would be "nurseries of wise and good men to adapt our modes of teaching to the peculiar form of government."[15]

Individualism, which took deep root in an expanding nineteenth-century America, was reflected on the campus. Strange new subjects, unheard of in the classical curriculum, were added. And students from less privileged backgrounds enrolled, in increasing numbers, in pursuit of new careers. The Enlightenment, the growth of scientific knowledge, the call of new vocations, plus geographical expansion—all of these extended the undergraduate college beyond the preparation of privileged youth for elite professions.

The historian Frederick Rudolph describes the optimism of nineteenth-century educators: "All were touched by the American faith in tomorrow, in the unquestionable capacity of Americans to achieve a better world."[16] He also illustrates the rise of a practical, hands-on orientation. Rensselaer Polytechnic Institute, one of the first technical schools in the country (founded in 1824), became "a constant reminder that the United States needed railroad builders, bridge builders, builders of all kinds, and that the Institute in Troy was prepared to create them even if the old institutions were not."[17]

Predictably, change was resisted. The Yale faculty fought doggedly against the proposition that each student "be allowed to select those branches of study which are most to his taste, which are best adapted to his peculiar talents, and which are most nearly connected with his intended profession."[18] This belief was heresy.

The famous Yale statement of 1828, the strongest and most influential curriculum declaration of its day, defended the proposition that nothing is more practical than good theory, nothing more useful than liberal education. "The course of instruction which is given to the undergraduates in the college is not designed to include *professional* studies," said the report. Specialization must come later, after the student demonstrated mastery of those branches of knowledge that "are the common foundation of all high intellectual attainments."[19] Training of the mind prepared students for duties in society.

But heresies have a way of becoming orthodoxies. In 1846, the corporation at Yale authorized the creation of a professorship of "agricultural chemistry and animal and vegetable physiology."[20] Union College offered modern languages and mathematics—and managed to attract a record number of students.[21] In 1850, the reform-minded president of Brown University, Francis Wayland, urged his faculty, without success, to build a curriculum "for the benefit of all classes."[22]

The historic Land Grant Act of 1862 wedded higher education to the practical arts. And Ezra Cornell, who started a university in Ithaca, New York, at the end of the Civil War, declared: "I would found an institution where any person can find instruction in any study."[23] Several years later, when the historian Henry Adams asked a student why he had come from the Midwest to Cambridge, Massachusetts, the answer was unambiguous: "The degree of Harvard College is worth money to me in Chicago."[24] Utility was in the saddle.

In 1869, Charles W. Eliot, in his landmark inaugural speech as president of Harvard, called for the end of the mandatory classical curriculum. "The endless controversies whether language, philosophy, mathematics, or science supplies the best mental training, whether general education should be chiefly literary or chiefly scientific," he began, "have no practical lesson for us to-day. This University recognizes no real antagonism between literature and science, and consents to no such narrow alternatives as mathematics or classics, science or metaphysics. We would have them all, and at their best."[25]

Having declared the curriculum open, Eliot moved Harvard quickly to an elective track. Within three years the college abolished senior-year requirements. Seven years later, juniors were liberated. In five more years, sophomores were freed. Finally, in 1897, Harvard requirements were reduced to a single year of freshman rhetoric.[26]

In Eliot's day the philosophical linchpin of the liberal arts college was to affirm that *formation* of the "whole student" was immensely more important than particular *information*. Thomas Babington Macaulay, the great nineteenth-century English historian, went so far as to suggest that no academic subject is intrinsically superior to another. The importance of the subject, Macaulay argued, depends upon two things: the external or utilitarian value assigned to it by society generally; and the purpose which the value serves. Thus,

> If instead of learning Greek, we learned the Cherokee, the man who understood the Cherokee best, who made the most correct and melodious Cherokee verses—who comprehended most accurately the effect of the Cherokee particles—would generally be a superior man to him who was destitute of these accomplishments.[27]

By the end of the nineteenth century, business leaders had joined academic reformers in opposing classical education. They argued that if a thorough mastery of any body of knowledge—and it didn't matter which—is the really formative element of a liberal education, why not study those bodies of knowledge that are commercially valuable? Andrew Carnegie, in characteristic candor, poked fun at the irrelevance of the undergraduate curriculum of his day:

> While the college student has been learning a little about the barbarous and petty squabbles of a far-distant past, or trying to master languages which are dead, such knowledge as seems adapted for life upon another planet . . . the future captain of industry is hotly engaged in the school of experience, obtaining the very knowledge required for his future triumphs. . . . College education as it exists is fatal to success in that domain.[28]

The curriculum of the twentieth-century college was open, geared to serving a nation of diverse immigrant backgrounds and an ever-growing variety of possible employment. Still, there were educators who worried about the absence of coherence. When A. Lawrence Lowell became president of Harvard in 1909, he introduced "distribution requirements" as a compromise between the rigidity of the old classical core and the randomness of electives.[29]

But Lowell's balancing act was less successful in practice than in theory. There arose a sharp distinction between the utility of the major and the fripperies of the distribution requirements; after all, it was the major that was most likely to lead to a career.

The tumultuous twentieth century brought with it two curriculum revivals that sought to breathe new life into the common core. The first coincided with the trauma of World War I, a time when the destruction of war and the death of millions of young people shook the foundations of Western idealism. Leaders were convinced that, through a revived general education, common problems could be defined and our common life renewed.

President Alexander Meiklejohn of Amherst College introduced in 1914 a survey course on social and economic institutions, a course in which students explored humanistic fields and gained "an 'orientation' to the larger world."[30] Soon thereafter, Columbia University launched its own required freshman course, called "Contemporary Civilization,"[31] which set a standard for many other institutions and is still being offered. Dartmouth and Reed followed suit, and new general education programs cropped up all across the country. At least thirty schools copied the Columbia or Reed designs.[32]

The most hotly debated experiment of the period was the University of Chicago plan, introduced by President Robert Maynard Hutchins. The Chicago plan was a bold departure from conventional procedures.[33] It embodied, in varying degrees, early college admission, great books, interdisciplinary courses, comprehensive examinations, and a fully required course of study.

The second general education revival came after World War II. It, too, reflected the shocked response of academics to ominous social and political events beyond the campus. Germany, that great center of scholarship, had spawned the barbarities of Nazism. Buchenwald and Auschwitz seemed to mock decades of lofty rhetoric about the ennobling and civilizing power of education. And then there was the atomic bomb. Could this genie of science, once unleashed, be harnessed to humane ends?

One harbinger of this revival was a one-year Western civilization course that flourished at Stanford University in 1939. And during the war, Denison University offered a core course entitled "Problems of Peace and Post-War Reconstruction."[34] Later, Wesleyan University in Connecticut introduced a year-long humanities seminar in which students explored the meaning of liberal education, the nature of man and society, and "man's interpretation of himself and his experience."[35]

But it was the 1945 Harvard report, *General Education in a Free Society*—informally called the "Red Book"—that became the national symbol of renewal. The authors defined their purpose as a "quest for a concept of general education that would have validity for the free society which we cherish."[36] They argued that in the curriculum, as in all parts of college life, a balance between individuality and community must be struck. "The two sides of the problem thus stand forth clearly," said the Red Book. "On the one, a need for diversity, even a greater diversity than exists at present in the still largely bookish curriculum . . . and on the other, a need for some principle of unity, since without it the curriculum flies into pieces and even the studies of any one student are atomic or unbalanced or both."[37]

Our present academic world would be unrecognizable to the men who founded Harvard College in 1636. The fixed curriculum of the colonial era is as much an anachronism today as the stocks in the village square. Separations and divisions, not unity, mark the undergraduate program. Narrow departmentalization divides the campus. So distinctive are the different disciplines in method and content, the argument goes, that there is no way to connect them in the minds of students. Knowledge is so vast and specialization so persistent that shared goals cannot be defined.

What the college confronts today is the need to make choices, to decide not only what each department stands for but what it stands for as an institution. The danger is that in a bid for survival, colleges will offer narrow skills training with a cafeteria of courses devoid of deeper meaning. If the college experience is to be worthwhile, there must be intellectual and social values that its members hold in common even as there must be room for private preferences. In this context one must ask: How is the balance to be struck between student preferences and institutional priorities? Can such a balance be struck?

There is, we believe, a way out of our dilemma. While preparing this report we repeatedly were reminded that two powerful traditions—*individuality* and *community*— have been at the heart of the undergraduate experience. These two priorities have defined throughout the years the boundaries of the collegiate debate about purposes and goals and within these traditions there is, perhaps, sufficient common ground on which a vital academic program can be built.

The focus on individuality, on the personal benefits and the utility of education, has a rich tradition in American higher education. Throughout the years, students have come to college to pursue their own goals, to follow their own aptitudes, to become productive, self-reliant human beings and, with new knowledge, to continue learning after college days are over. Serving individual interests has been a top priority in higher education.

On three separate occasions, from 1969 to 1984, undergraduates were asked to indicate the "essential" outcomes of a college education. From the first survey to the last, "training and skills for an occupation" and getting a "detailed grasp of a specialized field" moved from near the bottom to the top. In contrast, "learning to get along with people" and "formulating values and goals for life" became much less important (Table 9). The personal utility of education is affirmed. And to the extent that our universities and colleges have expanded enrollments and broadened curricula in response to individual interests, they, and the nation, can be justly proud.

But amidst diversity, the claims of community must be vigorously affirmed. By community we mean an undergraduate experience that helps students go beyond their own private interests, learn about the world around them, develop a sense of civic and social

Table 9   What Undergraduates Believe the "Essential" Outcomes from a College Education Should Be, 1969, 1976, 1984 (by percentage)

College Outcome	1969	1976	1984	1969–84
Learning to get along with people	76	69	65	−11
Formulating values and goals for my life	71	63	63	−8
Detailed grasp of a special field	62	68	70	+8
Training and skills for an occupation	59	64	73	+14
Well-rounded general education	57	58	60	+3

Source: The Carnegie Foundation for the Advancement of Teaching, National Surveys of Undergraduates, 1969, 1976, and 1984.

responsibility, and discover how they, as individuals, can contribute to the larger society of which they are a part.

Robert Bellah, co-author of *Habits of the Heart,* observes that "since World War II, the traditions of atomistic individualism have grown stronger, while the traditions of the individual in society have grown weaker. The sense of cohesive community is lost."[38] In an era when an emphasis on narrow vocationalism dominates many campuses, the challenge is to help students relate what they have learned to concerns beyond themselves.

Individuals should become empowered to live productive, independent lives. They also should be helped to go beyond private interests and place their own lives in larger context. When the observant Frenchman Alexis de Tocqueville visited the United States in the 1830s, he warned that "as individualism grows, people forget their ancestors and form the habit of thinking of themselves in isolation and imagine their whole destiny is in their hands." To counter this cultural disintegration, Tocqueville argued, "Citizens must turn from the private inlets and occasionally take a look at something other than themselves."[39]

We suggest, then, that within the traditions of individuality and community, educational and social purposes for the undergraduate experience can be defined. The individual preferences of each student must be served. But beyond diversity, the college has an obligation to give students a sense of passage toward a more coherent view of knowledge and a more integrated life.

Individualism is necessary for a free and creative society, and the historic strength of our democracy lies in its commitment to personal improvement and fulfillment. We need individualism but, at the same time, we must be mindful of the consequences of selfishness. It is appropriate, therefore, for educational institutions that are preparing students to be citizens in a participatory democracy to understand the dilemmas and paradoxes of an individualistic culture.

Just as we search culturally to maintain the necessary balance between private and public obligations, in education we seek the same end. The college, at its best, recognizes that, although we live alone, we also are deeply dependent on each other. Through an effective college education, students should become personally empowered and also committed to the common good.

PART

III

THE ACADEMIC

PROGRAM

5

LANGUAGE:
THE FIRST REQUIREMENT

The foundation for a successful undergraduate experience is proficiency in the written and the spoken word. Students need language to grasp and express effectively feelings and ideas. To succeed in college, undergraduates should be able to write and speak with clarity, and to read and listen with comprehension. Language and thought are inextricably connected and as undergraduates develop their linguistic skills, they hone the quality of their thinking and become intellectually and socially empowered.

When we speak of language we mean English. In an increasingly interdependent world, the mastery of a second or even a third language is an important collegiate goal. Still, the reality is that students will not be adequately prepared for American life if they cannot communicate effectively in English. The lack of this skill constitutes a formidable barrier that will severely limit a student's educational, social, and vocational options.

While language proficiency is the foundation of college-level education, we repeatedly heard faculty members complain that their students are unprepared to do college-level work. One frustrated professor put the problem this way: "Most of my freshman students are 'verbal,' but they can't clearly express an idea. As I read their papers I find some interesting thoughts scattered about, but frankly I have a tough time figuring out what they are trying to say!" A mathematics professor said: "There is a lot of talk around here about preparing more scientists and engineers, but the biggest problem I have with my students is getting them to read and write."[1]

The flood of complaints we heard about the language deficiencies of students was reinforced by our national survey. More than half the faculty nationwide rated the academic preparation of students at their institutions as only "fair or poor." This negative rating has increased 8 percentage points since 1976. Eighty-three percent of the faculty we surveyed also felt that today's high school students should be academically better prepared when they come to college and two thirds agreed that their institution "spends too much time and money teaching students what they should have learned in high school" (Table 10).

Faculty complaints are not new. Students have rarely lived up to the idealized expectations of their teachers. Two centuries ago, Charles Nisbet, an erudite and strict Calvinist who came to Dickinson College in Pennsylvania from Edinburgh in 1785, never did overcome his initial shock at the low state of American colleges and what he perceived to be the incompetence and indifference of his students. Nisbet wrote:

> The Rainy Weather by spoiling the Roads, has likeways retarded the Return of our Students, after the Vacation, so that I have waited this Week for them in vain. . . . Our Students are generally very averse to Reading or thinking, and expect to learn every thing in a short Time without Application. . . .[2]

Remediation has a long tradition too. In the nineteenth century, many colleges operated what were then called "preparatory departments" to provide secondary education before there were sufficient numbers of public high schools, as well as to deal with the deficiencies of many entering students.[3] But these departments were more like academies that offered content-rich courses—Greek, history, literature—to instruct students in precollege subjects unavailable to them in school. In contrast, remedial programs today teach incoming college students to read, write, and compute.

Table 10 Faculty Attitudes Toward Academic Standards and Student Quality in Four Types of Institutions, 1976–84

| | All Institutions | | | | Percent Agreeing in 1984: By Type of Institution | | | |
	1976	1984	Public	Private	Research University	Doctorate-Granting University	Comprehensive College	Liberal Arts College
The academic ability of the undergraduates at my institution is "fair or poor."	46	54	57	43	45	59	60	48
Teaching would be a lot easier here if students were better prepared before they were admitted.	NA	83	85	77	75	87	87	84
This institution spends too much time and money teaching students what they should have learned in high school.	NA	66	69	56	59	70	70	64
Present academic standards for undergraduate admissions should be "higher."	48	64	66	57	53	70	70	66
Present academic standards for bachelor's degrees should be "higher."	53	57	58	50	46	59	63	57

NA: Question not asked in 1976.

Source: The Carnegie Foundation for the Advancement of Teaching, National Surveys of Undergraduates, 1976 and 1984.

We are led to the inescapable conclusion that far too many of today's students lack a solid academic foundation—not just in their command of English, but in general education—and these deficiencies prove to be a serious barrier to academic progress. The faculty members, frustrated by the problem, often lower their expectations and, for relief, occasionally poke fun at student errors. Malapropisms and factual gaffes in students' work, passed around from professor to professor and even campus to campus, are a sure source of hilarity. Sadly, they also feed frustration, even cynicism, on campus.

As for the students, many have actually come to view college as a time for remediation. Alexander Astin of the University of California, Los Angeles, reports that in 1983 more than two out of every five freshmen said that going to college would "improve my reading and study skills," a figure that had nearly doubled in ten years. During the same period, the proportion of freshmen saying they will need tutoring when they get to college also has nearly doubled.[4]

Just how much time do colleges spend teaching students what they should have learned in school? The answer: quite a lot. Helen S. Astin, in reporting the situation at the University of California, Los Angeles, writes: "Though we admit only the top 12 percent of graduating high school seniors, half of all our new freshmen are placed in noncredit remedial math and English courses. The reality of working with underprepared students must confront everyone."[5]

A national survey of 250 higher education institutions revealed that 84 percent offer remedial courses in basic skills and roughly 15 percent of all freshmen at these colleges now attend at least one remedial class in English or mathematics.[6] In another national study, 85 percent of the colleges and universities surveyed agreed that the poor academic preparation of freshmen is either "very much" or "somewhat" a problem. Ninety-seven percent of these institutions evaluated the basic skills of incoming freshmen, and many are judged deficient: 28 percent in reading, 31 percent in writing, and 32 percent in mathematics.[7]

In our own study we found that all but two of our site visit colleges offer remedial work. The results are not encouraging. For example, we visited an 8 A.M. "developmental" English class at a southern college. The professor could not get students to volunteer answers to this question: Is the word "day" capitalized in "Christmas Day"? When it became obvious that the students simply wouldn't answer, and the teacher would have to take up the slack, she said, "You're either asleep or I'm explaining this fantastically well." Later, she told us, "We get all sorts of warm bodies in here. I've had students take this class three times."[8]

We conclude that American undergraduate education cannot be strengthened unless and until the academic deficiencies of entering students are candidly confronted. Top priority must be given to teaching English—essentially reading and writing—to incoming students who lack sufficient mastery of this basic academic tool. Failure to do so will leave them shockingly unprepared to do college-level work. This is unfair to both faculty and students.

As a first step, we urge that the reading and writing capability of all students be carefully assessed when they enroll. Those not well prepared in written and spoken English should be placed in an intensive, remedial course that meets daily during the first academic term. While offering credit, the course would not count toward graduation requirements. Students in this program should carry a reduced course load. It may be difficult for undergraduates to accept a course that doesn't meet graduation requirements at a time when nearly everything counts, but the problem is so serious, and the need is so great, that nothing less is good enough.

Almost all colleges already have a remedial program of some sort. But the academic gains of those enrolled have, at best, often been modest. Still, if the teaching time is concentrated, as we suggest, and if the teacher-to-student ratio is small, we remain convinced that a new and vigorous effort to overcome student deficiencies will be worth it.

While the need for remediational programs is a fact of life, we are convinced that the long-term answer is better precollegiate education. It is unacceptable to ask colleges to continue to play endless academic catch-up. Six weeks or six months of remedial work, even under the best of circumstances, cannot fully compensate for deficiencies that have built up during the previous twelve years of formal education.

What we need is better language training in the schools. We urge that every college and university enter into a partnership with surrounding schools to strengthen the teaching of English, especially in the early years. Colleges should work with schoolteachers to improve language teaching and the measuring of student progress. To pass a student from one grade to another *without* carefully monitoring and attending to his or her work perpetrates a cruel hoax. One failure leads to another; the student falls farther and farther behind and eventually may drop out or receive a meaningless diploma.

Young children have a special readiness for language. It is in the primary grades that they should learn to read and comprehend the main ideas in a written work, and write standard English sentences with correct structure, verb forms, punctuation, word choice, and spelling. Elementary school students should also learn to organize their thoughts around a topic, and present ideas orally, both in casual discussion and in more formal presentations.

Students, as they move to high school, should learn to write more clearly, read with greater comprehension, listen with more discrimination, speak with more precision, and, through critical thinking, develop the capacity to apply old knowledge to new concepts. We believe these goals can be more successfully achieved as college professors and high school teachers work together, through language workshops and year-round collaboration.

Just as high schools build on the early years, colleges must build on secondary education. Therefore, we recommend that all college freshmen, not just those with special problems, begin their undergraduate experience with a year-long course in English, with emphasis on writing. Clear writing leads to clear thinking; clear thinking is the basis of clear writing. Writing holds us responsible for our words and ultimately makes us more thoughtful human beings. As students put their ideas on paper, they improve their understanding and discover both the discipline and joy of self-expression. Guided by a good teacher, all students can become better writers, and in the process thinking becomes more precise.

We also underscore the point that good English usage must be reinforced by every professor in every class. We found that most college courses outside the English department do not give priority to writing. Examinations are usually restricted to multiple-choice answers, filling in blanks, and writing short summary statements. At one leading university, the writing skill of students majoring in science regressed from their freshman to their senior year, "since they received so few writing assignments and often lacked an incentive even to express themselves in complete sentences."[9]

"Writing across the curriculum" has become a popular label that makes an important point. The entire college, not just the English department, must help develop the student's capacity to weigh evidence, integrate knowledge, and express ideas with clarity and precision. Unless this occurs, gains will be lessened, if not reversed. We repeat, writing assignments and careful evaluation of writing should be made essential elements of every course.

The Bay Area Writing Project began in 1973 at the University of California, Berkeley, cooperating with surrounding schools with a modest grant from the National Endowment for the Humanities. Now it has evolved into the National Writing Project, with 117 university-based sites in forty-four states and in Canada, England, Finland, Sweden, and Australia. The purpose is to help teachers improve their teaching of writing. Teachers use their summer in-service training as a model for use in their classrooms as well as to instruct other teachers during the school year.[10] This procedure, directed originally toward teachers in the schools, has been adapted for use in higher education. College faculty should work with colleagues to critique examples of student writing and improve their own teaching, too.

At the University of Wisconsin at Madison, Professor Alger Doane has created "the writing studio" to give freshmen a better sense of the audience for whom they write. Students meet in groups of four and write for each other, rather than for the teacher. They assign themselves topics from daily journals and bring writing samples to each meeting. They work together on criticisms and revisions. Doane says "the students immediately begin to show in their writing such features as purpose, audience-directed organization, and clarity."[11]

Brown University offers the Writing Fellows Program, in which undergraduate tutors review the writing of fellow students in all subjects, not just English. At the request of professors, their tutors are assigned to classes, where they read papers, commenting on style and organization. Following this critique, students rewrite their papers and submit both the original and the revision to professors for final evaluation.[12]

The University of Texas at Austin has a language sequence that extends throughout the entire undergraduate program. Freshmen enroll in a composition course that includes the mechanics of language and basic rhetorical principles. The sophomore course is an introduction to British, American, or world literature. Juniors take a writing course in which the subject matter is drawn from their academic major. Seniors have a heavy technical writing component in which they direct their writing to an expert in their field.[13]

Eight years ago, the faculty of the College of Literature, Science, and the Arts at The University of Michigan approved new writing requirements for students from registration to graduation. After an evaluation of an essay required of all freshmen, the student is placed in a small tutorial class, an introductory composition class, or a group exempted from lower-division writing requirements. About 80 percent of the freshmen at Michigan are assigned to the introductory composition class. Another notable feature of the Michigan program is that all students must fulfill a thirty-six-page writing requirement in their major field during the junior or senior year.[14]

Professors at Michigan are now carrying the gospel of good writing to the schools. A school-college writing network extends all across the state.[15] What began as a pilot program has expanded, and today two hundred high schools are participants in this comprehensive language project.[16]

While stressing writing, we also urge that oral communication be an important part of the freshman language course. Historically, the study of the spoken word, or rhetoric, as it was once called, has been an essential element of education. The importance of speech is reflected in the classic works of Aristotle and Cicero. In the colonial period declamation was required of every student every year. Sophomores had a course on forensics and, before they graduated, seniors were expected to pass an oral examination.

In recent years the value of disciplined oral discourse has declined. At a leading private university in the Southeast, three fourths of the students in a senior course agreed that they could have completed a baccalaureate program at the institution without having ever spoken in class.[17] It should be remembered that we speak more than we write. Throughout our lives we judge others, and we ourselves are judged, by what we say and how we speak. The information age raises to new levels of urgency the need for all students to be proficient in the use of the spoken as well as the written word.

There remains a final consideration. Language study means much more than the mastery of technical procedures. Words are not merely formal tools; they represent the shared knowledge of a culture without which the potential for social cohesion is diminished. Therefore, the use of written and spoken symbols takes on meaning only as students are well informed and have important ideas to convey. We agree with E. D. Hirsch, Jr., professor of English, University of Virginia, that true language literacy is achieved only through "cultural literacy."[18]

In the eighteenth century, Dr. Samuel Johnson confidently assumed he could predict the basic core of knowledge possessed by an educated person, whom he called "the common reader."[19] Today it is hard to achieve agreement on the essential information to be shared, on what all students should know, and on what schools and colleges should teach as a part of common learning. But the task must be pursued. Without commonly held experiences and traditions we cannot communicate effectively regardless of the technical correctness of our language.

The undergraduate college has a unique mission to fulfill. The goals must be to affirm diversity and to explore, through language study, the commonalities as well.

6

GENERAL EDUCATION:
THE INTEGRATED CORE

Can the American college, with its fragmentation and competing special interests, define shared academic goals? Is it possible to offer students, with their separate roots, a program of general education that helps them see connections and broadens their perspective?

Today's undergraduates are products of a society in which the call for individual gratification booms forth on every side while the claims of community are weak. No less influential are the claims of job training, even at the cost of education for citizenship. A comment by a sophomore at a private southern university reflected the view of many with whom we spoke: "The main thing on everybody's mind right now is doing well enough to get out of college and get a job." The editor of the college paper said, "During the past few years students at this place seem to be a lot more interested in their personal plans than about what's happening in the world outside."[1]

Colleges exacerbate this tendency toward self-preoccupation and social isolation. We found during our study that general education is the neglected stepchild of the undergraduate experience. Colleges offer a smorgasbord of courses, and students pick and choose their way to graduation.

Too many campuses, we found, are divided by narrow departmental interests that become obstacles to learning in the richer sense. Students and faculty, like passengers on an airplane, are members of a community of convenience. They are caught up in a journey with a procedural rather than a substantive agenda. Faculty agree on the number of credits for a baccalaureate degree, but not on the meaning of a college education. Students, geared toward job training, complete courses, but general education is something to "get out of the way," not an opportunity to gain perspective.

When we asked undergraduates if general education course requirements should be raised, only one subject on the list, computer science, received strong support. History got the least backing (Table 11). Reflecting a predominant mood, a freshman said: "This year I have all these 'general education' courses to complete. I wish I could concentrate on what I really need to get a job."[2]

One professor, who has been teaching since 1961, summarized his view of today's students this way: "Most are polite and quiet. They don't challenge. Only a few march to a different drummer. They know that, even with effort, they may not attain the economic standing of their parents and past graduates. They are out to get a job, and they are willing to conform."[3]

Table 11   General Education Requirements: The Student View

	Percent Agreeing the College Should Require More		
	Total	Public	Private
Computer science	74	75	71
English composition	46	47	43
Mathematics	45	46	40
Science	34	35	28
Foreign language	34	35	30
The arts	28	28	26
Literature	26	27	22
History	24	25	21

Source: The Carnegie Foundation for the Advancement of Teaching, National Survey of Undergraduates, 1984.

But this is not the whole story. The picture is more mixed. While students are pulled by demands of a career and private concerns, they also spoke to us, often with deep feeling, about the need to put their own lives in perspective. We found a longing among undergraduates for a more coherent view of knowledge and, in quiet moments, they wondered aloud whether getting a job and getting ahead would be sufficiently fulfilling.

We also discovered that undergraduates, while drawn to their major, still are enthusiastic about those general education courses where great teachers link learning to contemporary issues. Almost without exception, classes such as these attract large crowds, a response that has nothing to do with showmanship or easy grading. Rather, it reflects an eagerness on the part of students to be taken seriously, to be well taught, and to be helped to define their larger commitments.

At one college in our study, an experimental core curriculum was being discontinued because it was too costly. It was the students who fought to keep it going. A junior said, "This is a liberal arts school, and this program really helped me get a well-rounded education." Another student told us: "This program stretched my mind. Without these general education requirements I would not have read important books."[4]

In our national survey, when we asked undergraduates how they felt about the overall contribution of general education, about three fourths of them said it "add(s) to the enrichment of other courses I have taken," and "help(s) prepare me for lifelong learning." A sizable percentage also felt that general education is *not* irrelevant "to the subjects that interest me most" and more than two thirds (68 percent) agreed that general education helps prepare people for jobs (Table 12). These responses may not constitute a ringing vote of confidence; still, they suggest that today's students are ambivalent. While concerned about careers, they also feel that education, at its best, should be something more than preparation for a job.

Table 12 Student View of General Education Courses at Public and Private Colleges and Universities: 1976 and 1984

	Percent Who Agree					
	Total		Public		Private	
	1976	1984	1976	1984	1976	1984
They add to the enrichment of other courses I have taken.	76	73	74	73	81	77
They help prepare me for lifelong learning.	NA	73	NA	72	NA	76
They are *irrelevant* to the subjects that interest me most.	31	38	33	38	26	35
They do *not* help prepare people for jobs.	32	32	32	33	28	28
They are mainly of interest to students planning to teach.	29	NA	30	NA	27	NA

NA: Question not asked in that year.

Note: In 1976, the above questions were addressed to courses in the humanities (e.g., English, history, and philosophy), as opposed to "general education" courses, as was the case in 1984.

Source: The Carnegie Foundation for the Advancement of Teaching, National Surveys of Undergraduates, 1976 and 1984.

Andrew Hacker, professor of political science at Queens College, City University of New York, in a thoughtful review of higher education writes about the deeper yearnings we found among students, a seriousness that is often masked by the training and credentialing functions that dominate campus life. Hacker states: "I am certainly prepared to grant that young people today do not read as much or as deeply as their elders would like. . . . Still, it would be a mistake to discount the intelligence and awareness of young people because many fail to express themselves coherently. They do possess a body of knowledge and understanding, and a politics as well, that will have to be uncovered and inspired if higher learning is to survive with any vitality in America."[5]

Given the push toward vocationalism and the fragmentation of academic life, we find it remarkable that the vision of common learning remains so powerful a part of the baccalaureate experience, not just among students, but, even more perhaps, among faculty and administrators. In our national survey of one thousand chief academic officers, more than half reported that, during the past five years, their commitment to general education has increased; only a small percentage said it has declined. These officials feel the same holds true for faculty. Among students, the increase in support for general education has, in the opinion of these administrators, been less substantial (Table 13).

Table 13   Perception of Academic Officers About Commitment to General Education, 1980–85

	Percent Reporting Status of Commitment		
	Decreased	Unchanged	Increased
Administration	3	39	58
Faculty	5	39	56
Students	15	60	25

Source: The Carnegie Foundation for the Advancement of Teaching, Survey of Chief Academic Officers, 1985.

Today, 95 percent of all four-year colleges offer some form of general education.[6] And since 1970, requirements in English, philosophy, Western civilization, third-world courses, and international education have modestly increased. The greatest increases have been in computer literacy, mathematics, and the arts. However, during the same period, foreign language and physical education requirements were reduced. Even with these changes, it should be noted that only three subjects—English, math, and the arts—are required by 60 percent or more of the colleges (Table 14).

Current trends are encouraging. We are impressed by the seriousness of students as well as by the resiliency of general education, for which the death knell has sounded more than once. Still, we are left with doubts about the quality of today's general education movement. During campus visits we found curriculum tinkering rather than genuine reform. We found that narrowly focused courses in English, science, and history often were easily relabeled "general education." And protecting departmental turf often seemed more important than shaping a coherent general education program.

Consider one example. A large western university in our study

Table 14 Course Requirements for General Education, 1970 and 1985

| | Percentage of Colleges Requiring at Least One Course in Selected Subjects | | |
Course	1970	1985	Change
English composition	77	85	+8
Physical education	59	51	−8
Mathematics	49	67	+18
The arts	44	60	+16
Philosophy/theology	44	50	+6
Foreign languages	42	34	−8
History of Western civilization	40	45	+5
International/global education	4	14	+10
Third world studies	3	7	+4
Computer literacy	1	21	+20

Source: The Carnegie Foundation for the Advancement of Teaching, Survey of Chief Academic Officers, 1985.

had abandoned all campus-wide requirements during what one administrator called "the chaos of the 1960s." There was, according to the dean of the college of liberal arts, "a kind of general understanding that students probably ought to have two semesters of English." Beyond that, they were on their own.[7]

Troubled by this lack of direction, the academic vice-president, in 1980, appointed a university-wide committee to look at the status of undergraduate education. After two years of study this committee, called the Commission on the Improvement of Undergraduate Education, submitted a report that began as follows:

> The university's undergraduate program has no common requirements. To some extent, this lack of a clear university-wide statement of expectations reinforces a perception that education is a collection of disciplines rather than the pursuit of a common goal. Further, in our judgment, the lack of any statement to a student about our expectation diminishes the student's perception of the importance of integrating a body of knowledge.[8]

In response, the commission, in a typical campus maneuver, called for the creation of yet another blue-ribbon committee, to define the core curriculum. Although this new group has met regularly since July 1982, progress has been glacial. When we were on the campus two years later, the only positive step that had been taken was a proposal to add requirements in English and mathematics. "We have a very distinguished group," a committee member told us, "but the work hasn't been very distinguished."[9]

Recently, the committee floated the idea of adding a foreign language requirement to general education and introducing a cluster of required "theme" courses. The suggestion predictably generated lively debate. One science professor remarked to our researcher, "I'm not opposed to a core curriculum in principle, but I think requiring a foreign language is unrealistic—one of my colleagues characterized it as something that would wind up in the joke column of *The New Yorker*. As for the 'themes' proposal, I have more sympathy with that intellectually, but I don't think it will fly either. There is too much disagreement around here about what the foundations of knowledge should be to support any requirement that is tightly structured."[10]

The only "realistic answer" to more general education, we were told by this professor, "is a gradual tightening of current requirements. There is no need for radical alteration. I think some members of the committee are just being hypocritical about wanting to go all the way with a series of required courses for everyone. They know that a reform like that would be institutional suicide. We'd have departmental warfare. Let's be realistic."[11]

The chair of the committee did not appear chagrined by the compromises and delays. "We're simply up against typical campus roadblocks." While remaining optimistic, he also reminded us, "There are a lot of forces working against general education—the fear of upsetting enrollments, disagreements about the meaning of liberal education—and most important perhaps, the problem of trying to design new thematic courses within a tight academic structure."[12]

The faculty at another mid-sized university we visited was more successful. A new curriculum was approved. The catalog states that, through this program, students become "well-educated, thoughtful, and responsible human beings, understanding themselves and the world around them."[13] But we found a disturbing gap between high expectations and reality. The "distribution" requirement now in place is typical of the programs at over 90 percent of the colleges and universities in the nation. All students at this college must now complete a course in English and mathematics, and at least one semester in foreign language. Beyond this, students select thirty units of credit from literally dozens of other courses spread among the humanities, natural sciences, and social science divisions.

On the surface, the new distribution arrangement seems rational and well balanced. Looking closer, we discovered that the natural sciences requirement can be met with courses that range from agricultural engineering to genetics to health education. In humanities, students can take anything from architectural history to Italian to philosophy. In the social sciences, course choices include dozens of options, from political science to sociology to economics.[14]

Each course, standing alone, may be first-rate. But it stretches the imagination to say that a blend of Italian, health education, and economics—or most of the other randomly selected combinations we observed—offers a general education worthy of the name. Through such a program, undergraduates pick and choose their way to graduation, using what the food service people call the "scramble system." This cafeteria-like arrangement offers a smattering of courses. Students move from one narrow department requirement to another, rarely discovering connections, rarely seeing the whole.

We conclude that general education urgently needs a new breath of life. More coherence is required to relate the core program to the lives of students and to the world they are inheriting. There is a need for students to go beyond their separate interests and gain a more integrated view of knowledge and a more authentic view of life.

In every field of study there is content to be covered—basic books and primary documents, the experiences of outstanding people, the ideas and events that have shaped the discipline. Students should study this content. Still, the great obstacle to general education is the fragmentation and specialization of the academy.

Academics live, as Michael Polanyi has reminded us, in "overlapping neighborhoods."[15] And general education is not complete until the subject matter of one discipline is made to touch another. Bridges between disciplines must be built, and the core program must be seen ultimately as relating the curriculum consequentially to life.

To achieve these ends, we suggest as one possible approach *the integrated core.* By the integrated core we mean a program of general education that introduces students not only to essential knowledge, but also to connections across the disciplines, and, in the end, to the application of knowledge to life beyond the campus. The integrated core concerns itself with the universal experiences that are common to all people, with those shared activities without which human relationships are diminished and the quality of life reduced.

In a complex, interdependent world we simply cannot afford to graduate students who fail to place their knowledge and lives in perspective. To deny our relationship with one another and with our common home, Earth, is to deny the realities of existence. Frank H. T. Rhodes, president of Cornell University, affirms the goal we have in mind. What we need, Rhodes said, "is not some new core curriculum based on the great books, not a new Chinese menu of distribution requirements . . . but rather a way to link the humanities directly to the concerns of humanity."[16]

We are encouraged by the prospect that, today, new academic alliances are being formed and that departmental majors are interdisciplinary insofar as knowledge crosses intellectual boundaries. Sociologists, psychologists, biologists, and chemists are seeking answers to similar questions. New disciplines are emerging at the points where old ones are converging. Literary critics use structuralist and psychological techniques; historians use anthropology and demography; linguists use semiotics; the theatrical arts show all these kinds of influences; there are similar crossovers in the sciences. The anthropologist Clifford Geertz, of the Institute for Advanced Study at Princeton, has gone so far as to describe these shifts in the world of scholarship as "an important change in the way we think about the way we think."[17]

Thus, the integrated core, while rooted in the disciplines, means overcoming departmental narrowness. It means a curriculum that encourages students to venture "across the disciplinary boundaries but not without a map in hand," to use Ann Hulbert's helpful formulation.[18] As students relate the content of one course to another, they begin to make connections, and in so doing gain a more integrated view of knowledge and a more authentic view of life.

We may accept the idea of an integrated core, but this is only the beginning. The crucial step is to translate the purpose into practice. What are common themes that cut across the disciplines? As one approach, we suggest seven areas of inquiry that, we believe, can relate the curriculum to experiences common to all people. Specifically, the following academic framework for general education may be useful:

- Language: The Crucial Connection
- Art: The Esthetic Experience
- Heritage: The Living Past
- Institutions: The Social Web
- Science: The Natural World
- Work: The Value of Vocation
- Identity: The Search for Meaning

It seems clear to us that an exploration of these universal experiences would be useful for helping students better understand themselves, their society, and the world of which they are a part. Here, then, are the themes we suggest.

Language: The Crucial Connection. The sending and receiving of sophisticated messages set human beings apart from all other forms of life. As humans, we take infinite pains to reflect on and interpret our experiences. We capture feelings and ideas with symbols and send them on to others through a process we call language. Language, in its many manifestations, is at the heart of understanding who we are and what we might become. What are the theories of the origins of language? How do symbol systems shape the values of a culture? How has language, through great literature, enriched our lives and enlarged our vision? What are the possibilities and problems introduced by the information revolution? Learning about the power of language in the human experience and becoming proficient in more than one language are, we believe, essential aspects of the integrated core.

> Cornell University offers a course called "Signs and Communication" that investigates how language relates to particular cultural codes; it identifies these codes, and explores how they work. The goal is to examine the symbol systems human beings use and investigate how language differs from one culture to another. Topics in the course include: the study of language, body language and signals, and social rituals. There is also a study of literature, television advertising, computer language, and architectural signs.[19]

> At Brown University, undergraduates can enroll in a course entitled "Language and Man." The course explores the nature of language and its role in human life. Among the areas covered are language theory, the biological foundations of language, the history and evolution of language, dialects, and language in social context. Students also examine how children acquire language, explore ethnicity and its relation to language, and examine linguistic features common to all languages.[20]

Art: The Esthetic Dimension. There are human experiences that defy the power of words to describe them. To express our most intimate, most profoundly moving feelings and ideas we use a more sensitive, more subtle language we call the arts. Music, dance, and the visual arts are no longer just desirable, they are essential. And the integrated core should reveal how these symbol systems have, in the past, affirmed our humanity and illustrate how they remain relevant today. Students need to understand the unique ability of the arts to affirm and dignify our lives and remain the means by which the quality of a civilization can be measured.

> Northeastern University offers a lower-division course entitled "Art and Society" that explores how societal forces and political philosophies are reflected in or are stated through the visual arts, particularly through painting and architecture. After a broad overview of several significant historical eras, the course focuses on the impact of these expressions during the past two centuries.[21]

> "What the Arts Have Been Saying Since 1800" is a course offered by the humanities division at Wake Forest University. Taught by a professor of history, the course is described as "an experiment in developing interpretive judgment and insight" for painting, music, and literature. Topics include "The Perception of Self," "The Perceived Loss of God," "Emerson and Art," and "The Problem of the Sinister in Art." Readings include works of Henry James, Goethe, T. S. Eliot, Edith Wharton, and Nadine Gordimer. The teacher of the course told us: "I consider all art as history. I want students to develop the capacity to perceive what a work of art is telling us about its time, what the creator was saying through his art."[22]

Heritage: The Living Past. The human species uniquely has the capacity to recall the past and anticipate the future. Through these remembrances and anticipations today's reality is shaped. In an age when planned obsolescence seems to make everything but the fleeting moment remote and irrelevant, the study of history can strengthen awareness of tradition, of heritage, of meaning beyond the present, without which there is no culture. It is imperative that all students learn about the women and men and the events and ideas that have contributed consequentially to our own history and to other cultures, too.

> The University of Southern Maine has offered an interesting course entitled "Three Crises in Western Culture: Civilization on Trial."

It examined three points in history when our view of the world and the understanding of our place in it profoundly changed. The three events studied were Socrates' trial in 399 B.C., the trial of Galileo in 1633, and the trial of Joseph K. in Franz Kafka's *The Trial*. Original writings were central to the study. Students read such works as Plato's *Apology*, Aeschylus' *Eumenides*, Freud's *On Dreams*, and Kafka's *The Trial*. [23]

Saint Anselm College, a four-year institution in Indiana, has a cluster of courses built on the theme "Portraits of Human Greatness." This interdisciplinary program, which views general education from a historical perspective, focuses on moral and ethical questions surrounding selected periods in history and studies the vocation of influential people. Two freshmen core courses at Saint Anselm cover nine ways by which "human greatness" historically has been described—from ancient times to the present. Recent units include a study of the warrior, the prophet, the philosopher, the lawgiver, the disciple, the knight, the townsman, and the medieval scholar, and a unit on Dante's *The Divine Comedy*, which is used to debate questions of God and humanity. Two other courses focus on the lives of noteworthy individuals. Most recently students studied Michelangelo, Martin Luther, Queen Elizabeth I, Cervantes, Pascal, Thomas Jefferson, Beethoven, Darwin, Lenin, Gandhi, Sartre, and Pope John XXIII. [24]

Institutions: The Social Web. Institutions make up the social fabric of life. We are born into institutions, we pass much of our lives in them, and institutions are involved when we die. No integrated core has been successful if it has not acquainted students with the major institutions—the family, the church, legislative and judicial bodies, for example—that make up our world. The curriculum we have in mind would look at the characteristics of institutions: how they come into being, grow strong, become oppressive or weak, and sometimes fail. The successful approach will always ask what institutions have to do with us, how we are influenced by them, and how we can direct our institutions toward constructive ends.

The University of Chicago offers an undergraduate course entitled "Presidential Government in America." Students explore the background, origins, and evolution of the executive branch of government; the personalities, ideologies, and leadership of selected presidents; the ways in which these leaders implement their policies; and the relationship of the president to his political and institutional environment, including Congress, the courts, public opinion, interest groups, and party and electoral politics.[25]

At Hampshire College, seniors are asked to complete a year-long project, roughly equivalent to honors theses. Through this self-directed study, students often explore in depth a single institution. Recently, one student studied a small community in Washington State that was trying to make decisions about environmental problems and a proposal to locate a ski resort there. The study was successful in pulling together environmental, ecological, and sociological information.[26]

Skidmore College offers a course called "The City." A variety of disciplinary perspectives is employed to help students explore urban life as well as some of the myths we hold about the metropolis. The course uses case studies to explore patterns of city life. The aim is to provide students with a general understanding of the nature of cities and a knowledge of the problems and questions confronting particular metropolitan areas today.[27]

Science: The Natural World. No core of learning is complete without introducing students to the ordered yet symbiotic nature of the universe. For this discovery, science is the key. It is through science that students explore the elegant underlying patterns of the natural world and begin to understand that all elements of nature are related. General education also should include a study of how science and technology are joined, and consider the ethical and social issues that have resulted from this merger. Scientific literacy for all students must be one of the college's most urgent and essential goals.

At Harvard University, the paleontologist Stephen Jay Gould teaches a course called "History of the Earth and of Life." The course includes a discussion of the historical development of scientific theories about the planet's history and moves to the physical history of Earth, examining plate tectonics, planetary geology, the beginnings of the continents, atmospheres and oceans, and the concept of continental drift. Biological history, another part of the course, focuses on Darwin's theory and its use as a model for the history of life.[28]

At Carleton College, the general education curriculum includes "The Rise of Modern Science," a course that covers the beginnings of science in the sixteenth and seventeenth centuries. After introducing students to the Aristotelian science, from which a transition was made, the course focuses on the writings of Galileo, Bacon, Newton, and others, illustrating both the mathematical and the experimental aspects of the new science. As the catalog puts it, "Both the breadth of approach and the subject matter make the course particularly suited as an introduction to the fundamentals of a liberal education."[29]

"Great Ideas in Science" is a general education course at The College of St. Catherine, in Saint Paul, Minnesota. This basic course focuses on scientific principles and the structure of the natural world. Students study concepts of matter, atomic and nuclear structure, and statistical mechanics, and the way these principles were determined. Ideas explored include general and specific relativity, radioactivity, the Big Bang theory of creation, and cosmography.[30]

Wellesley College has a course, "Technology and Society in the Third World," that looks at the impact of technology on developing nations. Recently students examined the Bhopal disaster and the "Green Revolution." One student said she had always thought of "high tech" development as a boon to underdeveloped countries. After taking the course, she knows "tractors require spare parts and gasoline, and that can promote greater dependence on the industrial powers." And she would be more inclined to question the long-term effects of a particular technology, not just the immediately visible ones.[31]

Work: The Value of Vocation. Except for a handful of individuals, no one can choose not to work. Everything we know about society suggests that work choices are exceedingly important in shaping the values and social relations of a time. The characteristics of a culture can, in fact, be defined by looking at work: who works; what work is valued; how it is rewarded; how do people use their leisure time? In an era when "rampant careerism" is alleged in every quarter, it is important for colleges to help students to consider the universal experiences of producing and consuming, and put their work in larger context.

Hamline University offers a general education course entitled "The Workplace: Experience and Reflection." The course is a winter interterm seminar in which the class meets daily to explore the ethical, esthetic, and historical aspects of work. Then, during the spring semester, students work at off-campus sites arranged by the career planning and placement office. The idea is to give undergraduates an experience in work related to their fields. Some jobs, for example, will be in historical societies and art museums. While they are working, students meet biweekly as a group, to reflect on their experiences. The course is team taught.[32]

"Work and Culture" is offered by the anthropology department at Central Connecticut State University. The course begins with an examination of the relationship between work and human evolution, including the development of tools and their influence on human physical and social evolution. Students compare work in agrarian and modern industrial societies. They look at how age, sex, and class dictate the sort of work one does in different cultures. Students consider how and why people make work choices. How does work influence their lives, their state of mind? How do they interpret the meaning of their work?[33]

Identity: The Search for Meaning. Ultimately, the aim of common learning is the understanding of oneself and a capacity for sound judgment. Knowledge is significant when it shows us who we are as individuals and as citizens, and touches the hopes and fears that make each of us both unique beings and a part of corporate humanity. Sound judgment at its best brings purpose and meaning to human lives. Who am I? What is the purpose of life? What are my obligations to others; what are theirs to me? The answers to these questions are notoriously elusive, but the questions are impossible to avoid. They are an essential part of an integrated core, a part of the search for identity and the quest for meaning.

> Princeton University, through its Program in Humanistic Studies, offers a course, "Psychology and Religion," that deals with issues of identity and the search for meaning by focusing on psychological theories such as Skinner's behaviorism and its relationship to the methodologies of James, Jung, and Erikson, plus Biblical texts drawn from Exodus and Job, and the religious perspectives of Luther, Buber, Tillich, and others.[34]

> At Randolph-Macon College, Ashland, Virginia, in the philosophy department a course called "Ethics" features readings from J. S. Mill, Kant, and ancient Greek writers, as well as modern ethicists. It seeks to clarify the students' thoughts on such issues as what sorts of persons we should be, what kinds of principles and actions we should affirm. Questions central to the inquiry include: What is a moral situation, a moral or ethical judgment or point of view? What are rights; who has them? Can they be justified? What are the implications of different ethical theories for the selves we are?[35]

In the shaping of an integrated core, we have suggested seven areas of inquiry that may, if properly developed, help students understand that they are not only autonomous individuals but also members of a human community. To weave these areas together can, we believe, enrich the lives of students, broaden their perspective, and relate learning to wider concerns. Some of these themes may call for special interdisciplinary or thematic courses. In other instances, existing departmental courses in English, history, sociology, or science, if broad in their purpose, may effectively fill the bill.

There are other strategies, of course. The essential goals of general education can be achieved in a variety of ways. In our national survey of academic deans we asked them to identify a college or university in the nation where, in their opinion, general education is succeeding. The five most frequently cited institutions were, in the order named: Harvard University, University of Chicago, Alverno College (Wisconsin), St. Joseph's College (Indiana), and Brooklyn College of the City University of New York. In a review of these widely approved and yet greatly varied programs, we found many courses—both discipline based and interdisciplinary—that focused on the core fields of language, science, social institutions, history, the arts, and the rest.

But here we add a word of caution. It would be a mistake, we believe, to slip existing courses into a general education curriculum unexamined. The title of a course may sound appropriate, and the catalog description may be appealing. But the way the course is actually taught may, in fact, promote specialized, not general, education. The central question is not whether the curriculum selected is old or new, disciplinary or thematic—but whether students are helped to see integration across the disciplines and discover the shared relationship common to all people. In such a program, the academic disciplines should be viewed as a means to a larger end.

One other point. Thus far, we have spoken mainly of general education *courses*. But the goals of the integrated core can be achieved in other ways as well. We know of several colleges, for example, where general education seminars are held in residence halls and student lounges. At one college, week-long colloquia and a year-long convocation series are scheduled. Recently, Ohio Wesleyan University made a campus-wide commitment to study the theme of the nuclear threat. Special colloquia were held; lecturers came to campus; faculty helped students with special readings, joined them in seminars, and advised them as they completed a project—a film, a videotape, or an essay.[36] We suggest that all colleges set aside special days throughout the year when the campus, as a community, would bring faculty and students together from the separate departments to focus on topics related to the goals of common learning.

The mid-year term also may be used to enrich the integrated core. When the so-called 4-1-4 calendar was introduced about thirty years ago, it offered a marvelous opportunity for innovation. Although hundreds of institutions now have such a calendar, the inter-term is often simply a vacation period or a time when independent study is pursued. We urge that the mid-year period be considered a general education term and be used to explore integrative themes.

Eckerd College in Florida offers a course during its January term called "Continuity and Change," taught by a professor of economics and a recently retired executive of an international energy company. The emphasis is on technical changes in the last forty years, plus forces that have molded the business and corporate environment. Demographic, social, and ethical issues that are likely to affect the future of the economy and the general well-being of the nation, as well as the future of the students, are featured. The mid-term at the college offers integration.[37]

We repeat: General education is *not* a single set of courses. It is a program with a clear objective, one that can be achieved in a variety of ways. And while there may be great flexibility in the process, it is the clarity of purpose that is crucial.

In writing to a group of undergraduates, the late Charles Frankel, former chairman of the National Center for the Humanities, said: "If you have a liberal education . . . you will live at more than one level. You won't simply respond passively to events, and you won't be concerned about them *only* personally. At least sometimes you will see your fate, whatever it is, as an illustration of the human condition and of the destiny of man."[38] This is the vision of the integrated core.

Finally, the general education sequence, regardless of its structure, is not something to "get out of the way." Rather, it should, we believe, extend vertically, from the freshman to the senior years. And the integration of knowledge should also touch the major, as students move from depth to breadth and bring questions of value and meaning to their field of special study. In a properly designed baccalaureate program, general education and specialized education will be joined.

7

SPECIALIZATION:
THE ENRICHED MAJOR

"What's your major?"

If there were a contest for the most popular question on the American campus, that would be the winner. The latest edition of the *College Blue Book* lists more than six thousand different majors and the number is rapidly expanding. From Sun Belt colleges to universities in the Ivy League, careerism dominates the campus.

At most colleges in our study, we found the baccalaureate degree sharply divided between general and specialized education. Students overwhelmingly have come to view general education as an irritating interruption—an annoying detour on their way to their degree. They all too often do not see how such requirements will help them get a job or live a life.

This unhealthy separation between the liberal and the useful arts, which the curriculum and the faculty too often reinforce, tends to leave students poorly served and the college a weak and divided institution. We take the position that if the undergraduate experience is to be renewed, general and specialized education must be viewed as contributing to common, not competing, ends.

Most students agree that pursuing a special field of study, one that leads to a career, is the main reason for going to college—and for staying, too. Over a third of the undergraduates at public institutions and slightly fewer of those at private ones say that if college did not increase their prospects for employment they would drop out.[1]

The push toward career-related education has come to dominate most campuses and, during the past fifteen years, it has dramatically increased. At almost all colleges in our study, new vocational majors have been added and old ones have been split up into smaller pieces. One East Coast university had just one major in forestry in 1965. By 1975, forestry had become a separate college offering four different majors. By 1985, when we visited the institution, the college had seven majors in this division, including three specialties in horticulture alone: fruit and vegetable horticulture, ornamental horticulture, and turf-grass horticulture.[2]

Another university we visited offered only one major in business administration in 1965. The faculty, in response to marketplace demand, dramatically expanded the program. Last year we found not one, but twenty-one, business-related majors. Here's the list: administrative office management; business and office education; domestic public administration; employee services and industrial recreation; fashion merchandising; finance; foods and nutrition in business; general business; health services administration; international public administration; labor relations; management; management information systems; marketing; marketing and distributive education; occupational safety and health; operations management; organizational and mass communications; personnel management; professional accounting; and societal relations in business and industry.[3]

These examples reflect the pattern nationwide. Between 1968 and 1984, the percentage of baccalaureate degrees awarded in business, computer science, engineering, and the health professions increased, while the percentage of degrees awarded in traditional liberal arts fields, especially foreign languages and the physical and social sciences, went down along with education degrees, reflecting, among other things, changes in the job market and new career options for women (Table 15).

The shift toward business and away from the liberal arts has been described as the new vocationalism in higher education and, based on the preferences of today's students, it seems likely that, in the

Table 15 Baccalaureate Degrees in Selected Disciplines as a Percentage of Total Baccalaureate Degrees Conferred

	1968	1973	1978	1981	1984	Change 1968 to 1984
Biological sciences	5	5	6	5	4	−1
Business	13	14	18	22	24	11
Computer science*	0	0	1	2	3	3
Education	21	20	15	12	10	−11
Engineering	6	6	6	8	10	4
Fine arts	4	4	4	4	4	0
Foreign languages	3	2	1	1	1	−2
Health professions	3	4	7	7	7	4
Physical sciences	3	2	3	3	2	−1
Social sciences	19	17	12	11	10	−9

*Degrees in computer science were less than 1 percent of all baccalaureate degrees awarded in 1968 and 1973.

Source: U.S. Department of Education, National Center for Education Statistics, *Digest of Education Statistics, 1970*, p. 89; *Ibid.,* 1976, pp. 111–16; *Ibid.,* 1980, pp. 120–24; *Ibid.,* 1983–84, pp. 113–17; data for 1984, U.S. Department of Education, Center for Statistics, unpublished surveys of "Earned Degrees Conferred."

short term, this pattern will persist. In 1970, when entering freshmen were asked about their preferred majors, the largest percentage chose "arts and humanities." In 1985, the percentage choosing this field had declined by more than half. During the same period, physical science showed a similar decline. In contrast, the percentage of freshmen who identified business as their intended major increased from 16 to 27 percent. Today, business is the most popular field of undergraduate study (Table 16).

For years, "specialization" has been the watchword for employers, too. In spite of impressive speeches by corporate leaders, when it is recruitment time on campus, business and engineering majors are often chosen first. The director of career development at one college told us she had talked with an executive at the local manufacturing plant about placing a bright English major. The executive said he would not even talk to the woman until she had taken some business courses.[4]

Students, in their search for a secure future, have read the signals all too literally, and the liberal arts have taken a back seat to the more

Table 16   Percentage of Entering Freshmen Intending to Major in Selected Fields of Study, 1970–85

Intended Major	1970	1975	1983	1984	1985	Change 1970 to 1985
Arts and humanities	21	13	8	8	8	−13
Biological sciences	4	6	4	4	3	−1
Business	16	19	24	26	27	+11
Education	12	10	6	7	7	−5
Engineering	9	8	12	11	11	+2
Physical science	6	4	3	3	2	−4
Professional occupations*	X	X	14	14	13	−1
Social science	9	6	6	7	8	−1

*Includes architecture, home economics, library science, nursing, and related health professions.

X: Professional occupations category not comparable in years 1970 and 1975 with years later than 1980.

Source: Alexander Astin and associates, *The American Freshman: National Norms for Fall 1970* and other selected years (Los Angeles: Cooperative Institutional Research Program), 1970, p. 41; 1975, p. 44; 1983, pp. 46–47; 1984, pp. 48–49; 1985, pp. 48–49.

practical, career-related, training. But there are signals that the pendulum may be swinging back. "I sense a shift in interest toward people with more generalist backgrounds and less practical, specialized, technical training," said Christopher Shinkman, the former director of Stanford University's placement office. "Employers recently have begun looking harder for liberal arts people."[5]

A survey of 2,813 businessmen who require computer skills in their operations revealed that reading ability, reasoning skills, and personal enthusiasm rank far more importantly than technical training for new employees.[6] A study by Northwestern University shows that many major companies plan to increase their hiring of liberal arts graduates by some 20 percent.[7]

Caught in the crossfire of competing interests, many campuses still are torn between careerism and the goals of liberal learning. At one college we visited, members of the faculty complained bitterly about the way the baccalaureate degree, as one professor put it, "is now the property of the professional schools and controlled by accrediting committees." In contrast, a professor of marketing said, "I have nothing at all against students taking courses in literature and the arts. But those things they can pick up on their own later in life if they're interested. My students tell me what they're here for is to get a good practical education that will serve them in the working world."[8]

A history professor told us he was "deeply offended" by his college's policy of adding majors at "the whim" of local business interests. He said, "The administration is destroying any hope that this will become a respected educational institution. They are trying to create a multiversity, all things to all people, and when you do that, quality education suffers." In response, the president said "the college risks losing political support if it does not respond to community needs. If financial leaders want more business courses, we'll have more business courses."[9]

At another college an English professor described the conflict this way: "There really is the 'two cultures' phenomenon on this campus. The two sides have a hard time talking to each other. Today there is some superiority emanating from the technical side. They feel confident these days. And you hear it from students, too, who say their professors are continually speaking disparagingly about the humanities, degrading the people who teach it."[10]

The head of the faculty senate spoke still more bluntly: "It seems obvious that someone should bring together the humanities and technical faculty for a 'peace conference.' Everyone should be checked for weapons at the door. The amount of misunderstanding and hostility crackling between the 'two cultures' is amazing and, considering our liberal arts mission, probably destructive. Each side needs somehow to be convinced that they are working for similar objectives."[11]

In our national survey of faculty we found attitudes about specialized and general education split almost down the middle. On one hand, 45 percent of the faculty reported that they would prefer teaching courses that focused on "limited specialties," rather than those that covered a wide variety of material. On the other hand, about half the faculty said that undergraduate education in America would be improved if there were *less* emphasis on specialized training and more on liberal education. About 40 percent agreed that the typical undergraduate curriculum has suffered from the specialization of faculty members. Then again, about half the faculty said they prefer teaching students who have a clear idea of the career they will be taking (Table 17).

Table 17   Faculty Attitudes Toward Specialized Education

	Percent Who Agree
I prefer teaching courses which focus on limited specialties to those which cover a wide variety of materials.	45
Undergraduate education in America would be improved if there were less emphasis on specialized training and more on broad liberal education.	53
The typical undergraduate curriculum has suffered from the specialization of faculty members.	41
In my undergraduate courses I prefer teaching students with a clear idea of the career they will be taking.	47

Source: The Carnegie Foundation for the Advancement of Teaching, National Survey of Faculty, 1984.

This ambivalence reflects, we suspect, a deeper conflict among faculty over goals. We found, for example, that on some campuses, faculty opposed new career-related majors because they were considered "too novel" or "too new." Overlooked in such debates was the fact that most disciplines that now have status within the academy—modern languages, laboratory sciences, for example—were themselves once considered too novel for the academy to embrace. Professor Frederick Rudolph reminds us that at the turn of the century, "At [the University of] Chicago chemists fought zoologists over disputed scientific territory, and economists fought sociologists as both laid claim to statistics. History and classics fought for control of ancient history at Harvard."[12] We conclude that the "newness" of a proposed field of study is not a sufficient reason for its rejection, nor should tradition alone be used to justify holding to an existing major.

We also found a resistance to new majors not just because of newness, but because the graduates would work in less prestigious fields. We heard it argued, for example, that it is all right to prepare students to be doctors, but not nurses. To educate future college teachers is applauded, but to prepare students to teach in elementary school is considered a less worthy task. To dig ruins of the past as an archeologist is considered a respectable career objective, but to work with ruined lives in an urban jungle as a social worker is a less well-regarded field of study. Lost in these debates was the recognition that college graduates, instead of being demeaned by all but the prestigious professions, can, in fact, lift up a job and give it meaning.

But the most heated curriculum debates we encountered focused not on the newness or the status of a major, but on whether the proposed program was too "job-related." Here the battle lines were most sharply drawn. Many faculty members, especially those at liberal arts colleges, voiced the opinion that it is inappropriate for colleges to offer majors that are primarily "vocational." At one faculty meeting we attended, a science professor declared that the college would be "demeaned" if it offered programs that lead directly to a job. At a small college in the Northwest, the faculty recently voted down a proposed major in computer science. "It doesn't belong in the curriculum in the liberal arts. It's tied too closely to a job," we were told.[13]

Again, what we found missing in these discussions was the recognition that a university education has always been considered "useful." Samuel Eliot Morison reminds us that the first formal universities were "distinctly purposeful."[14] There was a utility to learning and students enrolled to prepare themselves for what was considered worthy work. The University of Salerno was a medical school and the universities that followed in its wake—Bologna, Paris, Oxford, Cambridge—offered only four courses of study— law, medicine, theology, and the arts. The first three were explicitly vocational, and law was the most popular of all the medieval studies.[15]

The practical nature of the medieval university was portrayed vividly by C. P. Snow in a short narrative history of Cambridge University. Students, he wrote, studied a curriculum that would seem to us "arid, valueless, just word chopping." They attended classes in "cold, comfortless, straw-strewn rooms," some "in bitter poverty and half starved." They did this for one motive; "if they could get their degree, jobs lay ahead. Jobs in the royal administration, the courts, the church; jobs teaching in the schools—the fees were not light, and the teachers made a good living. The training was in fact vocational, and jobs lay at the end."[16]

The point is that all students, regardless of their major, are preparing for productive work. As with engineering and business and computer science, a student who majors in English or biology or history will, it is assumed, someday become employed and use what he or she has learned for some useful end. Even the most traditional colleges expect their graduates to move on to careers. And a great embarrassment for a department occurs when its graduates "cannot get placed."

This is not to suggest that colleges become vocational schools; nor does it mean that every kind of career preparation is appropriate for the baccalaureate degree. In response to marketplace demands, many institutions are offering narrow technical training and providing credentialing for occupations, devoid of rich intellectual content. Therefore, in judging the merits of a major, the issue is not the newness, or status, or even the utility of the program. Rather, the basic test of a proposed major is this: Does the field of study have a legitimate intellectual content of its own and does it have the capacity to enlarge, rather than narrow, the vision of the student?

We conclude that career preparation in the undergraduate experience means more than a job. At its best, such an education will help students not only to be technically prepared but also to discover the personal and social significance of work. Thomas F. Green puts the challenge this way:

> . . . if we are to understand the relationship between education and work we need to make a *sharp distinction between work and job.* There is an enormous difference between the person who understands his career as a succession of jobs and a person who understands the succession of jobs he has held as all contributing to the accomplishment of some work. . . . Work is basically the way that people seek to redeem their lives from futility. It, therefore, requires the kind of world in which hope is possible, which is to say, the kind of world that yields to human effort.[17]

The challenge then is to enlarge lives by bringing meaning to the world of work. And the special task of the undergraduate college is to relate the values of liberal learning to vocation. Therefore, what we propose, as a centerpiece of the undergraduate experience, is the *enriched major.* By an *enriched major* we mean encouraging students not only to explore a field in depth, but also to help them put their field of special study in perspective. The major, as it is enriched, will respond to three essential questions: What is the history and tradition of the field to be examined? What are the social and economic implications to be understood? What are the ethical and moral issues to be confronted?

Here then is the heart of our curriculum proposal: Rather than view the major as competing with general education, we are convinced that these two essential parts of the baccalaureate program should be intertwined. Through such a curriculum the student can move from depth to breadth as departments put the specialty in larger context. If a major is so narrow and so technical that it *cannot* be discussed in terms of its historical and social implications, if the work in the proposed field of study cannot be a broadening experience, then the department is offering mere technical training that belongs in a trade school, not on a college campus, where the goal is liberal learning.

And yet we found that in many fields, skills have become ends.

Scholars are busy sorting, counting, and decoding. We are turning out technicians. But the crisis of our time relates not to technical competence, but to a loss of social and historical perspective, to the disastrous divorce of competence from conscience. Alfred North Whitehead wrote about "the unimportance—indeed, the evil—of barren knowledge."[18] Knowledge, Whitehead argued, becomes important only when we *use* it, and, we might add, apply it to humane ends.

Professionals in almost every field—doctors, journalists, lawyers, businessmen, computer specialists, biochemists, stockbrokers—once they begin to practice their craft, must respond to questions that relate not just to the "what" and "how" of the field, but to the "why" as well. Specialists must make judgments that are not only technically correct but also include ethical and social considerations. And the values professionals bring to their work are every bit as crucial as the particularities of the work itself.

But the foundation of an advanced service society is quality, not quantity. A television set is a complex instrument, but producing high-quality sets in large numbers is much easier than producing high-quality programming. Designing high-powered automobiles, fast trains, and supersonic airplanes requires technological skills, but we are far from designing environments and transportation systems that effectively serve human needs. And, given the escalating rates of divorces compared to happy, solid marriages, it looks as though putting a microwave oven in every kitchen is easier than having a congenial dinner.[19]

In an editorial titled "How to Make People Smaller Than They Are," Norman Cousins wrote:

> The doctor who knows only disease is at a disadvantage alongside the doctor who knows at least as much about people as he does about pathological organisms. The lawyer who argues in court from a narrow legal base is no match for the lawyer who can connect legal precedents to historical experience and who employs wide-ranging intellectual resources. The business executive whose

competence in general management is bolstered by an artistic ability to deal with people is of prime value to his company. For the technologist, the engineering of consent can be just as important as the engineering of moving parts.[20]

Can the undergraduate experience be viewed as an integrated whole? Again, it was Whitehead, in his famous essay "The Aims of Education," who declared that "there can be no adequate technical education which is not liberal, and no liberal education which is not technical. . . . Education should turn out the pupil with something he knows well and something he can do well."[21] We are confident that the goals of general education, when properly defined, can be accomplished through the major. The liberal and the useful arts can be brought together in the curriculum just as they inevitably must be brought together during life. Such linkage should be cultivated in all disciplines, and be exemplified in the lives of those who teach them.

Consider these examples: Students specializing in computer science might be introduced to the history of technology and the social impact of the information revolution. English majors could be asked to explore the roots of language and consider how symbol systems can be creatively used or dangerously abused. Those in architecture, genetics, industrial chemistry, and television production might be asked to examine the social and ethical implications of their work. The pre-engineering student would understand that beyond technical skills there are concerns for the physical environment to be considered.

During our study we found both good and bad examples. One college, for example, has a textile management major in which fifty-four semester hours of textile courses—"Yarn Structures and Form," "Textile Costing Inventory Control," and "Fabric Structure"—were required. Courses such as these consume about 40 percent of a student's time; business courses take another 16 percent. A total of 56 percent of the student's program is devoted to this major.[22]

It is difficult to believe that this laundry list of courses represents a legitimate discipline. Much of this can be better learned on the job, and specialized information is too often imparted without an intellectual framework. Course descriptions speak only of "skills"—the sort of statement one finds in trade school pamphlets and brochures. Nowhere is the student encouraged to view the specialty in larger context. As now organized and taught, the program does not make the grade as an enriched major.

In contrast, we found at a large state university a journalism major in which students are being offered breadth in a field that is often considered narrow. In this program there are courses on the history of communication and the ethics of journalism. The dean said, "I feel strongly that an undergraduate program is for people who are not experienced enough to be sure of what they want. Not all of the students here are primarily interested in journalism as a career. We have at least fifteen a year who go to law school. We do not owe a student just a ready-made formula for career training."[23]

Like this journalism major, the business major at another university is also known for its enrichment. "It's a big part of our reputation," says the Director of Undergraduate Programs. "As a faculty, we have decided, several times, to keep the undergraduate program very general, to look at the larger context, and not get down to the technical aspects of management. We don't want narrowly trained undergraduates—we think we're honing minds here. They should see business as a social enterprise."[24]

At Northeastern University, both humanities and professional school faculty have long been concerned with the narrow orientation of their students. The colleges of Pharmacy, Business Administration, and Criminal Justice have now each hired at least one humanist, and the social science departments have increased offerings in policy areas relevant to the professional schools. Communication between traditionally isolated colleges of the university has increased, and faculty research has developed out of themes presented in these new courses.[25]

Stanford University has a program in human biology that introduces students to policy problems, such as population and hunger, pollution, conservation of natural resources, and the costs and delivery of health care. In addition to traditional requirements in biology and statistics, students take either health or environmental policy courses and complete a supervised project that involves them in a community service agency. Faculty are drawn from the medical school and traditional departments of the university.[26]

Worcester Polytechnic Institute in Massachusetts has completely revised its undergraduate engineering program. The new "WPI Plan" is designed to educate "technological humanists." The institute states its educational philosophy as follows:

> The learning of facts without values can no longer be acceptable. Scientists and engineers must be able to evaluate the consequences of modern technology and of their own decisions in the world we live in. Social scientists and humanists, on the other hand, must develop a greater understanding of the basic forces of technology.
>
> We need people today who can understand both technology and its social implications, who understand their machines and also have an awareness of their place in the human spectrum. Specialization must be tempered with interdisciplinary breadth, for the solutions to the problems of our technological world demand minds of wide scope.[27]

Sir Eric Ashby, the noted British educator, wrote: "The path to culture should be through a man's specialism, not by by-passing it. . . . A student who can weave his technology into the fabric of society can claim to have a liberal education; a student who cannot weave his technology into the fabric of society cannot claim even to be a good technologist."[28]

As the major begins to intersect with the themes of common learning, students can return, time and time again, to considerations of language, heritage, social institutions, and the rest. At a college of quality when a major is so enriched, it leads the student from depth to breadth and focuses not on mere training, but on liberal learning at its best.

In the end, integrating the liberal and the useful arts depends every bit as much on people as on programs. Courses alone do not bring coherence. Faculty must provide the enlightening and integrative foundation so essential to a successful undergraduate experience. They should not only be devoted to their disciplines but also embody and exemplify in the classroom the spirit of a liberal education.

PART

IV

A TIME
TO LEARN

8

FACULTY:
MENTORS AND SCHOLARS

The curriculum does not carry the full burden of collegiate education. Teachers, of course, are critically important. Members of the faculty control the academic rules, shape the curriculum, and help create the climate for learning on the campus. Through their professional priorities and in their relationships with students, professors sustain or weaken the intellectual and social environment of the college.

At a time when college teaching seems to be more criticized than praised, we were impressed by the large number of faculty who are deeply committed to their tasks, and who talk enthusiastically about the satisfactions of teaching. These colleagues spoke often of liking undergraduates and generously gave time to students outside the classroom. One professor said: "It's great to see students come back and say they've used what we taught them. It's good to know that we have some influence on their future. If I didn't believe that, I wouldn't have gone into the academic profession in the first place."[1]

A history teacher described his job as "the best in the university." He enjoyed working with ideas, and felt the satisfaction that comes from being engaged in an important and rewarding task. But he hesitated when we asked him what it meant to be a college teacher. "At cocktail parties, people invariably ask what you do, and when I say I'm a professor, they say, 'Oh, do you teach?' . . . For some reason I feel I'd get more respect if I said I'm a scientist or scholar," he said. "They think teachers wear tweed jackets with patches on the elbows, puff on pipes while sitting with their feet on the desk listening to some kid verbalize the grass imagery in *Heart of Darkness.*"[2]

A psychology professor, who also spoke enthusiastically about his students, went on to say that "professionals on this campus are pulled in two directions. Teaching is important, we are told, and yet faculty know that research and publication matter most." A professor of English at a Midwest university made this comment: "We faculty members now find ourselves under attack at the very point which has always seemed most secure to us, and in which we have taken the most pride. Our fields of scholarly training and specialization are the basis of our claims to expert knowledge and hence to intellectual authority."[3]

There is, we found, a tension on most campuses over the priorities of teaching and research. Faculty members like to teach and yet the American professoriate has been profoundly shaped by the conviction that research is the cornerstone of the profession. James Morgan Hart, an American academic who studied at the universities of Berlin and Göttingen in the 1860s, described the model that influenced, with enduring consequences, higher education in this country. He wrote: "The [German] professor is not a teacher, in the English sense of the term, he is a *specialist* [emphasis added]. He is not responsible for the success of his students. He is responsible only for the quality of his instruction. His duty begins and ends with himself."[4]

The influence of the German professoriate, though not entirely successful in displacing the collegiate model, has shaped dramatically our academic culture. The explosive growth of knowledge that began in the nineteenth century led to academic specialization. The empirical values of science came to be considered essential for disciplined inquiry. And holders of the Ph.D. organized themselves, by academic disciplines, into departmental structures.

After World War II, competition for dollars and young scholars enormously increased as grants from Washington encouraged universities to put more and more emphasis on research. The curriculum proliferated. On many campuses, graduate programs overshadowed undergraduate education, despite the fact that undergraduate tuition was the lifeblood of the institution.

As universities became more research oriented, faculty members reduced their teaching commitments. More time was devoted to scholarly pursuits. The consequence is that, today, only 8 percent of the faculty at research universities and 19 percent at doctorate-granting universities spend eleven or more hours each week in undergraduate instruction. And at the research institutions, 26 percent of the faculty spend no time teaching undergraduates. In contrast, 38 percent of the faculty at liberal arts and 36 percent at comprehensive colleges spend at least eleven hours each week teaching undergraduates (Table 18).

Table 18 Average Number of Hours per Week Faculty Devote to Classroom Instruction in Undergraduate Courses (percent responding)

Type of Institution	None	1–4	5–10	11–20	Over 20
All institutions	14	21	38	25	2
Research universities	26	35	30	8	1
Doctorate-granting universities	14	24	41	19	2
Comprehensive universities and colleges	8	13	41	36	2
Liberal arts colleges	3	13	43	38	3

Source: The Carnegie Foundation for the Advancement of Teaching, National Survey of Faculty, 1984.

It is misleading, however, to think of the time devoted to teaching only in classroom hours. The time devoted to teaching also involves preparation time, the marking and evaluation of assignments, record keeping, and, of course, the time devoted to private consultation with students. If these hours are considered, the total picture is radically different.

Small liberal arts colleges may have a culture of their own. Faculty may teach more and spend more time with students. But even these institutions live in the shadow of the research university.

They value good teaching but are likely to reward most handsomely those members of the faculty who have scholarly reputations. A paper read at a national convention nets more praise than a splendid lecture to undergraduates. A published article in a prestigious journal or a major book is valued most of all. A senior professor at a small Midwest institution put it this way: "When I first came here we were told to spend time with students. To get tenure you had to teach. Now, every college professor under age sixty has felt the sting of contempt directed toward what was once called the 'vocation' of undergraduate teaching."[5]

This pressure to publish, while found to one degree or another in all types of institutions in our study, was especially apparent at those universities or doctorate-granting institutions that see themselves as "being in transition." The goal, as an administrator at one such institution put it, is "to be in the top twenty, or certainly in the top fifty." Meanwhile, the same institutions enroll large numbers of undergraduates, and members of the faculty—especially young faculty members—often feel caught in the middle.

Derek Jones, a popular teacher of German at a large public university in our study, exemplifies the problem of priorities unresolved. Jones came to his current assignment as a non-tenure-track instructor of German language and literature. After several years of teaching he was appointed assistant professor in a tenure-track position. Jones, who says he was never much interested in trying to publish in his specialty, spent most of his time teaching—and he taught well.

A typical year was 1981, in which—not counting summer courses—he taught thirty-seven hours of language classes, with 205 students enrolled. He supervised another twenty-four hours of classes taught by teaching assistants. In the fall semester, he taught two sections of elementary German, one section of intermediate German, one section of German conversation, and a graduate course on German-language teaching.

Jones also has been language coordinator of the German department for several years. In addition, he is undergraduate adviser for the department's majors, and he has led several student-faculty trips to Europe. Jones's résumé shows several articles in professional journals. During our campus visit he told us, "You always hear that researchers make the best teachers, but they only recognize one kind of research in this department—formal literary scholarship. Now, my research area is the first twenty-five years of the nineteenth-century literature. How could concentrating on that make me a better teacher? I'm a language teacher and coordinator. Every hour I spend in the library writing is an hour I'm not working on my other key assignments."

Jones's original tenure bid was supported by his department head and the departmental promotion and tenure committee, by the College of Arts and Sciences, and unanimously by the Council of Deans. The German department head was especially supportive, calling Jones the "backbone" of the department, insisting that his teaching and advising ability, and his large teaching and service load, combined to outweigh his limited research record. But the university-wide tenure committee, while "recognizing that Dr. Jones is carrying a very heavy teaching and administrative load," denied tenure on the grounds of "inadequate scholarship."[6]

We found this conflict between scholarly productivity and other campus duties to be especially conspicuous at institutions that define themselves as "emerging." The goal is to be ranked among the "top fifty" or "top one hundred" research institutions in the nation, or at least to move up the prestige ladder another rung or two. Professor Burton Clark has reminded us that "the unguided imitative convergence of universities and colleges upon the most prestigious forms is an enormous cultural component in higher education."[7] A teacher at one such campus told us: "The junior faculty around here are under enormous pressure. The ambition to imitate this single model has been distorting the mission of too many institutions. In some ways, it's harder to work at a place that's up and coming. They're trying to build a reputation on the backs of the exploited new faculty. The people who are setting these standards could never, ever meet them themselves."

In a sharp rejoinder, the chief academic officer told us, "The very best teachers that I have ever seen are those who are also on the leading edge of the research, and that is axiomatic." In fact, simply raising the issue of "rewards for teaching" prompted him to deliver a long lecture against professors who say they "don't do research because they say they want to concentrate on teaching."

He continued, "At this place, it's demanded of young professors that they produce good research and do good teaching, and it should be. And if someone says he doesn't have the time to do good research along with his teaching, the university will have something else to say about that, because he's only working at partial capacity. Now, he may say he's spending all his time working with students, but what about the people in his department spending all their time with students *and* doing research?"

This administrator offered an image of the "100-percent teacher" as a mossback who "longs for the university of the 1950s," as he put it. "The faculty member who doesn't publish is under no stress—he teaches his class, sits down in his office with his feet on the desk, and has a nice chat with his students."

In another part of the interview the administrator added: "These guys want to be paid the same as their fellow workers who are putting out the research and the good teaching—and that's what I find objectionable. The researcher is putting out a hell of a lot more than the '100-percent teacher,' and he deserves to be paid more for it."

We then asked why the inverse is true—why it seems permissible to dedicate full time to research and to ignore teaching. "Because that's the greenback dollar bill—that's the big buck. And in the long run no department can afford to be without a strong research team. Now, at the same time, within that strong research team, you'll always have good teachers. Because if they're good researchers, I claim that you will find a significantly higher proportion of good teachers there too. However, it's not the other way around."[8]

The teacher in the colonial college was responsible for the "formation" of his students and the German university professor was responsible for the advancement of his discipline. In contemporary American higher education the conflict over the value to be assigned to teaching and research has never fully been resolved. In a recent editorial in *Science,* Norman Hackerman, former president of Rice University, writes pointedly about the tension over priorities within the modern university. There is, he says, "an exhausting attempt by each field, each institution, each individual, to be number one. I have no interest in stifling ambition but intend, rather, to suggest that the process of *educating individuals,* because of the relative anonymity associated with it, has not maintained its proper preeminent position" (emphasis added).[9]

Still, it does little good to exhort faculty to "return to teaching," as if they delight in avoiding students. Faculty who pursue research are acknowledging the realities of academic life and of good scholarship as well. With few exceptions, young professors know that if they wish to gain tenure or an appointment at a highly rated institution, they will need to achieve distinction not by good teaching but by an impressive record of research and publication. In our national survey of college professors, 75 percent said that it is very difficult today to achieve tenure in their department without publishing.

How to strike a balance between teaching and research? There is, we believe, more than one response. We have in the United States today research universities, community colleges, and, in between, a luxuriant growth of doctorate-granting institutions, comprehensive colleges, liberal arts campuses, and specialized institutions—all of which have their own culture, with different goals, a different mix of students, and separate definitions of academic work. We should celebrate and encourage this diversity as a source of strength in the total system of American higher education.

It seems reasonable to conclude that at the research university, as well as at a selected number of what have been called "research colleges," scholarship, research, and publication should continue to be central criteria by which faculty performance is measured. The advancement of knowledge is crucial and these institutions must reward professors who define and explore authentic academic problems, who, in short, do top-quality research and contribute to scholarship in their fields. Those who join these institutions should be held to high research standards and one must ask: If not within the higher learning academy, where should the bulk of basic research in a free society be conducted and rewarded?

At the same time, research institutions also must aggressively support good teaching. After all, at large universities, where much of the research is conducted, two thirds or more of all students are undergraduates, and the push to publish, without an equal concern for teaching, can have a chilling effect on the classroom and be shockingly detrimental to the students. Christopher Jencks and David Riesman, in their important book *The Academic Revolution*, starkly describe the price that is paid when teaching is neglected:

> No doubt most professors prefer it when their courses are popular, their lectures applauded, and their former students appreciative. But since such successes are of no help in getting a salary increase, moving to a more prestigious campus, or winning their colleagues' admiration, they are unlikely to struggle as hard to create them as to do other things. . . . Many potentially competent teachers do a conspicuously bad job in the classroom because they know that bad teaching is not penalized in any formal way.[10]

We conclude then that, at every research university, teaching should be valued as highly as research, and good teaching should be an equally important criterion for tenure and promotion. To expect faculty to be good researchers and good teachers is a demanding standard. Still, it is at the research university where the two come together, and faculty, at such institutions, should contribute effectively to both.

At many research universities, the title Distinguished Research

Professor is in place. We recommend that institutions also extend special status and salary incentives to those professors who not only are productive scholars but who are, in addition, outstandingly effective in the classroom. We are aware that such a provision is only a modest step. But this recognition, sparingly given, will signify that the campus regards teaching excellence as a hallmark of success and that superior research and superior teaching must flourish side by side.

How should the balance be struck at the other institutions, which range from doctorate-granting institutions to liberal arts colleges? On these campuses we urge great flexibility. Some campuses may give priority to research, others to teaching, and still others may provide a blend of both. Even within a single institution or department there may be different priorities, as well as from one department to another. Decisions in this matter should be tied to mission. Throughout, however, wherever undergraduates are taught, teaching excellence must be an essential expectation.

The president at one university, in commenting on the tenure debate at his institution, took this position: "This campus should be a place where both great teachers *and* great researchers function side by side. We should have the confidence to say, 'Look, you're a great researcher and we are eager to have you here doing what you do best.' " He then added, "We should also be able to say to a colleague, 'You are terrific with students, but you are not publishing. Still, we want you to help us perform an important mission on the campus.' "[11]

This suggestion that not every faculty member is, or should be, a researcher reflects, we found, the preference and the work patterns of professors. Our survey of five thousand faculty members revealed that 42 percent of those at four-year institutions devote fewer than five hours a week to research; 17 percent admit to none at all (Table 19). Further, 55 percent have never published a monograph or book (in 1976 it was 62 percent). Twenty-two percent say they have never published in a professional journal, and almost 30 percent

Table 19   The Average Number of Hours per Week Faculty Devote to Research (percent responding by type of institution)

Type of Institution	Hours per Week Devoted to Research				
	None	1–4	5–10	11–20	Over 20
All institutions	17	25	26	17	15
Research universities	8	13	24	26	29
Doctorate-granting universities	11	27	29	18	15
Comprehensive universities and colleges	23	32	27	12	6
Liberal arts colleges	33	36	19	10	2

Source: The Carnegie Foundation for the Advancement of Teaching, National Survey of Faculty, 1984.

report that "they are not now engaged in scholarly research that will lead to publication" (Table 20).

Again, however, the pattern differs from one type of institution to another. Thirty-eight percent of the faculty at liberal arts colleges have never published in a professional journal and about half are not now engaged in scholarly research that will lead to publication. In contrast, at research universities, only 11 percent of the faculty have never published, and only 12 percent are not now engaged in scholarly research (Table 20).

What all of this seems to suggest is that although research pressures are very real, a considerable gap exists between the reward structures of the profession and the preferences of professors. Members of faculty, in conversation, often spoke glowingly of their time with students and indicated that this brought them the most reward. Further, in our faculty survey 63 percent reported that their interests "lie toward teaching as opposed to research." Even at research universities, almost 40 percent of the faculty showed a strong preference for teaching. And over half of the faculty at all types of institutions agreed that "teaching effectiveness, not publication, should be the primary criterion for promotion" (Table 21).

We conclude then that the time has come to recognize that the American professoriate is a profession with many cultures. There is the research university that has, we believe, a special mandate to sustain basic and applied research, offering all students, both gradu-

Table 20 Faculty Research and Publication, 1975 and 1984 (percent responding)

| | All Institutions | | | | 1984: By Type of Institution | | | |
	1975	1984	Public	Private	Research University	Doctorate-Granting University	Comprehensive College	Liberal Arts College
Never published or edited a book or monograph	62	55	53	62	48	51	59	67
Never published in a professional journal	28	22	20	31	11	18	29	38
Not now engaged in scholarly research that will lead to publication	29	28	25	37	12	20	37	49

Source: The Carnegie Foundation for the Advancement of Teaching, National Surveys of Faculty, 1975 and 1984.

Table 21 Faculty Attitudes Toward Teaching and Research: 1975 and 1984 (percent agreeing)

	All Institutions 1975	All Institutions 1984	Public	Private	Research University	Doctorate-Granting University	Comprehensive College	Liberal Arts College
					1984: By Type of Institution			
My interests lie toward teaching as opposed to research.	70	63	60	73	39	63	75	85
Teaching effectiveness, not publication, should be the primary criterion for promotion.	70	58	54	70	34	53	72	83
In my department it is very difficult to achieve tenure without publishing.	54	69	74	53	92	85	54	35

Source: The Carnegie Foundation for the Advancement of Teaching, National Surveys of Faculty, 1975 and 1984.

ates and undergraduates, high-quality teaching. There are liberal arts and comprehensive colleges, where the mission is primarily teaching undergraduates, although a handful of these colleges—the so-called research colleges—may also follow the research model. In between we see great flexibility, in which institutions and departments with colleges and universities may decide to give priority to teaching or to research or to a blend of both.

But here an important distinction should be drawn. While not all professors are likely to publish with regularity, they, nonetheless, should be first-rate *scholars*. We understand this to mean staying abreast of the profession, knowing the literature in one's field, and skillfully communicating such information to students. To weaken faculty commitment to scholarship, as we define it here, is to undermine the undergraduate experience, regardless of the academic setting.

Further, the results of such scholarship should be made available for judgment. There are many ways to do this: In addition to publishing books, monographs, or articles in journals, a scholar may write textbooks or perhaps be asked to review and assess recent key developments in one's field. Regardless of the criteria used, scholarly activity should be evaluated by peers. How else can we judge whether a faculty member is staying professionally alive?

This is the point: Scholarship is not an esoteric appendage; it is at the heart of what the profession is all about. All faculty, throughout their careers, should, themselves, remain students. As scholars, they must continue to learn and be seriously and continuously engaged in the expanding intellectual world. This is essential to the vitality and vigor of the undergraduate college.

Sustaining scholarship highlights another important concern of this study: There is, we conclude, an urgent and growing need for faculty to be renewed. Although many members of the faculty like what they are doing and say that if they had it to do over they would become a college teacher, we also found 41 percent are less enthusiastic about their work today than when they began their careers (Table 22). And about half say they are now considering or would seriously consider another *academic* position if one were offered. Forty-six percent say they would consider a *nonacademic* position if one came along (Table 23).

Many of today's faculty joined the profession to be productive scholars and then, following in the footsteps of their mentors, to move from campus to campus, up the professional ladder, gaining recognition. Today, the prospects for such mobility and advancement are restricted. One humanities professor who has had tenure for several years said: "If I were to stay on this campus much longer I would atrophy—and many of my colleagues have."[12]

Table 22   Faculty Attitudes Toward Their Professional Career (percent agreeing)

	1975	1984
I am more enthusiastic about my work now than when I began my academic career.	NA	59
I often wish I had entered another profession.	NA	20
If I had it to do over again, I'd not become a college teacher.	NA	22
I feel trapped in a profession with limited opportunities for advancement.	NA	27
I am considering another line of work because prospects for academic advancement seem limited now.	NA	23
My job is the source of considerable personal strain.	36	40
My institution has serious financial problems.	58	49
In the next five years I expect that some of the tenured faculty here will lose their jobs due to lack of funds.	35	27
The teaching load at my institution is "better" today than it was five years ago.	24	21
Department morale at my institution is "better" today than it was five years ago.	30	25
The intellectual environment of my institution is "fair or poor."	51	51

NA: Not applicable.

Source: The Carnegie Foundation for the Advancement of Teaching, National Surveys of Faculty, 1975 and 1984.

Table 23 Faculty Attitudes Toward Changing Their Jobs, 1975 and 1984 (percent agreeing)

| | All Institutions | | 1984: By Type of Institution | | | | | |
	1975	1984	Public	Private	Research University	Doctorate-Granting University	Comprehensive College	Liberal Arts College
I would consider another *academic position* if one were to come along.	53	52	54	46	54	52	51	47
I would consider a *nonacademic position* if one were to come along.	42	46	46	44	42	44	48	49

Source: The Carnegie Foundation for the Advancement of Teaching, National Surveys of Faculty, 1975 and 1984.

The last statement could have been made by faculty members in any era. A change of setting, after four, six, eight years, has always been considered good for the curriculum vitae and the circulation of the blood. But young professionals now are frozen out of or into positions that originally were viewed only as transitional. The result is a restlessness and a low-grade frustration among many mid-career academics. The profession is *A National Resource Imperiled,* as one significant report has put it.[13] The turnover of short-term "gypsy" scholars has become a source of particular distress.

Increasingly, faculty burnout is being talked about in higher education. The undergraduate college, which depends so much on vitality in the classroom, must be served by faculty members who can be renewed throughout their careers. And yet, we found that such an obvious and important practice as setting aside a portion of the budget for faculty development is rare. We strongly recommend that every college commit itself to the professional growth of all faculty and provide them with opportunities to stay intellectually alive.

The sabbatical leave is the most common form of faculty renewal, but we found that sabbaticals are far from universal and leaves are rarely available for junior faculty. We urge that a sabbatical leave policy be available at every institution, with the understanding that such leaves will be competitively awarded and will be used in ways that will promote faculty growth and assume benefits to the institution and its students.

A variety of other incentives will be needed. Specifically, we recommend that funds be made available to help teachers develop new ideas and improve their pedagogical procedures. These grants —to be administered by a campus-wide faculty committee—should favor those who engage in undergraduate instruction. We also urge that all colleges have a grant program for faculty research. The Andrew W. Mellon Foundation has helped nearly eighty colleges to establish such programs for faculty development, among them Carleton College in Minnesota. The goals are to advance knowledge, serve the departments, and strengthen the faculty members' professional careers. After five years of competition, the signs are promising. Twenty-eight Carleton faculty members, nearly 20 percent, have won competitive awards.[14]

Faculty development programs might also include exchange arrangements and guest lectureships, which would move faculty from one campus to another. While modest funds from the college's operating budget should be set aside to support such projects, we strongly recommend that private foundations and corporate donors help underwrite their costs.

Since 1980, The Bush Foundation has funded a variety of faculty development programs at colleges and universities in Minnesota, North Dakota, and South Dakota. Projects include released time for faculty during the academic year or during the summer for reading, studying, and consultation with colleagues; travel grants to attend curriculum seminars or to meet with outstanding faculty at other institutions; and funds to finance visiting professorships.[15]

The Associated Colleges of the Midwest, a consortium of liberal arts colleges, arranges faculty exchanges each year. Professors teach and do research at other colleges and specialized institutions. They can, for example, spend time at the Newberry Library in Chicago, teach and conduct research at Oak Ridge National Laboratory, or travel to the Wilderness Field Station in northern Minnesota. Others go off for a semester or a year at off-campus centers in Costa Rica, Japan, London, Yugoslavia, or Florence.[16]

The National Faculty Exchange program enables college teachers from 130 affiliated organizations to work at other institutions. This nonprofit network is administered by Indiana University and Purdue University at Fort Wayne. Institutions become members by paying a small annual fee. More than seventy faculty and staff placements have been made since the program began.[17] We recommend that clusters of colleges all across the country organize Regional Faculty Exchange Networks.

Further, we recommend that every college and university give public recognition and special awards to outstanding teachers. Since 1974, students, faculty, and alumni of the Boston University community have been able to show their appreciation for excellence in teaching by nominating faculty members for the Metcalf Cup and Prize and the Metcalf Awards. Endowed by a gift from Dr. Arthur G. B. Metcalf, chairman of the Boston University Board of Trustees, the Metcalf Cup and a $2,500 prize are awarded each year to one professor. The Metcalf Awards are $1,000 prizes given to one or more finalists in the competition for the Metcalf Cup and Prize.[18]

In the end, faculty renewal calls for leadership as well as initiative by department chairs, who assign priorities to their colleagues. It is often in the department that the priorities for young professors are fixed. Today's departmental structures fragment the curriculum and isolate faculty members from one another. The academic profession urgently needs leaders who are concerned about the whole curriculum. We need leaders who will help build academic bridges on the campus. Department chairs should provide such leadership. Because department chairs are so important to faculty development, we recommend that campuses pay more attention to the regional seminars or workshops conducted specifically for department chairs to prepare them for leadership with their faculty.

No examination of the professoriate would be complete without considering the part-time teacher. In the past, college teaching was viewed somewhat romantically, perhaps, as a lifetime calling. A growing practice in American higher education is to hire instructors without prospect for tenure, creating in the process a permanent "under class" of temporary faculty members who are often insecure and unconnected to the college.

Approximately 25 percent of all faculty in four-year colleges and universities are employed part time. On some campuses, the percentage is much higher. Sixty percent of those we surveyed report an increase in part-time faculty at their colleges during the past five years. And almost half the faculty (47 percent) feel that these people are taking jobs that otherwise would be filled by full-time teachers.[19]

Part-time faculty operate under unfavorable conditions: no office, lack of time on campus, usually hired on short-term contracts. Because of a fragmented schedule, it is difficult for them to develop deep institutional commitments, and their connections with other faculty and with students are tenuous at best. The spirit of community is weakened.

On a large urban campus a few of the large number of part-time faculty were praised; but mostly we heard complaints: "These people are hard to find after class." "They don't know how the college works." One student said, "I have an uneasy feeling about some of these part-time people. They come in from other places with no commitment to the college. It seems like they never have time to stay after class and talk; you can make an appointment, but you have to work your schedule around theirs, not like most professors here who will see you any time."[20]

Part-time teachers are beneficial economically and can enrich the campus. One university recruited the director of planning in the environmental protection agency, the chief of homicide detectives, and the stage manager at the local theater to teach courses because they had knowledge in specialized subjects not available in the regular faculty.[21]

There are, however, some central educational questions to consider: What is the impact of part-time faculty on the spirit of community on campus? Is it possible for undergraduate students to be effectively served if large numbers of their teachers show up only briefly on campus?

It is our position that a balance must be struck between full- and part-time faculty. Specifically, we propose that no more than 20 percent of the undergraduate faculty be part time and that when part-time faculty are used, it is essential that their employment be educationally justified.

In this *tour d'horizon* of faculty life, we have considered teaching and research, faculty renewals, and points of tension in the professorial career; strengths also should be noted. Most reassuring perhaps is the fact that in none of our case studies did we identify a single instance of violation of basic faculty rights. And faculty respondents to our national survey confirmed that "the administration here strongly supports academic freedom." We also found that most faculty, in spite of frustration and complaints, still are deeply committed to their profession.

The condition of teaching is, in short, a pattern of contradictions. We found faculty committed to the enterprise, in spite of eroding incomes and quality of campus life. We found continuing commitment to the disciplines and little dissatisfaction with the curriculum. Faculty, while strongly identifying with a common culture, live within disciplines and work at institutions that have sharply contrasting values and traditions. While great prestige comes from research and publications, many faculty members prefer teaching, and we suspect that many endure personal discontentment about the conflict which they hardly dare to voice. There is a yearning for community, although each individual goes on in his or her individualistic competitive way.

How does this portrait of the professoriate relate to the quality of the undergraduate experience? Clearly, faculty must remain intellectually alive, stay abreast of developments in their fields, and enjoy the respect and attention of their peers. But the joy of teaching, of engaging the intellect of students, and the satisfaction of participating in the building of an institution of higher learning—these, too, can and should be a source of fulfillment as great as seeing one's name in print in the pages of a professional journal or hearing the applause of one's fellow scholars at a professional meeting.

Kenneth E. Eble, of the University of Utah, recently urged that faculty "seek to broaden definitions of professional competence and humanize the means by which we arrive at such judgments. Put less stress on evaluating what we have done and more on stimulating what we might do. Do less counting of our own and our colleagues' publications and more thinking about what we do day-to-day which will never be published. Do less longing to arrive at the higher goals of academe and more about making wherever you are a liveable and interesting and compassionate community."[22] We conclude that where such conditions are found, students will be well served and the undergraduate college will truly be a community of liberal learning.

9

CREATIVITY IN THE CLASSROOM

At a freshman psychology lecture we attended, 300 students were still finding seats when the professor started talking. "Today," he said into the microphone, "we will continue our discussion of learning." He might as well have been addressing a crowd in a Greyhound bus terminal. Like commuters marking time until their next departure, students in this class alternately read the newspaper, flipped through a paperback novel, or propped their feet on the chairs ahead of them, staring into space. Only when the professor defined a term which, he said, "might appear on an exam" did they look up and start taking notes.[1]

What we found in many classrooms was a mismatch between faculty and student expectations, a gap that left both parties unfulfilled. Faculty, concerned with scholarship, wanted to share ideas with students, who were expected to appreciate what professors do. This appreciation might exist in graduate or upper-division courses, where teachers and students have overlapping interests, but we found that often this was not the case in lower-division courses.

"If you're batting .666 on attendance, you're doing well," one faculty member complained, implying that if only two out of three students attend a class, it was a success. Another asserted: "Students don't seem to have the attention span they used to. It's hard to hold their interest. You practically have to do a song and dance, and I won't do that." An English teacher described the learning climate on his campus as one of "intellectual meekness."[2]

As for students, they are remarkably conscious of grades, willing to conform to the formula for success. A sophomore in a pre-med program said she wanted her courses to be spelled out "with no surprises. My goal is to get a good background so I can pass the MCAT [Medical College Admission Test] and I'm not interested in hearing about the professor's Ph.D. dissertation."[3]

"A college degree isn't enough," said one honors student. "You've got to have a good GPA to get into graduate school, or get a first-rate job." Another commented: "People at this college are very résumé-conscious. Undergraduates are afraid of controversy. They hesitate to participate in vigorous give and take on any topic. The main thing is to prepare for the exam."[4]

If faculty and students do not see themselves as having important business to do together, prospects for effective learning are diminished. If students view teachers as distant and their material as irrelevant, what could be a time of exciting exploration is reduced to a series of uninspired routines.

The most discouraging comment came from a professor who said he *liked* the passivity of students. "With these students, not everything has to be proven. . . . Some people say this is a return to the fifties. Perhaps, and that isn't all bad. . . . We didn't feel we knew it all and neither do they. For the first time in a while, I don't feel a generation gap."[5]

This "no hassle" attitude was vividly revealed in the classroom at a prestigious Northeast college. Students in a Gothic fiction course had been asked to read all of Peter Straub's novel *Ghost Story*. When they assembled the following Monday morning, only six of the sixty students in a large lecture hall raised their hands when asked who had done the reading. A few volunteered that they were halfway through the novel, but most admitted that they hadn't cracked the book. The professor then took all of his ninety-minute lecture to review the plot. Some students took notes. At the end of class he apologized: "I'm sorry if I spoiled the finish for those of you who haven't gotten there yet." But no one looked disappointed. They'd just received all the information they needed for an upcoming test and wouldn't have to read.[6]

A science professor stated this frustration: "How am I to cover difficult and important material when students are unwilling to really work? Sure, they'll cram for tests but they want to be spoon-fed, and when I try to get them interested in more substantial matters only a few respond. I'm pretty discouraged with students."[7]

Students are just as quick to switch the blame to their professors. One student said, "Why should I be interested in the class if the professor acts bored?" Another student agreed and added, "There's nothing worse than my biology professor, who acts as though he's doing us a big favor by teaching us about photosynthesis. Believe me, he's not doing me a favor." Still another student said, "Most of my professors are great. But I have one who makes it clear that he'd rather be in his laboratory conducting research than standing in front of two hundred students."[8]

At a large university with many teaching assistants who handle labs and discussion sections, students resent the lack of attention from the professor, suspecting (correctly) that only the T.A. will see and grade their work during the course of the quarter. In particular departments, foreign teaching assistants are a problem. Mathematicians, according to the arts and science dean, are "hard to hire in this city, unless they're foreign students who can barely speak English."[9]

Students are quick to praise their teachers, too. One said, "I love my history professor. I don't even like history but he makes it so interesting that I really want to go to class." Another said, "I like the professors who have a sense of humor. They come into class, joke around a little, and then start the lecture." Students also praise their professors for being available after class. Another student: "The professors here will go out of their way to find time to see if you need help or want to discuss something." Said another: "This college has a good academic reputation. So, I knew the classes were going to be hard. I didn't know they were going to be as hard as they are, though. Still, that's why I'm here!"[10]

One sophomore said, "My biology teacher is the worst. He is all biology. He comes in and starts talking. It's like he's not even human." She continued, "But my French teacher is great. He comes into class, talks informally with us before he begins the lecture. I feel like he really gets to know his students." A senior engineering major said, "The best teachers are those that really care about their students. I've never had a professor who wouldn't find time to talk with you after class, but some professors really make an effort to get to know their students. I also like professors who act like they're interested in what they're teaching."[11]

This mixed response, the ambivalence we found to teaching and learning, was reinforced in our national survey. Most students are quite satisfied with the teaching on their campus, but the pressure to get good grades diminishes their enthusiasm. Almost two thirds say they are under great pressure to get high grades; about one third feel it is difficult to get good grades and still "really learn something." Forty-three percent of today's undergraduates also say that many students at their institutions succeeded by "beating the system" rather than by studying (Table 24). The cheating on assignments, the term papers students buy, the shortcuts to duplicating homework assignments—all enhance the cynicism of students and erode the quality of education.

Do professors take a personal interest in the academic progress of their students? At liberal arts colleges 73 percent of the students feel they do. The proportion dropped to 59 percent when all institutions were counted. On the matter of classroom participation, we found that 81 percent of liberal arts college students feel they are encouraged to "discuss their feelings about important issues"; but that's true for only 66 percent of the total sample. Students at liberal arts colleges are also far more satisfied with the teaching they re-

Table 24 Student Attitudes Toward Course Grades, 1976 and 1984 (percent who agree)

	All Institutions 1976	All Institutions 1984	Public	Private	Research University	Doctorate-Granting University	Comprehensive College	Liberal Arts College
						1984: By Type of Institution		
I am under a great deal of pressure to get high grades.	58	64	66	59	71	62	63	55
It is difficult both to get good grades and really learn something.	36	34	35	31	41	33	31	32
Many successful students at my college make it by "beating the system" rather than by studying.	50	43	44	37	43	43	44	36

Source: The Carnegie Foundation for the Advancement of Teaching, National Survey of Undergraduates, 1976 and 1984.

ceive. And a higher percentage of these students believe their teachers look out for their interests.

On a nonacademic level, students at liberal arts colleges are more inclined to seek personal advice from professors than are students at all institutions. When asked whether professors encourage them to participate in classroom discussion, 91 percent of the students at liberal arts colleges said yes—10 percent more than undergraduates at all colleges and universities (Table 25).

Class size, like so many other aspects of teaching and learning, varies from one type of institution to another. Twenty-nine percent of the students at research universities report that "most" or "all" of their classes have more than one hundred students enrolled; at liberal arts colleges only 1 percent of the students report having most or all classes of this size. At the other end, only 5 percent of students at research universities said they had *no* classes larger than one hundred students. At liberal arts colleges, it was 80 percent (Table 26).

We also discovered that, for most undergraduates, the freshman and sophomore classes (often the general education sections) are the ones most likely to be overloaded. Further, we found that at large institutions these classes are often taught by graduate assistants or junior professors. Forty-one percent of the students we surveyed report that "general education courses are rarely taught by the best faculty members in the departments in which they are given." And 37 percent said, "General education courses reflect the interests of the faculty" rather than of the students (Table 27).

We concluded that one important way to measure a college's commitment to undergraduate education is to look at class size in general education. Do these courses enroll hundreds of students? Are they taught by senior professors? Do students have an opportunity to meet with their teachers? A college or university that does not give top priority to the basic undergraduate courses is not fully committed to excellence in education.

A significant number of students we interviewed said they had

Table 25 Students' Appraisal of Their College Professors and Teaching, 1976 and 1984 (percent who agree)

	All Institutions		1984: By Type of Institution					
	1976	1984	Public	Private	Research University	Doctorate-Granting University	Comprehensive College	Liberal Arts College
Overall, I am satisfied with the teaching I have received.	69	71	68	81	68	68	71	85
There are professors at my college who take a personal interest in my academic progress.	63	59	57	68	52	56	61	73
Professors at my college encourage students to discuss their feelings about important issues.	NA	66	63	74	59	63	67	81
On the whole, I trust the faculty here to look out for students' interests.	75	75	72	84	71	72	75	88
There are professors at my college whom I feel free to turn to for advice on personal matters.	53	39	36	49	30	37	41	54
Most of my professors encourage students to actively participate in classroom discussion.	NA	81	79	88	74	79	83	71

NA: Question not asked in 1976.

Source: The Carnegie Foundation for the Advancement of Teaching, National Survey of Undergraduates, 1976 and 1984.

Table 26 Frequency of Classes Larger Than 100 Students (percent of undergraduates reporting)

	All Institutions		Public	Private	Research University	Doctorate-Granting University	Comprehensive College	Liberal Arts College
	1976	1984				1984: By Type of Institution		
All	1	1	2	1	3	2	1	1
Most	9	11	13	4	26	14	4	0
Several/few	54	52	58	28	66	68	46	19
None	36	36	27	67	5	16	49	80

Source: The Carnegie Foundation for the Advancement of Teaching, National Survey of Undergraduates, 1976 and 1984.

Table 27 Students' Evaluation of General Education at Their College (percent who agree)

	Total	Public	Private	Research University	Doctorate-Granting University	Comprehensive College	Liberal Arts College
General education courses are rarely taught by the best faculty members in the departments in which they are given.	41	43	32	47	45	39	28
General education courses reflect the interests of the faculty and departments rather than broad student interests.	37	38	35	34	35	41	31

1984: By Type of Institution

Source: The Carnegie Foundation for the Advancement of Teaching, National Survey of Undergraduates, 1984.

no objection to being in a large lecture course; others, however, strongly favored small classes that allow discussion. A math professor in a small university went so far as to say that if he had been introduced to mathematics in the kind of large, distracting lecture hall he himself was teaching in, he would never have continued to study the subject.[12] We strongly urge, therefore, that the finest teachers should teach freshmen, and that undergraduate classes should be small enough for students to have lively intellectual interaction with teachers and fellow students.

In the early American college the primary method of instruction was recitation, a process in which students repeated from memory, often verbatim, textbook assignments. For disputation, students defended or attacked a proposition in Latin, the required language both in and out of class.[13] By the mid-eighteenth century, the lecture by teachers occasionally supplemented student recitations. Lectures were, however, a talking textbook as instructors read slowly and students copied down what was said, word for word.

The lecture slowly replaced recitation and disputations. There was new knowledge to be conveyed, and it became more difficult to call on all students in the enlarged classes. Another sign of the times: The blackboard was first used by a teacher at Bowdoin College about 1823.[14] And experiments with the seminar, a German import, were introduced in the mid-nineteenth century. According to Arthur Levine, in his significant *Handbook on Undergraduate Curriculum*, it was in 1869 that Charles Kendall Adams tried the seminar at The University of Michigan. "Seven years later it became a staple in the curriculum at Johns Hopkins. . . . A discussion class, designed to supplement lecture instruction originally called the 'conference quiz section,' was created at Harvard in 1904."[15]

Today, the lecture method is preferred by most professors. With few exceptions, when we visited classes, the teacher stood in front of rows of chairs and talked most of the forty-five or fifty minutes. Information was presented that often students passively received.

There was little opportunity for positions to be clarified or ideas challenged.

There are times, of course, when lecturing is necessary to convey essential issues and ideas and also to handle large numbers of students. At other times, such a procedure seems inappropriate, especially when the class is small and much of the material being presented is available in the text.

When discussion did occur in classes we visited, a handful of students, usually men, dominated the exchange. We were especially struck by the subtle yet significant differences in the way men and women participated in class. This situation persists despite the ascendancy of female enrollments on most campuses.

Women now make up over half of all undergraduate enrollments and they get the majority of all bachelor's and master's degrees. In 1963 about half of all women undergraduates majored in education. In 1983 only 15 percent were doing so. They receive 32 percent of the academic doctorates awarded, 25 percent of those in medicine, and 33 percent in law.[16]

Still, in many classrooms women are overshadowed. Even the brightest women students often remain silent. They may submit excellent written work, and will frequently wait until after class to approach a teacher privately about issues raised in the discussion. But it is the men who seem most often to be recognized and talk most in class. Not only do men talk more, but what they say often carries more weight. This pattern of classroom leaders and followers is set very early in the term.[17]

We agree with Mortimer Adler's conclusion that "all genuine learning is active, not passive. It involves the use of the mind, not just the memory. It is a process of discovery in which the student is the main agent, not the teacher."[18] And all students, not just the most aggressive or most verbal, should be actively engaged. It is unacceptable for a few students to participate in the give and take with teachers while others are allowed to be mere spectators.

On a related matter, we frequently were struck by the competitive climate in the classroom. Since as a democracy we are committed to equality of opportunity, and since in a vital society we need some way of bringing talent forward, we use, both on and off the campus, the calculus of competition to stimulate ambition and achievement. We must do this, or else we lack essential leadership in all areas of life.

However, if democracy is to be well served, cooperation is essential too. And the goal of community, which is threaded throughout this report, is essentially related to the academic program, and, most especially, to procedures in the classroom. We urge, therefore, that students be asked to participate in collaborative projects, that they work together occasionally on group assignments, that special effort be made, through small seminar units within large lecture sections, to create conditions that underscore the point that cooperation is as essential as competition in the classroom.

The undergraduate experience, at its best, means active learning and disciplined inquiry that leads to the intellectual empowerment of students. Professor Carl Schorske, at Princeton University, says that the test of a good teacher is "Do you regard 'learning' as a noun or a verb? If as a noun, as a thing to be possessed and passed along, then you present your truths, neatly packaged, to your students. But if you see 'learning' as a verb!—the process is different."[19]

While the college teaching we observed was often uninspired, we still found exciting examples of outstanding teaching at many institutions. One professor of English spoke to our site visitor as follows: "At this college there's a lot of emphasis on teaching and there's a lot of good teaching. I like that because teaching is my real vocation. I feel most strongly about that." Another professor also enthusiastically endorsed his role as teacher: "This college is not filled with many academic bright lights. Students work hard and they really care about their studies. The fact that many are 'average' doesn't bother me. My favorite image of a teacher is that of the midwife encouraging students, coaching them. What you really do in the classroom is help students come to know their own mind—

become independent thinkers. These students have potential, but they have to have more confidence academically. It's our job to bring it out of them."[20]

One Monday morning, at a New England college, we visited an "Introduction to Philosophy" course. The subject for the day was a problem from Thomas Aquinas: If God is all-powerful and all-good, how can there be evil in the world? The students offered answers: because salvation must be achieved through suffering, because Adam's sin produced suffering, because God just set the world in motion and didn't know how everything would turn out. "You're revising the premise," the professor responded to the last answer. "Your God is not all-powerful, he's only good-intentioned."[21]

A student asked: "Why would you worship a God who is not all-powerful?" "Why not?" asked another. And so it went, with many hands raised and ideas flowing so fast that the professor had to intervene often to sort out key points and keep the discussion on course. "Today's students are poorly equipped to deal with questions about ethics," he told us later. "I think they're unaccustomed to reasoning." Yet, he persisted in engaging students in active forms of inquiry, providing them experience in addressing questions of ethics and challenging them to learn.[22]

At a public institution in the West, we visited a mid-afternoon class in European history, with about one hundred students. The day's lecture was on the influence of the writings of the French philosophers on the enlightened despots of the eighteenth century. "Did Voltaire and Diderot favor a radical reconstruction of society?" the professor asked.

"No, they just wanted to reform society in some ways," a student answered.

"What ways?" the professor probed.

"To make it more rational."

"How can people be made more rational?"

"Through education."

"Did the Enlightenment writers want to introduce mass public education?"

"No, they still favored the aristocracy."

"Why was that?"

This exchange continued through a discussion of how uniform legal codes developed. The professor lectured briefly, highlighting key themes, but he never stopped asking penetrating questions—and expecting thoughtful answers.[23]

In an upper-division Constitutional law class the professor used the "case method." Each student had been assigned to read summaries of a series of cases dealing with the president, Congress, and the courts. Guiding the discussion, the teacher would name a case and tell a student to give him "the principles we can take from this example." The classroom discussion was lively, with the instructor making it a point to call on different students instead of waiting for them to respond. He occasionally digressed from the set format with interesting historical asides, discussing, for example, Earl Warren's role in the internment of Japanese citizens during World War II. He also tried, when possible, to tell students what was going on in the Supreme Court right now that related to the issues and cases they discussed.[24]

In a class in the history of modern music, we watched the instructor, through a combination of knowledge, enthusiasm, humor, recordings, and exercises, keep the class engaged—even excited—through a ninety-minute session on the early technique in the music of Arnold Schönberg.[25] In a freshman chemistry class, the professor spent the entire period on problem-solving techniques, hoping to break students of the habit of "looking for plug-in formulas" to solve problems.[26]

In a seminar called "Women in Literature," some students who were obviously not impressed with *Jane Eyre* were kept intellectually engaged through a compelling and at times humorous lecture style. "So she faints. Why? Look, you can't have a nineteenth-century novel without somebody fainting. All right? All right."

Then: "Okay, let's go through some of your objections to the novel. The diction is first on the list, right?"[27]

At a New England college, we visited a course in French literature conducted entirely in French. The seventeen students enrolled had read Rousseau's *Discourse on the Origin of Inequality* for homework. In class, the professor asked questions about the style and substance of the work: What does Rousseau say is the basis of human inequality? How would people label Rousseau were he to present his ideas today? What was the source of evil for Rousseau? For whom was he writing? What was his tone? Students seemed generally comfortable with discussing the work in French and were able to pinpoint passages from the text to illustrate their answers.[28]

The professor corrected their grammar and pronunciation from time to time. One student, for example, spoke as if *l'amour du bien-être*—love of comfort—were the same as *l'amour*—love. The professor asked her to translate the words literally into English, and she figured out her mistake for herself. But the professor's main emphasis was at least as much on creativity, on original thinking, as on the mastery of French.[29]

The central qualities that make for successful teaching can be simply stated: command of the material to be taught, a contagious enthusiasm for the play of ideas, optimism about human potential, the involvement with one's students, and—not least—sensitivity, integrity, and warmth as a human being. When this combination is present in the classroom, the impact of a teacher can be powerful and enduring.

Good teaching also means careful evaluation of the student. And yet it is for this important task most teachers are not well prepared. They usually test as they were tested, asking students to put check marks or short answers on a piece of paper. The evaluation procedures now in place often give priority to memory over imagination and cramming over creative thinking. Learning is diminished. One student told us, "We have a test in here every week and that's all I think about. Who's my competition?"[30]

We strongly urge that faculty seminars be held on student evaluation to help teachers become better in assessment, to learn how to give students careful and concise criticisms, and to help them understand the strengths and weaknesses of their performance. Again, special emphasis should be given to rewarding students for group effort in which they have to depend on one another to complete an assignment.

The evaluation of teachers is also the mark of a good college. A systematic assessment of instruction will yield important information about classroom performance, help faculty discover how their course is received, and suggest how the instruction might be improved. Yet, most colleges have only internal arrangements and at only one institution among those we visited was the idea of formal and regular evaluation being considered. The faculty member who is heading the project said, "I used to teach at a college where evaluation was an accepted part of the system. But here it's an uphill battle all the way."[31]

Those opposing teacher evaluation at this college took the position that there is plenty of informal evidence available. For example, an education professor pointed to students' scores on teacher certification exams and took pride in the fact that they were among the top 5 percent in the state, year after year. A psychology professor claims he gets many phone calls asking him to recommend students because of the department's reputation for quality. In the business division, a faculty member said that area companies are happy with the performance of their "new hires." No need to check further, we were told.

Still, if teaching is to assume the status it deserves, the performance of each teacher in each classroom should, we believe, be formally assessed. The procedure should begin with senior faculty members, who evaluate their peers through interviews with students and colleagues and through occasional visits to the classroom.

Students also have an important role to play. At Princeton University a faculty evaluation program was introduced in 1969. Today, all students fill out an evaluation form for all faculty in all courses.

This form includes an "open-ended" question in which students are free to make additional comments. Student evaluations at Princeton are used for tenure review, and also provide feedback to each teacher.[32]

Perhaps the best critique of teaching is for the teacher and students occasionally to step back and evaluate while the course is still in progress. As professors pause to talk openly about what is going on, students will be encouraged to react, and through such openness teaching and learning will improve. In one class we visited, the professor began with a discussion of the last class meeting, which he felt "had not gone very well." Students were asked to give their opinions about the session. A healthy exchange followed. The goals and procedures of the class were candidly discussed.[33]

The key question is this: Can good teaching be taught? Not everyone who enters the classroom will feel at home and, yet, all too frequently it is assumed that anyone with an M.A. or a Ph.D. can teach. Andrew Hacker states the problem well: "Graduate schools provide little or no aid, since they regard their mission as training scholars who will not be judged as educators. Even teaching assistants, [Frederick] Rudolph says, are 'thrown into a classroom at undergraduates' without advice or supervision. On the whole, college teaching is self-taught. Only rarely will a tenured professor be told that his or her performance can stand improvement."[34]

Teacher preparation should begin in graduate school as graduate assistants work with mentors who carefully critique their work. They should be helped in their teaching procedures and be trained to give helpful oral and written comments in anticipation of their work with students later on.

Junior professors also should get guidance. At the University of Georgia, young professors elect to take part in a year-long teaching fellows program. Each fellow is an assistant professor in a tenure-track position, with one to three years' teaching experience. The goals are to bring these young teachers in touch with senior colleagues known for good teaching and to underscore the institution's commitment to good teaching.[35]

Even seasoned teachers can improve. The Center for Teaching and Learning at Harvard has, for years, worked with faculty who voluntarily participate in the program. The teaching procedures of these faculty members are critiqued through observation, self-evaluation, and the viewing of videotapes of actual classroom instruction.[36] Harvard's Bureau of Study Council also has a library of several hundred audiotapes that present important incidents in the classroom. With the guidance of a skillful mentor, aspiring teachers or even experienced professors learn how pedagogy can improve and how, for example, the first class meeting of a new semester can set the tone. These nonthreatening tapes offer a powerful way for faculty to sharpen their skills and monitor their attitudes.

Northwestern University's Center for the Teaching Profession has a similar program. Faculty from many colleges and universities have used the Center's materials—booklets, surveys, films—to become more effective teachers.[37] At Stanford University, a handbook is presented to junior faculty members and teaching assistants to help them better organize their classes and their teaching materials.[38]

In the end, the most important teaching may go on outside the classroom. At one college in our study, the faculty member named most frequently by everyone as the most outstanding on the campus is a science professor who has taught at the institution for twenty-two years. He is frequently found on the campus from 7:30 in the morning until early evening, and his involvement with students is something in which he believes. One senior who enrolled in this professor's anatomy and physiology course described the class and instructor in this way: "I took the class because I needed it for my major, and have found it is much tougher than I expected—he really makes you work, but I respect him for that. . . . I think he just wants us to be the best we can be. He also shows a genuine concern about his students, and he cares whether we are learning something, whether we pass the course or not . . . I always see him out on the campus, talking to kids, and you can tell he worries about them and about the school."[39]

But how far does the relationship extend? Not all faculty are comfortable with the idea of becoming open enough to be fully known to students. A senior professor at a prestigious eastern university defined his role as follows: "I'm a scholar. I have important information to convey, and it's the responsibility of these students to hear what I have to say and use what they find helpful. I have neither the time nor inclination to spend endless hours reviewing what I have already covered or spoon-feed them."[40]

Is the teacher to be a mentor? Is the faculty member's responsibility toward his "client" comparable in scope to that of professionals in medicine or law? For every court case, there is a lead attorney; for every patient, an attending physician; for every audit, a partner-in-charge. Lose a case, maim a patient, or botch an audit and there is no question upon whom the responsibility lies.

Even at the best colleges, no one faculty member assumes, indeed can assume, the comprehensive responsibility toward an individual student that an attorney or physician has for a client or patient. Only at the graduate level, or occasionally in tightly organized academic departments, are such connections made. Why? In part, because learning is an active exercise in which the student must play the lead role. No one can learn for him. Also, in part, because the faculty responsibility is a collective one. No one faculty member can teach all that the student needs to know or guide him or her singlehandedly toward the desired educational outcome. Further, there is danger in viewing students in a paternalistic fashion. Indeed, such a stance is especially ludicrous in an age when students are more mature, and when more than a few are as old as their professors. The danger, however, in a system in which all are said to be responsible is that *none* can be held accountable for what happens or does not happen to the students during the decisive years of undergraduate education.

In such a climate, students are rarely provided the opportunity to question, to challenge, to explore their doubts, introduce new assumptions, and have such contributions carefully critiqued. These are the conditions out of which genuine learning will occur.

Here then is our conclusion. Good teaching is at the heart of the undergraduate experience. All members of the faculty should work continually to improve the content of their courses and their methods of instruction. This means "digging below the level of course syllabi to analyze what students are learning. It means studying the different modes of instruction to determine what each accomplishes. It means using the literature on student learning and development to inform changes in the context and delivery of the curriculum."[41]

The undergraduate college, at its best, is an institution committed to knowledge, backed by wisdom—a place where students, through creative teaching, are encouraged to become intellectually engaged. With this vision, the great teacher is challenged not only to transmit information but also to enrich and inspire students, who will go on learning long after college days are over.

10

RESOURCES:
PRINTED PAGE AND PRINTOUTS

At a college of quality there is a wide range of learning resources that enrich and extend classroom instruction and encourage students to become independent, self-directed learners.

The brochure at one college we visited described the library as the "focal point of learning on the campus."[1] And yet, despite the idealism expressed in this statement, we found the library at most institutions in our study to be a neglected resource. If the college did *not* have a library, faculty and students might worry. But since the library is always there, it is easily ignored.

The attitude on many campuses was summarized by one thoughtful librarian, who said: "As long as faculty members don't complain, as long as the size of the collection and other standards meet a level acceptable to accrediting agencies, the administration is happy to let the library alone."[2] One administrator went so far as to predict that in twenty-five years the library will be as obsolete as the unused chapel.[3]

Today, about one out of every four undergraduates spends *no* time in the library during a normal week, and 65 percent use the library four hours *or less* each week. Nearly one quarter reported spending just one to two hours there each week. This means that about half of all the undergraduate students spend *no more than two hours* in the library every week (Table 28).

We found that the library is viewed by most undergraduates

Table 28 Hours Undergraduates Spend Studying in the Library in a Normal Week

	All Institutions	Public	Private	Research University	Doctorate-Granting University	Comprehensive College	Liberal Arts College
None	27	28	25	29	31	26	22
1–2 hours	24	24	24	18	26	26	27
3–4 hours	14	14	13	14	12	15	14
5–10 hours	20	20	20	22	17	20	19
11–20 hours	11	10	13	12	11	9	11
21+ hours	4	4	5	5	3	4	7

Source: The Carnegie Foundation for the Advancement of Teaching, National Survey of Undergraduates, 1984.

simply as a quiet place to study. A freshman told us that "there is no other good place to study on this campus. Something's going on in the dorm room 'round the clock, and my roommate plays records all the time. I go to the library to get some peace and quiet. I don't check out books, but at least I can concentrate for a while."[4] Over half of the the students never use the library to consult specialized bibliographies or to read a basic document referred to by an author. About 40 percent never use the library to "run down leads" or to look for further references (Table 29).

Harvie Branscomb, in a 1940 study of college libraries, found that some of the blame for the underuse of the library might be attributed to librarians themselves, who, he felt, had come to place so much "more emphasis on acquisition and preservation of library materials than on the use." But faculty, Branscomb said, "are making only a very limited use of the library in their teaching work." The reason, then, that students use the library so little was simple: "They do not use the library's books because in a great deal of their work they do not have to; they can do quite acceptable work, in some cases possibly better work, without doing so."[5]

This gap between the classroom and the library, reported almost a half century ago, still exists. After visiting dozens of classrooms on

Table 29 Student Use of Library Services at Comprehensive Colleges and Universities

	Frequency of Use by Percent of Students							
	Very Often		Often		Occasionally		Never	
	Public	Private	Public	Private	Public	Private	Public	Private
Developed a bibliography or set of references for use in a term paper or other class assignment	10	11	23	27	41	46	27	16
Found some interesting material to read just by browsing in the stacks	7	7	17	16	42	44	35	33
Ran down leads, looked for further references that were cited in things read	4	4	12	12	42	46	43	38
Used specialized bibliographies (such as Chemical Abstracts, etc.)	4	4	9	9	26	32	61	56
Went back to read a basic reference or document that other authors often referred to	1	2	7	7	35	38	57	53
Used library as a quiet place to read or study materials you brought with you	17	15	22	23	47	48	15	14
Used the card catalog to find what materials there were on some topic	13	12	25	28	48	50	14	10
Asked the librarian for help in finding material on some topic	5	4	16	14	54	57	26	26
Read something in the reserve book room that was assigned by a faculty member	7	9	16	21	38	44	39	26
Used indexes (such as the Reader's Guide to Periodical Literature) to journal articles	8	9	20	23	43	47	28	22

Source: Higher Education Research Institute, 1982; composite comparative data from surveys between 1979 and 1982.

campuses, we were struck by the infrequency with which the library was referred to. Textbooks dominate the teaching and only occasionally was the library mentioned, and then in the context of a special reading that was "on reserve." Typical was this comment of one professor, who told the class at the beginning of the semester: "I've put several books on the reserve shelf that you should read this term. But you'd better grab them early because they usually disappear." The advice drew a nervous chuckle from students.[6]

We also found that budget cuts often hit the library first. Today only about half of all the four-year-college libraries in the country meet the minimum academic standards of the American Library Association. Collections, staff, budgets, and service come up short on every count.[7] The recommended minimum expenditure, of 6 percent of the general and educational budget, is achieved at very few institutions. The average library expenditure has held steady at under 4 percent of the institutional budget for more than eight years.[8]

At a mid-sized southeastern college we visited, the library had 55,000 volumes, 440 periodicals, and 11 newspaper subscriptions. Last year this college, which enrolls some 1,000 undergraduates, spent only $15,000 on new books, $6,000 to rebind existing holdings, and $12,000 on periodicals.[9] The total expense translates to about $33 per student—little more than the cost of one hardcover volume for each student, and far below the national average expenditures of $216 per student.[10]

In desperation, one faculty member on this campus proposed that each division set aside 10 percent of its annual budget for library purchases. He wanted to encourage his colleagues' commitment to improving the library. In response, one division chair said, "Departmental money is in short enough supply." He refused to give up another 10 percent of "his" budget. "The library," he said, "is someone else's problem."[11]

There is a still larger concern. To exhort students to use the library is useless if they do not prize a book, and many undergraduates, even when they come to college, have never been introduced to the joy of reading. Parents do not read to children, and a study by the National Assessment of Educational Progress reported that high school seniors actually spend less time reading books than fourth-graders.[12]

It is our position that the undergraduate college should work closely with surrounding schools and with community libraries to help strengthen library holdings, and provide continued training for school and community librarians. Colleges also should open their own libraries to teachers and selected high school students.

At most high schools in the nation, book budgets are disgraceful. In 1983, in the country as a whole, the median rate of expenditures for books for school libraries was $3.71 per pupil, a fraction of the cost of one new hardcover book. While the price of children's books has risen 30 percent since 1978, the average per-pupil expenditure for books has increased about 7 percent.

Especially alarming is that, in many high schools, the library has become little more than a study hall or detention center. Most students are given little training in the use of the library or appreciation of the literary riches that can be found there.

The college library must be viewed as a vital part of the undergraduate experience and every college should establish a basic books library to serve the specific needs of the undergraduate program. This core of book holdings should include those original, classic sources and contemporary writings that relate to general and specialized education in the baccalaureate program. The book acquisition budget should be adequate to both build and maintain this basic library. And a Basic Books Library Committee should be named to monitor the quality of the library's holdings for undergraduate education. The library staff should be considered as important to teaching as are classroom teachers. Since the library expresses the philosophy of education and the distinctive characteristics of a college, its role should be to "bring students, faculty and books together in ways that would encourage learning, intensive scholarship, and casual browsing."[13]

We further recommend that every undergraduate student be introduced carefully to the full range of resources for learning on the campus. Students should be given bibliographic instruction and be encouraged to spend at least as much time in the library—using its wide range of resources—as they spend in classes.

We also conclude that support for the purchase of books should be increased, and we urge that at large multipurpose institutions, where the library budget is used heavily to support specialized collections, an adequate portion of the budget be clearly designated for general education. It is not unreasonable, we believe, for a minimum of 5 percent of the total operating budget of the college to be available for library support.

The undergraduate college also has a special obligation not only to support the library adequately, but in a larger sense to sustain the culture of the book. Colleges should celebrate the book and schedule activities each year that feature books and reading—bringing authors to the campus, for example—or they can have seminars in which faculty members talk about books that were influential in their lives.

At stake here is the quality of learning; and unless students read and have a love of books, unless the habit of reading is firmly established by the time students graduate from college—preferably reinforced by the habit of *buying* books—there is little chance for it to develop once occupation and family cares take over. On the other hand, if students get into the habit of reading books independently, colleges may not need to worry so much about covering all the education that most students require before graduation. Learning will be lifelong.

For the library to become a central learning resource on the campus, we need, above all, liberally educated librarians, professionals who understand and are interested in undergraduate education, who are involved in educational matters, and who can open the stacks to students, create browsing rooms, reform the reserve book system, help distribute books throughout the campus, and expand holdings in ways that enrich the undergraduate experience.

The librarian also must extend learning resources on the campus and be a leader in linking the campus libraries to knowledge networks far beyond the campus. The library may not be "obsolete in twenty-five years," as one administrator predicted, but surely, because of technology, the scope and method of its work will change —a dramatic revolution already under way.

Before 1981, *Library Literature*, the monthly index for all aspects of the profession, did not even have an entry for microcomputers. Today, more than fifty periodicals on library technology alone are published in the United States.[14] On many campuses, especially those with large library holdings, computers are now considered a necessity. *The Washington Post* recently reported: "The catalog at Yale's main Sterling Library contains over 13 million entries. With a sea of new books and journals being published every year, most university libraries, like those at Yale, are putting their card catalogs on computer data bases."[15] Last year, at the main facility of the New York Public Library, hundreds of familiar wooden card catalog cabinets with well-worn index cards were replaced by up-to-date computer terminals.

On campuses from coast to coast, it is now commonplace for undergraduates to find electronic catalogs. Students can search for books using the traditional author, title, or subject approach, and in a variety of other ways, using, for example, key words. What's more, students can gain access to the on-line catalog by a terminal placed anywhere—in the library, in a dormitory room, or at home.

Library networks also now extend nationwide. In 1981, the Online Computer Library Center began as a computer-based bibliographic data cooperative for 50 Ohio libraries; since then, it has expanded, with 6,000 member libraries in the United States and nine other countries. Fifty-six percent of the membership consists of college and university libraries. In addition to storing more than 11 million bibliographic records, Online now provides services including interlibrary loans and acquisitions.[16]

Even with increased library budgets, colleges cannot have, as permanent holdings, all of the publications that may be needed by faculty and undergraduates. To broaden their services, we urge that every college and university link its library to one or more computer-based learning networks. As such connections are made, undergraduates, quite literally, have the world of learning at their fingertips.

Many students coming to the campus are already comfortable with the computer keyboard. One third report that high school provided instruction in the use of computers. Almost one half also said they had used a computer in college. Interestingly, only 16 percent of part-time students report having had such instruction, reflecting, we suspect, that they are part of an older population. Nearly 75 percent of all undergraduates feel their college should require undergraduates to take more computer courses (Table 30).

For many college students, the ubiquitous computer has become the number-two pencil on campus. In 1972, the Carnegie Commission reported that "4.5 percent of enrolled students have had instructional experience with the computer."[17] Four years later, almost one third of all surveyed undergraduates said they have used a campus computer facility to analyze data or to learn programming.[18] Our recent national survey reveals that almost half of today's students are using campus computing facilities.[19]

Recent estimates suggest that in 1985 from 300,000 to over 500,000 microcomputers were in use in American colleges. About a dozen colleges now ask their students to buy personal computers along with textbooks. And "about two-thirds of all colleges and universities were providing financial assistance to students or faculty in buying computer hardware."[20] The campus has gone from the printed page to printouts.

When Drew University in New Jersey began to supply all freshmen with personal computers in the fall of 1984, incoming students used the machines in their first week on campus to write freshman seminar papers and to finish a chemistry-laboratory test. Alan Candiotti, the associate professor of mathematics who directs

Table 30 Undergraduates' Computer Experience and Their Appraisal of Computer Instruction in the College Curriculum (percent responding "yes")

	All Institutions 1976	All Institutions 1984	Public	Private	1984: By Type of Institution — Research University	Doctorate-Granting University	Comprehensive College	Liberal Arts College
My high school provided instruction in the use of computers.	NA	33	32	41	42	31	29	39
I have used the campus computer facility for analyzing data or learning to program.	32	48	47	52	49	53	45	51
My college should require undergraduates to take more computer courses.	NA	74	75	71	71	76	76	71

NA: Question not asked in 1976.

Source: The Carnegie Foundation for the Advancement of Teaching, National Survey of Undergraduates, 1976 and 1984.

Drew's academic computing program, said that he "had dinner at the dorm and asked the freshmen about using their computers. It was," he said, "like asking them if they were using their chairs."[21]

Drew's applications increased by 49 percent after the requirement was announced, and the SAT scores of incoming students rose as well, increasing nine points each on the verbal and math sections. The cost of the required computers at Drew is covered by a 14.2-percent tuition increase, which includes the work stations as well as funds for computer laboratories, administrative costs, and faculty computers.[22]

Something called a "scholar's work station" may be the next big step in computing on the campus. The first universities to receive such units are MIT, Carnegie-Mellon, and Brown. With the help of computer manufacturers, these universities will channel nearly $200 million into their computer networks, linking thousands of the new computer stations on the campus.[23] Some call this machine a "3-M," because it has one million bytes of memory, handles one million instructions per second, and has a display screen that measures one million pixels—or, one million of the miniscule dots that make up a television picture.[24]

About the time these dazzling projects were being launched, a computer system was installed at a small college we visited—but this system couldn't possibly spark envy. The director of computer services is a professor whose course load for the last nineteen years has included anatomy, zoology, and biology. His new job keeps him at work at least fifty hours each week. When he decided that the college could use another computer, he brought in his own machine.[25]

Despite the limits, the professor has put together two small computer "systems" at this college. Seven terminals are available for student use and eight are scattered throughout administrative offices. This one faculty member did all the programming for the computers, and he also teaches students to use them. The system was funded with $60,000—two thirds of which came from a federal government Title III grant, and the remaining $20,000 from the college.[26] Those are the extremes: the wired campus, and the colleges with a terminal or two.

Higher education no longer merely anticipates a revolution in computer use; the revolution is under way. According to Steven Muller, the president of Johns Hopkins, "We are, whether fully conscious of it or not, already in an environment for higher education that represents the most dramatic change since the founding of the University of Paris and Bologna . . . some eight or nine centuries ago."[27]

Educators with long memories will say, "Here we go again." They recall that virtually every new piece of education hardware has been oversold, misused, and eventually discarded. "Technology breakthroughs" fill storerooms on the campus. They gather dust, unused after twenty years or more. Perhaps the only tool that caught on—beyond the chalkboard—was the overhead projector, a simple, manageable little box used to throw an image on the wall for the whole class to see.

If we look back, technology revolutions have come and gone because the hardware has been better than the content. Consider instructional television. Programs of twenty years ago were little more than "talking heads" that offered the worst features of classroom teaching and none of the excitement of the new medium. Further, technology revolutions bypassed education because teachers were bypassed in the process.

This time it may be different. Today, on many campuses we found teachers more actively involved in the use of computers and, with their help, programming has improved. Professor Harry Holland's fine arts classroom is free of oil and turpentine smells; no easels stand under the muted lighting, no dropcloths beneath the students' feet. Instead, the aspiring artists sit in a semicircle and stare at computer screens. One student touches a metal stylus to a pressure-sensitive electronic pad; as she does so, the colors displayed in the lower third of the screen mix to her specifications. She can choose from 256 colors in this computerized palette created by her professor and blend them with the others in hundreds of subtle combinations. When the shade satisfies her, she uses the stylus to transfer it to the abstract drawing waiting farther up on her screen.[28]

Next to her, another student works on a black-and-white self-portrait. Still another experiments with the pointillist style, putting hundreds of tiny dabs and dots of color together to create a picture. Holland himself uses the stylus with ease, moving between the menu of line, shape, and color and his own abstract drawing. He considers the computer just another artist's tool, a technological paintbrush that expands his creative possibilities.[29]

Stanford historian Carolyn Lougee has created a computer program about Louis XIV that involves role playing for her students. In this game, played on Apple Macintoshes, the class takes on the persona of a young Frenchman in 1638. Their goal: to become rich and prestigious. Each student "collects rents and grain from the tenant farmers on his land, tries to buy an advantageous position at court . . . tries to get in with the right clique at court, and woos various maidens." The game, which engages the students and provides a glimpse of another society, has "also brought out some startling behaviors: More than one student has plotted to have his peasants starve so as to drive up the price of his grain."[30]

English professor Robert Chapman recently wrote that his evaluation of student compositions has improved due to computer use. He says, "I have found, because I am still doing some papers by hand, that I really am better and more thorough and expressive, a more helpful critic, on the computer. It flows out of me just amazingly. I always felt the process of taking the paper and writing on it was quite remote. The paper does not give me the space and fluidity."[31]

And rhetoric professor Jacqueline Berke at Drew reported that, because of word processors, "our understanding of the way people write—the stages, the process—has changed. The phase of writing that is actually most important is revision. Yet how much time does the poor student give to revision?" She remembers a comment from a student's journal: "The computer makes revision a playground instead of a punishment."[32]

But despite all of the rich, exciting possibilities—and achievements—we are troubled by the trends. On many campuses, libraries are directed with no connection to other learning institutions on the campus. Computer centers operate in isolation. And most classrooms do not yet integrate the resources of these facilities. To improve the undergraduate experience—and strengthen the community of learning—the challenge is to build connections. The strategy we have in mind is to link technology to the library, to the classroom, and—in the end—to college goals.

To achieve such integration, college administrators "will have to do much more than shower their campuses with expensive equipment," as Harvard's president Derek Bok put it.[33] Three specific recommendations are proposed: First, computer hardware should not be purchased before a comprehensive plan has been developed, one that covers personal computers, information services, and the use of technology by the institution. Second, the college also should devise plans for faculty involvement, both for programming and instruction. Finally, we urge that every college have a high-level committee to plan for the integration of all learning resources on the campus.

Looking down the road, we see that the day may come when every undergraduate student will have a "scholar's work station." At such a console students might study the anatomy of the human body, conduct science experiments, design buildings, stress-test the Brooklyn Bridge, or view, on the screen, the world's greatest art gallery. In such a world, the computer would extend the classroom, and the undergraduate experience would be enriched.

Still, caution is advised. The growing use of computers may both expand imagination and restrict it. While using technology, students also need to understand how society is being reshaped by our inventions, just as tools of earlier eras changed the course of history.

There is a danger that greater credibility will be given to data than to ideas and that scholars will mistake information for knowledge. The challenge is not only to teach students how to use the new technology but also to encourage them to ask when and why it should be used. And this calls for continuing personal interaction.

Sir Eric Ashby, the British educator and scholar, speaks eloquently of the human side of education. He reminds us that:

> Five centuries of the printed book have not diminished the need for the lecture, seminar, and tutorial. In most fields of knowledge— even in science and technology—the intuitive value judgment, the leap of imagination, the processing of data by analogy rather than by deduction, are characteristic of the best kind of education. We know no way to elicit these except through dialogue between the teacher and the pupil. The most precious qualities transmitted from teacher to pupil are not facts and theories, but attitudes of mind and styles of thinking.[34]

Technology, in whatever form, should not be allowed to erect barriers that isolate teachers from students, or to restrict creative thought, or to hamper the free flow of ideas from one person to another. Television can take students to the moon and to the bottom of the sea. Calculators can solve problems faster than the human brain. And computers can instantly retrieve millions of information bits. Word processors can help students write and edit. And the classroom can be a place where the New York Philharmonic comes live from Lincoln Center.

But television, calculators, word processors, and computers cannot make value judgments. They cannot teach students wisdom. This is the mission of the undergraduate college, and the classroom should be a place where students are helped to put their own lives in perspective, to sort out the bad from the good, the shoddy from that which is elegant and enduring. For this we need great teachers, not computers.

PART

V

CAMPUS

LIFE

11

LIFE OUTSIDE THE CLASSROOM

The undergraduate college should be held together by something more than plumbing, a common grievance over parking, or football rallies in the fall. What students do in dining halls, on the playing fields, and in the rathskeller late at night all combine to influence the outcome of the college education, and the challenge, in the building of community, is to extend the resources for learning on the campus and to see academic and nonacademic life as interlocked.

The early American college did not doubt its responsibility to educate the whole person—body, mind, and spirit; head, heart, and hands. Faculty members were recruited from men who believed that in serving the cause of truth they were also serving the cause of faith. Student life was tightly regulated. Classroom, chapel, dormitory, playing field—all these areas of college life were thought of as connected.

Not that the relationship between college rules and student conduct was worked out easily or maintained without a struggle. Teenagers then, as now, were inclined to test the limits of tolerance. Throughout the colonial period, and continuing until after the Civil War, there were periodic uprisings in response to oppressive rules and the chronic complaint of "atrocious food." According to Fred and Grace Hechinger, in their important book *Growing Up in America*, Henry Thoreau's grandfather, when a student, confronted a tutor with this demand: "Behold our Butter stinketh and we cannot eat thereof. Now give us we pray thee Butter that stinketh not."[1] In American higher education some things never change.

Religion was a centerpiece of the early college. The historian Dixon Ryan Fox describes how piety marked the beginning of each day at Union College in New York:

> [The] ringing of the Chapel bell called sleepy boys to "repair in a decent and orderly manner" without running violently in the entries or down the stairs, to prayers that were to open the day. We can see the college butler on a cold pitch-black winter morning at his post beside the pulpit stairs, when the officers file in, holding his candle high so that the president may safely mount to read the scripture lesson from the sacred desk, to petition the Almighty on behalf of the little academic group.[2]

Some professors were not happy with the rigidity of nineteenth-century campus life and, most especially, with their proctor and detective duties. James McCosh at Princeton confessed: "I abhor the plan of secretly watching students by peeping through windows at night, and listening through keyholes."[3] Still, most academic spokesmen retained faith in the moral uplift generated by the college. "It was a faith undergirded by the notion that mental discipline was provided by a complex of theological, moral, psychological, and behavioral factors whose vagueness was more than offset by the power of popular convictions."[4]

In this climate, chapel was used, not just for morning prayers, but also as the place where reprimands were meted out and confessions made. During the 1870s, little Mount Union College in Alliance, Ohio, had trouble containing student rebelliousness against the rules. The majority of the infractions were drinking, cursing, gambling, card playing, and leaving campus without a signed excuse. Mount Union's campus historian reports as follows: "Unless the infractions were of an unusually serious nature, most of the major offenders, after a severe reprimand from the faculty, were required to appear publicly in chapel and reaffirm their loyalty to the college and pledge to obey all the rules (taking no mental reservations)."[5]

During the nineteenth century, American higher education grew. The grip of religion was weakened, and scholarship among the professoriate took precedence over piety. In 1869, Harvard decided to break the link between academic status and student conduct. The classroom was the place of learning and social life was viewed as less consequential to the goals of education. Ranking, henceforth, would be based on course grades alone. The parallel use of delinquency demerits based on behavior was struck down. Here is how Frederick Rudolph commented on the significance of this development:

> What now mattered was intellectual performance in the classroom, not model behavior in the dormitory or the village tavern. A commitment to the needs of scholarship meant that the universities expressed their purposes no longer in chapel, no longer in the senior year with the president on moral and intellectual philosophy.[6]

Still, the American college did not fully free itself of the vision of educating the whole person. Until well into the twentieth century, chapel attendance was required at many institutions, both public and private. Residence hall living was still monitored by the college. Women, in particular, received heavy doses of regulation. There was ambivalence, to be sure, but in enrolling a student the college clung to the tradition that its responsibility went beyond the classroom. However, since faculty oversight was now limited to scholarly concerns, a cadre of specialists—registrars, chaplains, advisers, house mothers—emerged to guide student life.

The 1960s brought dramatic changes to the American campus. Rules were weakened. Residence halls became coed and often were almost off limits for administrators at the college. Required attendance at chapel services and campus-wide convocations were abolished on most campuses. Students, it was argued, should be treated as adults.

Today, we found on many campuses an uneasy truce. Students still have almost unlimited freedom in personal and social matters.

Conduct is generally unguided. And yet, administrators are troubled by the limits of their authority, and there is a growing feeling among students that more structure is required.

There are 168 hours in a week. If the student takes 16 credit hours, and spends 2 hours in study for each credit hour of instruction (a generous estimate!), that means 48 hours of the week are devoted to academics. If 50 hours are assigned to sleep, that leaves 70 hours in the student's life unaccounted for, a block of time greater than either sleep or academics.

How do students spend their time outside the classroom? Here is a partial answer. Our survey of undergraduates revealed that almost all students work. Although researchers have reported that some work can, in fact, be beneficial to the academic and social progress of the student, work can also be excessive. We found, for example, that almost 30 percent of all full-time students and 84 percent of all part-timers work 21 or more hours a week while attending college. And as tuition costs go up, the number of hours students work is likely to increase (Table 31).

Table 31   Hours Spent Working by Employed Undergraduates in a Normal Week by Enrollment Status (percentage agreeing)

	Total	Public	Private	Research University	Doctorate-Granting University	Comprehensive College	Liberal Arts College
			Full-Time Undergraduates				
10 hours or less	29	25	42	31	22	26	47
11–15 hours	20	21	17	26	21	18	12
16–20 hours	22	23	18	21	28	21	15
21–35 hours	21	23	14	16	19	26	14
36+ hours	8	8	9	6	10	9	12
			Part-Time Undergraduates				
10 hours or less	2	2	2	3	4	2	2
11–15 hours	4	5	2	6	2	4	1
16–20 hours	10	10	9	11	7	11	6
21–35 hours	14	16	7	8	18	17	3
36+ hours	70	67	80	72	69	66	88

Source: The Carnegie Foundation for the Advancement of Teaching, National Survey of Undergraduates, 1984.

What else engages them? Thirty-one percent of the students report devoting more than ten hours a week to informal conversation with other students. Fourteen percent spend more than ten hours a week in front of the television set. (In the student union of one university we visited, the big-screen television set attracts the largest crowd during the noon hour for "All My Children.") The typical student does leisure reading between one and two hours a week. About one fourth say they spend no time studying in the library each week. Organized sports consume the least amount of student time. Almost half devote no time to cultural events, and the same proportion do not participate in any organized student activity (Table 32).

Table 32   Number of Hours Students Spend Each Week on Selected Activities
(by percent responding)

Activity		Hours per Week					
	None	1–2	3–4	5–6	7–8	9–10	11 or more
Talking informally to other students	3	19	16	13	9	9	31
Watching television	13	22	18	14	11	8	14
Leisure reading	23	35	17	11	6	4	4
Talking to faculty members	26	56	11	4	1	1	1
Studying in the library	27	24	14	9	5	6	15
Attending campus cultural events	46	36	11	4	1	1	1
Participating in organized student activities (other than athletics)	50	26	10	6	3	2	3
Participating in intramural sports	70	16	8	3	1	1	1
Participating in intercollegiate athletics	93	1	*	*	1	1	4

* = less than 1 percent

Source: The Carnegie Foundation for the Advancement of Teaching, National Survey of Undergraduates, 1984.

Few students, we found, participate in intercollegiate athletics. Still, they love to cheer. On many campuses sports are the big event, and football and basketball games often sell out well in advance.

One large university we visited has an 82,000-seat, multilevel stadium that is visible from virtually all parts of the campus. It was defined by one observer as the "emotional core" of the university.

Adjoining this huge edifice are a twenty-five-court tennis center and a student recreation center, complete with basketball courts, volleyball courts, handball courts, weight rooms, and a swimming pool. A coliseum serves as the home of the basketball team as well as the site of other campus activities, including concerts and lectures. Farther west are track, football practice fields, baseball and rugby fields, and a golf driving range and practice greens.[7]

The athletic center completes the picture. The lobby of this modern shrine is filled with trophy cases for the seventeen intercollegiate sports that are played here. The cases overflow with symbols of success. The walls are lined with photos of star athletes and memorable moments in the university's athletic history. To say that the institution is proud of its athletic teams is an understatement.

On this campus, students don't just get excited about the games, one observer told us, they "go crazy" about their sports programs. Many travel hundreds of miles each Saturday to watch the game and attend pep rallies in massive numbers. They wear university sweat shirts, hats, and shoes and wave pennants and place bumper stickers on their cars and decorate other parts of their autos with memorabilia.[8] Spectator sports seem to be the best way to build a sense of community on most campuses today.

Intercollegiate athletics have been called a "deified monster" on American campuses, going far beyond considerations of health or physical fitness, or just plain fun. Often such programs are the means by which a school acquires a reputation, discretionary funds, and even endowment. "It takes athletics to sell a university" is how one president describes his school's approach to sports. At another university—one that "fields the best teams money can buy," as students and faculty express it—the president expects to raise $6.8 million a year from football alone.[9]

In 1929, The Carnegie Foundation prepared a report entitled *American College Athletics.* It revealed that higher education, almost sixty years ago, was being poisoned by a corrupt and corrupting system. In speaking about the destructive influence of big-time athletics the report said: "More than any other force, [athletics have] tended to distort the values of college life and to increase its emphasis upon the material and the monetary. Indeed, at no point in the educational process has commercialism in college athletics wrought more mischief than in its effect upon the American undergraduate. And the distressing fact is that the college, the Fostering Mother, has permitted and even encouraged it to do these things in the name of education."[10]

The words of this report are as apt today as in 1929. If the situation has changed, it has been for the worse. Several universities we visited have had athletic scandals. At one, the football program went through a major crisis in the late 1970s. Seventy violations of the National Collegiate Athletic Association rules, including the creation of a $35,000 "slush fund" for recruiting, resulted in N.C.A.A. probation and a two-year ban on television appearances and bowl games.[11]

Scandals may be the exception, but even on campuses that live by the rules we found that sports frequently dominate the schedule. Class time, term papers, research in the library—all of these are sacrificed for practice, for travel, and for games. On too many campuses the issue is money, not school spirit. Undergraduate athletes are used as fodder for a competitive machine that pleases the alumni and corporate boosters but violates the integrity of the college and has little, if anything, to do with education.

In the light of the shocking abuses that surround intercollegiate athletics we should reflect on the sentiments of the former president of Stanford, David Starr Jordan, who spoke on the subject over eighty years ago. Jordan said:

> Let the football team become frankly professional. Cast off all the deception. Get the best professional coach. Pay him well and let him have the best men the town and the alumni will pay for.
> Let the teams struggle in perfectly honest warfare, known for what it is and with no masquerade of amateurism or academic ideas. The evil in current football rests not in the hired men, but in

academic lying and in the falsification of our own standards as associations of scholars and men of honor.[12]

The tragedy is that the cynicism that stems from the abuses in athletics infects the rest of student life, from promoting academic dishonesty to the loss of individual ideals. We find it disturbing that students who admit to cheating often excuse their conduct as being set by college example, such as athletic dishonesty. Again, the 1929 Carnegie report states the issue clearly: "It is the undergraduates who have suffered most and will continue most to suffer from commercialism and its results. . . . Commercialism motivates the recruiting and subsidizing of players, and the commercial attitude has enabled many young men to acquire college educations at the cost of honesty and sincerity."[13]

Integrity cannot be divided. If high standards of conduct are expected of students, colleges must have impeccable integrity themselves. Otherwise the lessons of the "hidden curriculum" will shape the undergraduate experience.

Colleges teach values to students by the standards they set for themselves. But we believe real reform will come only when a wave of moral indignation sweeps the campuses. Perhaps the time has come for faculty and students at universities engaged in big-time athletics to organize a day of protest, setting aside a time to examine how the purposes of the universities are being subverted and how integrity is lost.

Further, we strongly urge that intercollegiate sports be organized and operated to serve the student athletes, not the institution. Success in class must be the most important objective. At the same time, respect for one's opponents and rules of sportsmanship and fair play must dominate the program.

We also propose that when serious athletic violations are discovered, the accreditation status of the institution should be revoked—along with eligibility status for the National Collegiate Athletic Association. It is ironic that one hears that a university has lost its athletic eligibility but never hears that a college has been on accreditation probation or suspended because of unethical behavior in athletic procedures or in its abuse of students.

We suggest further that presidents of universities and colleges begin to say publicly what they acknowledge privately: that big-time sports are out of control. Campus leaders can meet with each other and agree to a process of cutting back expenditures for recruitment and training, and they can continue to get involved in National Collegiate Athletic Association deliberations. By reaching agreements within various conferences, we can begin scaling back on the commitment to big-time athletics, without individual schools' jeopardizing their public standing.

Further, boards of trustees have an absolutely critical role to play. When a president who wants to fire a coach is told by trustees that his own job is jeopardized if he acts, it seems apparent that the integrity of the institution has been lost.

Against the backdrop of scandals in intercollegiate athletics, intramural sports and recreation are emerging as an encouraging option. Already, 30 percent of the undergraduates participate in such sports and the number appears to be growing. Many students are also keeping fit through jogging, aerobics, lap swimming, weight training, and the like.

At one university we visited, the department of intramurals has a budget of $350,000, drawn from the institution's general fund. Sixty-five percent of the students participate in some program. Over 176,000 students, many of them repeat visitors, were counted in the recreation building during a single academic year. The intramural department offers some forty sports programs, including softball, basketball, volleyball, track, wrestling, and water polo.[14]

According to one student who has played on three intramural teams, "If somebody wanted to, he could play intramurals every afternoon for the whole semester because there are so many teams. Regular exercise is now a way of life for many."[15] We urge every college to develop a comprehensive, well-supported program of intramural sports, one that serves all students, not the select few. We further urge that the intramural program be given top priority when budget decisions about athletics are made and the recreational facility space is assigned.

Most encouraging is the emerging emphasis on wellness. More and more colleges see health and body care as an important educational objective. This, in our opinion, should be a high priority on every campus. The chairman of the intramurals department at one college said the emphasis on wellness is no fad: "Our students are in better shape than they were in the seventies, and there is a new awareness of the importance of caring for the body."[16]

At a large public university on our tour, over two thirds of the students participate in a university-sponsored "wellness program," which includes health education and fitness training. The project also prepares a group of students to be "health promoters" and sends them back to their residences to help others. These "health promoters" study everything from birth control and sexually transmitted diseases to nutrition and how to cope with stress. They not only counsel fellow students, but maintain a first-aid kit and post health information on bulletin boards to keep students abreast of current medical news. We urge that every college consider educating a core of senior students who, in turn, would educate their fellow students through informal seminars about health, nutrition, and first aid.

Health concerns have moved into the cafeteria, too. Menus are now being more closely supervised by dieticians and scrutinized by the students. Health food and vegetarian sections are now standard fare at almost every well-run college in the country. And students are actively involved. Haverford College has a "napkin bulletin board"—a place where students scrawl their reactions to the food on a napkin and tack it up before they leave the cafeteria. Before the day is over, the dietician has posted a reply.[17]

We urge that all students be helped to understand that wellness is a prerequisite to all else. They should be taught about good food, about exercise, and should begin to understand that caring for one's body is a special trust. Further, a professional nutritionist should advise the campus food service and also be available for students as a part of the campus health service. A procedure for students to evaluate the food service also should be available on the campus.

Finally, we suggest that leaders of students' health centers work directly with their counterparts in food service, intramural athletics, residence hall supervision, student government, and even the academic administration to assure that the institution's "wellness" program has the resources and endorsement of the whole campus.

Athletics, health education, and food service are all of direct concern in a college community seriously committed to a quality undergraduate experience.

College life is clearly more than lectures, classes, convocations, and sports events. Wedged in between large group events there must be open spaces—moments when students can spend time alone or relax with one or two close friends. Students need solitude and intimacy as well as togetherness; and they should be able to choose their privacy and their companions without institutional constraint. Open space is needed for recreation, free expression, and student-initiated activities. Indeed, the most exciting activities we found on campus were informal ones, projects organized by students, whether religious, social, political—center, left, or right. On one mid-sized campus, for example, we found women's rights organizations, a gay and lesbian student group, the Liberty Lobby, the Young Americans for Freedom, Save the Whales, and animal rights advocates. None of these was very large, but they had been organized by loyal advocates who were sufficiently vocal and cohesive to make their mark.[18]

Religious groups are among the fastest-growing organizations on many campuses. At one Midwest state-sponsored college there are religious meetings—revivals, study groups, or songfests sponsored by Christian organizations—almost every night at the student union. These assemblies are very diverse theologically and socially. The Maranathas, Campus Crusade, and the Navigators are evangelical. A middle-of-the-road organization called Ichthus tries to "serve all Christians on the campus." There is the Hillel House for Jewish students and the Newman Club for Catholics. The Ecumenical Campus Ministries, sponsored by the mainstream Protestant denominations, has a rather small following among undergraduates ("If it weren't for their building, you wouldn't know they were here," says one active Christian).[19] Student involvement in religion, which seems to be experiencing a renewal, cuts across all denominations and religious faiths.

In our student survey, we found ambivalence regarding religion and church attendance. It revealed that about three out of four college students believe there is a God who judges people, but only 42 percent say that most students on their campus are religious. And only 30 percent say that they, personally, are more religious now than when they first came to college.

By comparison, 14 percent of the faculty we surveyed consider themselves "deeply religious" and 45 percent view themselves as "moderately religious." Nearly one third say they are "largely indifferent to religion," and only 7 percent say they are "basically opposed to religion" (Table 33).

Table 33   Faculty and Undergraduate Appraisal of Their Religious Conviction: 1976 and 1984 (percent agreeing)

		1976	1984
I consider myself "deeply religious."	faculty	15	14
	students	15	15
I consider myself "moderately religious."	faculty	45	45
	students	54	63
I am largely "indifferent to religion."	faculty	33	34
	students	26	19
I am basically "opposed to religion."	faculty	7	7
	students	5	3

Source: The Carnegie Foundation for the Advancement of Teaching, National Survey of Undergraduates, 1976 and 1984.

As for politics, most students characterize themselves as middle of the road or moderately conservative. They are less likely to characterize themselves as liberals but they consider themselves more liberal than their parents. In contrast, 42 percent of the faculty classify themselves as left of center. Thirty-one percent are either moderately or strongly conservative (Table 34).

Table 34 Political Orientation of College Students, Their Parents, and Faculty: 1976 and 1984

		Left	Liberal	Middle of the Road	Moderately Conservative	Strongly Conservative
Students: How would you characterize yourself politically?						
	1984:	2	23	39	31	5
	1976:	4	34	39	21	2
Students: How would you characterize your parents?						
	1984:	1	10	34	43	12
	1976:	*	11	31	46	11
Faculty: How would you characterize yourselves?						
	1984:	6	36	27	27	4
	1976:	6	38	28	25	3

*= less than 1 percent

Source: The Carnegie Foundation for the Advancement of Teaching, National Survey of Undergraduates and Faculty, 1976 and 1984.

We found that on most campuses the conservative viewpoint is getting a better hearing these days. Over the past four years, more than fifty right-wing "alternative" publications have emerged on college campuses. Funded largely by the Institute for Educational Affairs, these publications attack what their supporters see as the "entrenched liberal bias" on the campus. A striking example is the *Dartmouth Review,* which comments, "We've noticed that women who claim sexual harassment often tend to be low on the pulchritude index," and refers to study programs on women, blacks, and Native Americans as "victims' studies."[20]

The Young Conservative Foundation, Inc., a Washington-based organization, is encouraging students on at least one hundred campuses to protest their schools' investments in companies that do business with the Soviet Union and are, according to the foundation president, "for a few pennies marketing the value of the free world."

The group stresses that its effort is not a response to recent anti-apartheid protests, the extent and organization of which they say indicates that the KGB was "without question" involved.[21] A junior at George Washington University who joined the Progressive Student Union and helped form Women's Space, a peace group, says she's been labeled a "radical." The membership of the group is fifteen. "I know that more than fifteen people agree with us," she says, "but because of apathy or fear, they don't show up at meetings."[22]

Despite the drift toward conservatism, today's students still hold a wide spectrum of beliefs. Although only one in three agrees that capital punishment should be abolished, nine out of ten believe more effort should be made to improve relations between the United States and the Soviet Union. There is also strong support for nuclear disarmament, hand-gun control, environmental protection, and abortion (Table 35).

Table 35 Attitudes of College Students on Selected Political and Social Issues (percent agreeing)

	1976	1984
More effort should be made to improve relations between the United States and the Soviet Union.	NA	93
Nuclear disarmament should be given high priority by our government.	NA	76
A woman should have the freedom to choose whether or not to have an abortion.	NA	76
I would support stronger environmental legislation even at the expense of economic growth.	84	76
Laws should be enacted to control hand guns.	NA	72
The United States is spending too much on national defense.	56	57
Current unrest in Central America is caused by internal poverty and injustice rather than external political interaction.	NA	54
Our leaders are doing all they can to prevent nuclear war.	NA	52
Capital punishment should be abolished.	40	24

NA: Question not asked in 1976.

Source: The Carnegie Foundation for the Advancement of Teaching, National Survey of Undergraduates, 1976 and 1984.

Thus, the student activities picture in the American college, like the rest of the undergraduate experience, is mixed. On the one hand, the formal structures of student life—student government, convocations, and the like—do not seem to be working very well. Only a handful of students are involved, and those who are often seem driven by their own special interests. On the other hand, a lot of informal, less structured activities are flourishing. Students are getting together as private campus citizens, to push their own separate causes.

Self-generated activity adds vitality to the campus, and we could argue that informal student organizations are sufficient. After all, students are adults. They are understandably more committed to organizations that are flexible, responsive, and "cause related," as one student put it.

But even though open time and private space are crucial, a college, we believe, must be something more than a holding company of isolated enclaves. We found it significant that even with athletics and all of the student-sponsored projects, almost two out of five of today's undergraduates still say they do *not* feel a sense of community at their institution. At liberal arts colleges it is only one out of five (Table 36).

We conclude that the effectiveness of the undergraduate experience relates to the quality of campus life. It is directly linked to the time students spend on campus and to the quality of their involvement in activities. In summarizing the research, Alexander Astin reports that participating in almost any type of extracurricular activity, involvement in honors programs, and undergraduate research projects are factors significantly affecting the students' persistence in college. It is not an exaggeration to say that students who get involved stay enrolled.[23]

The campus cannot be satisfied if students separate themselves from one another or, worse, reinforce stereotypes and prejudices. Therefore, even at large complex institutions, with their autonomous units, the goal should be to build alliances between the class-

Table 36 How Undergraduates Evaluate Community at Their College (percent agreeing)

	All Institutions	Public	Private	By Type of Institution			
				Research University	Doctorate-Granting University	Comprehensive College	Liberal Arts College
I feel a sense of community at this institution.	61	58	74	63	58	57	80

Source: The Carnegie Foundation for the Advancement of Teaching, National Survey of Undergraduates, 1984.

room and campus life, to find group activities, traditions, and common values to be shared. What we seek is a climate in which loyalties can be strengthened. The college cannot be a parent; but neither can faculty and administrators turn their backs on life outside the classroom, where there is so much learning that either enhances or diminishes the quality of the undergraduate experience.

At an East Coast college we visited, dorms have "living rooms," a fact that pleases students. Students like to sit near the fireplace and socialize. Last December, the director of resident life organized "fireside forums" in the dorms. Forum topics reflected the pressure students feel before exams: "overcoming test anxiety," for example. Forums were also held on social themes. Recently, someone came from Amnesty International to talk about political prisoners and human rights.[24]

Other colleges have suspended classes for a day in order for the entire campus community to discuss a topic of campus-wide concern. Other meetings, of smaller groups, take place in the evenings in various campus settings. At an East Coast public university we visited, students on a December evening could choose among a lecture, "Apartheid in South Africa," sponsored by the women's studies department; a series of one-act plays directed by members of a theater class; and an Egyptian film with English subtitles sponsored by the government department.[25]

Such cultural activities add greatly to the intellectual life of a college community. They have potential for enlarging much of what students are learning in their formal courses. Yet, it was disappointing to observe on most campuses that these kinds of programs receive little support from the faculty. Students are rarely reminded of them, and few efforts are made to connect these out-of-class educational events to ongoing classroom teaching. In a college of quality, the faculty will understand the importance of encouraging student participation in campus cultural events. They, too, will be active participants, and will attempt to tie their teaching to them whenever possible. In this way, they can contribute to the kind of learning community we wish to support.

Beyond these modest examples, the bringing together of the entire campus community remains the larger vision. Is it possible for the modern campus, with all of its separations and divisions, to find points of common interest? Can students feel both the excitement and responsibility that come from being an active member of a community of learning?

There are all-college convocations. Careful planning can provide such a series on campus that will be a vital force, stirring discussion and controversy, reflection and commitment. For example, Washington University in Saint Louis has such an assembly series every Wednesday morning, featuring poets, artists, political leaders, and others who draw large audiences and help to revitalize the community.

Commencements and alumni weekends can have an equal influence, as can concerts on the campus. And occasionally a college can be brought together to support a worthy cause. Several years ago the State University of New York at Brockport hosted the National Special Olympics. The whole campus came together in a project that stirred inspiration and lifted the vision of both faculty and students.

Carl Schorske, in a brilliant study of creative communities, describes Basel, Switzerland, in the nineteenth century as a place where civic and university creative activities were inextricably interlocked. Professor Schorske said, "The primary function of the university was to foster a civic culture . . . and the city state accordingly assumed, as one of its primary political obligations, the advancement of learning."[26]

If a city can stir a creative, intellectual climate, if merchant families can foster civic culture, what about the intentional community we call a college? While leaving space for privacy and individual interests, we believe there can be celebrations and traditions that tie the institution together and that, through shared experiences, intellectual and social integration on the campus can occur. At such a college all parts of campus life are brought together into what we have called a community of learners.

The college of quality remains a place where the curricular and cocurricular are viewed as having a relationship to each other. At a time when social bonds are tenuous, students, during their collegiate years, should discover the reality of their dependency on each other. They must understand what it means to share and sustain traditions. Community must be built.

12

A HOME AWAY FROM HOME

Late in the summer of 1986, housing officials at the University of Wisconsin–Milwaukee stopped taking requests for dorm rooms after six hundred names were on the waiting list.[1] Two years ago, at the University of Oregon, the waiting list for housing was considered a novelty; this fall hundreds of students who registered for campus housing were turned away.[2] At the University of North Dakota in 1983, one hundred students were housed in a local motel, despite the fact that the previous year the school had just opened a new dormitory.[3]

The popularity of residential living has sparked a crisis. Students are heading back to campus housing, and doubling up (sometimes tripling up) in rooms.[4] At one liberal arts college we visited, students were being shuttled back and forth from a Comfort Inn on the main highway while renovations on the oldest residence hall on campus were rushed to completion.[5]

For 40 percent of the undergraduates we surveyed, college is, quite literally, a home away from home; for freshmen, the rate is much higher (Table 37). Over two thirds of the students enrolling at public four-year colleges live in dormitories during their freshman year. And at private universities, 86 percent of the freshmen are residents, while at the private colleges the campus residency rate among freshmen is approximately 80 percent.[6]

The new enthusiasm for campus living is a paradoxical turn-

Table 37 Undergraduates' Living Arrangements, 1984 (percent responding)

	1984
Live on campus	40
Commute	60
Live off campus without parents	38
Live with parents	22

Source: The Carnegie Foundation for the Advancement of Teaching, National Survey of Undergraduates, 1984.

about. Just fifteen years ago, most requirements that students had to live on campus were abolished. The courts have since ruled that students cannot be forced to live in campus housing simply because colleges need the money.[7] Freedom of choice notwithstanding, today's students are showing a strong preference for college-owned housing. They prefer the convenience and social interaction and the comparative economy of such arrangements.

Despite some grumbling about overcrowding, noise, heat, and hot water, most of the undergraduates we talked with said dorm life is "just great." The typical residence hall is now coed. "Special interest" and "quiet" floors are available, and the freedom to decorate common areas and refurbish the rooms are options enthusiastically supported by students. Add to this the fact that most of the restrictions on residential living have been lifted.

Still, it seems remarkable that students, many of whom had their own rooms at home, can live amiably in close quarters with someone who, until recently, had been a total stranger, but most seem to do so.

There are, of course, exceptions. One junior told us, "My worst experience in college involved walking in on my roommate when he and his girlfriend were, to put it politely, passionate on my couch. He had the nerve to get mad at me for being so inconsiderate, when 'I knew he had a guest.' " And a sophomore complained, "I almost left this place one night when my roommate, after a binge on Oreos and beer, threw up all over the bathroom floor and left it there for six hours before he cleaned up."[8]

Crude and careless behavior notwithstanding, most students not only adapt but also make some of their best friends in campus housing. A senior about to graduate commented, "I have lived in the tin cans for four years. They are noisy, they are old, the showers are a mess, and it's hard to study there, but I wouldn't want to move for anything in the world. The social life is absolutely great."[9]

In most of the residence halls we visited, rules prohibit disorderly conduct and the use of illicit drugs (which isn't to say they don't occur), but otherwise students may do pretty much as they please.

If there is one regulation that raises the ire of students everywhere, it is visitation restrictions, though these rules, if there are such, are often unenforced. In the men's dorms, according to one male resident, "women come and go at all hours of the day and night." And one woman student told us, "My boyfriend stays all night in my room all the time. My roommate and I just work something out, and she doesn't mind. . . . This college needs to get out of the Dark Ages."[10]

On one fairly typical campus, "quiet hours" are in effect from 7 P.M. until 8 A.M. However, loud noise from stereos and parties can be heard at all hours. The director of housing at another college told us that some rooms are "unbelievably filthy," with enough old food, papers, and miscellaneous garbage to be health and fire hazards. Her office has announced that it will begin monthly inspections of dorm rooms. This college also seeks to restrict visits from members of the opposite sex between the hours of midnight and 11 A.M. on weekdays and between 2 A.M. and 10 A.M. on weekends.[11]

College students today take for granted life-styles that twenty years ago might have gotten their parents, when in college, admonished or expelled. Sexual freedom is just assumed. Says a woman dormitory resident at a small college in the Southwest: "Oh sure, they have regulations, but nobody follows them. My freshman year, we had a fire drill in here on the weekend because somebody set a trash can on fire. It was about three in the morning. And from every single room in the fourth-floor women's wing, a guy came out. Every single room—I'll never forget that!"[12]

Several colleges in our study have rigid rules about student conduct in general and sex in particular. But even at one tiny religious college in the Southeast that explicitly forbids "fornication" as well as "wearing shorts outside of the gym," sexual activity doesn't surprise campus authorities. Says the school's psychologist: "As for sex, there is enough of it. One of our students did a survey that showed there wasn't that much difference in sexual activity between here and the university four miles away. If someone is interested in sex, he can probably find it here."[13]

We found during campus visits that residential living is, in fact, one of the least well-guided aspects of the undergraduate experience. Students are given a room on campus, but frequently they are not prepared for what is too often a casual and sometimes chaotic part of campus life. Personal freedoms are generally unrestricted, and thoughtless actions create difficulty for others. Responsibility for residence hall living has been delegated so far down the administrative ladder that leaders on the campus have little idea about what goes on in these facilities—unless there is a big crisis.

On most campuses residence hall responsibility is "turned over" to student personnel officials and then is delegated again to a Resident Assistant, typically a college student who lives in the dorm and serves as a supervisor and counselor to other students. These "R.A.s" confront daily the realities of dormitory life. Beyond the ordinary, day-to-day hassles, they must deal with accidents, abuse of alcohol, depression, and questions about birth control and abortion. It is a twenty-four-hour job, one that involves not just "keeping order" and finding light bulbs, but becoming deeply involved in shaping the lives of students and helping the college accomplish its most fundamental goals. And yet, on most campuses the president of the college would be hard pressed to name one resident assistant.

Eileen Stewart, an R.A. at a church-related college we visited, said, "I don't seem to get anything done, but I'm busy all the time."

For someone who doesn't get anything done, she has a demanding job: "This is a Christian school and every sort of problem that exists in the world exists here, and most have to do with identity—growing up, and male-female relationships. Because of the size of the school, it's like a family. If I hear one roommate bad-mouthing another, I will call her in for a talk. And if there is a student with a real socialization problem—a loner—I'll help her reach out to others."[14]

Stewart's apartment is right behind the main desk in the lobby of her dorm. Often she has a student talking with her or resting in her living room. "The most important aspect of living in the dorm," she says, "is learning how to give, and how to give up a certain amount of privacy. When I see a student who is upset, or maybe too tired from studying, I tell her to go take a nap on my couch for a few hours. I tell her she'll feel better."[15]

Another college we visited houses R.A.s on each floor. An R.A. whose floor is made up largely of freshman males told us that he sees himself partially as a "lookout" for students who are having trouble fitting in. "The more introverted you are, the harder it can be here. If I see someone like that, I try to approach them, mention things that are going on, maybe invite them to some frat parties."[16]

Not every dormitory has R.A.s as willing to get so involved, nor does every student want that sort of attention. But counseling and guidance pressures often are intense as R.A.s are asked to play parent, big brother or sister, counselor, disciplinarian, and a myriad of other roles—all for room and board.

We find it troubling that college students are given such a weighty assignment when key college administrators, and especially members of the faculty, frequently are far removed from the day-to-day lives of students. We strongly urge that colleges and universities provide intensive workshops for students who agree to serve as resident assistants. We recommend further that R.A.s have mentors who meet with them regularly and supervise their work. We also urge that every campus have appropriate health and psychological support services available to which students can be referred. Finally, we recommend that resident assistants be reimbursed adequately for their important work.

During campus visits we found that at almost all colleges and universities alcohol is overwhelmingly the drug of choice and the drug of greatest damage. In 1977, half of the college students polled favored decriminalization of marijuana; today the figure is 23 percent.[17] Although the use of marijuana and hallucinogens has decreased significantly in the last decade, the national survey of drug abuse reported that at least 75 percent of the nation's college students drink.[18] According to our survey of undergraduates, 42 percent of the respondents say that alcohol is a problem on the campus (Table 38).

Table 38   Student Assessment of Campus Alcohol Abuse (percent responding)

	All Institutions	Research University	Doctorate-Granting Institution	Comprehensive College	Liberal Arts College
Alcohol abuse is a serious problem on this campus.	42	48	45	38	36

Source: The Carnegie Foundation for the Advancement of Teaching, National Survey of Undergraduates, 1984.

While faculty members and administrators do not mention cocaine in discussing drug use, students do: Several undergraduates described one fraternity whose affluent members routinely spend several hundred dollars a weekend on cocaine and who inflate ticket prices of the spring formal in order to factor in a $15,000 drug budget.[19] Thirty percent of all college students have tried cocaine by the time they have been graduated, according to a study conducted by The University of Michigan for the National Institute on Drug Abuse. The report explained that cocaine use is popular on college campuses because of the drug's availability and the students' underestimation of the drug's danger.[20]

At a prestigious university in the deep South, we were told that drinking is probably the most popular "unofficial student activity" on campus. A student services dean estimated that between 6 and 10 percent of its undergraduates are alcoholics and in need of serious treatment; another 30 to 40 percent are serious weekend abusers of alcohol.[21]

On another campus, we learned that though the state drinking-age law (nineteen for beer and wine, twenty-one for liquor) is strictly enforced both at campus events and in bars, students say that eighteen-year-olds drink too, usually in their dorm rooms. Federal legislation has resulted in a new state law, raising the drinking age to twenty-one, yet college officials have agreed with students that the change in minimum age has not stopped student drinking, only displaced it.[22]

We found that what to do for those who drink too much has become an urgently discussed issue on most campuses in our study. At one small college in the East, the dean of students and the chaplain said that much of their counseling time is spent with students who have alcohol-related problems. Pushed to the wall by a number of legal and social factors, colleges are being forced to rethink one of college folklore's legends—the boozing, boisterous undergraduate. According to the chaplain, alcohol abuse had been "hushed up" in the past, but last year the college had an "alcohol awareness" week to bring the problem out in the open.[23]

Campus counseling centers have become a vital part of the response to alcohol abuse. The counseling center on one of our site campuses recently hired a Substance Abuse Coordinator, who set up a peer counseling program to deal with both drinking and drug problems. At another institution, the head of the counseling center reports that students with drinking problems are usually sent to him by faculty and staff members or even friends who had spotted the problem. Sometimes, however, students come in on their own when it becomes clear to them that drinking is interfering with their studies.[24]

On other campuses, administrators have decided that the alcohol issue should be ignored or quietly condoned. Says one administrator: "Students are going to drink regardless. We'd rather control and supervise it here than have them drive off campus and maybe end up hurting someone."[25]

A college in a northern state where the legal drinking age is twenty-one still has no regulations about underage drinking in the dorms. When the legal counsel for the college advised the board of trustees of their vulnerability in case of accident, the majority view of the trustees was: "Even if we took a stand, they'd just keep drinking." The president at another college, which had failed even to declare itself on the alcohol question, took this position: "We'd be less liable in the courts than if we were on record with a rule we didn't enforce."[26]

What we found particularly disturbing is the ambivalence college administrators feel about their overall responsibility for student behavior. Most of the college leaders with whom we spoke had an unmistakable sense of unease—or was it anxiety? Many were not sure what standards to expect or require. Where does the responsibility of the college begin and end? Where is the balance to be struck between students' personal "rights" and institutional concerns?

In just thirty years, colleges have gone from being parent to clinician. No one would argue that they can or should return to the days when young women were locked in, when lights were out at 11:00 P.M., and when to be caught with a bottle of beer was to risk suspension or expulsion. But does this mean that there are no standards by which conduct can be measured—or that colleges have no obligations to their students? Unclear about what standards to maintain and the principles by which student life should be judged, many administrators seek to ignore rather than confront the issues.

We found students less confused. In our national survey, about half of today's undergraduates said they support a code of conduct on the campus; at liberal arts colleges it was 60 percent. A slightly higher percentage of undergraduates said that known drug offenders should be suspended or dismissed. This is a dramatic increase since 1976. About 60 percent of the students also agreed that the drinking age in all states should be raised to twenty-one (Table 39).

We also heard students say that they would like the college administration to exert more control over boisterous fraternity parties. And several faculty members we talked with have reservations about how well dormitory life supports such important values as civility and academic achievement.

This is not to suggest that students are calling for tight control. The awkward compromise they seek was best captured in an interview that John Millett, former president of Miami University, Oxford, Ohio, had with a young woman at De Paul University, who told him, "We'd like you to understand one thing. We don't want the university to interfere *in* our lives, but we want someone in the university to be concerned *with* our lives."[27]

Lloyd Averill, in his book *Learning to Be Human,* perceptively notes a permanent truth about the human condition: A community is not just a collection of individuals. He cites Edward Shils and Michael Young, who say a community "is, more fundamentally, a group of persons acquiring their significance by their conformity with standards and rules from which they derive their dignity." Within such a community, "there is a recurrent need in men to reaffirm the rightness of the moral rules by which they live or feel they ought to live."[28]

It is our position that a college needs standards not just in academic matters, but in nonacademic matters, too. Such standards should clarify the expectations of the institution and make rules understandable. More importantly, they also can help to define the character of the college as a learning community.

Standards regarding simple courtesy and the rights of others are good examples. Private space should be respected and honored by peers. Loud noise should not be allowed. Sexism, racism, and religious bigotry are offenses to the dignity of other human beings. They violate everything a college stands for. They are wrong.

Table 39 Undergraduate Attitudes Toward Moral Issues on Campus

	All Institutions			1984: By Type of Institution				
	1976	1984	Public	Private	Research University	Doctorate-Granting University	Comprehensive College	Liberal Arts College
Colleges should provide a code of conduct for students.	NA	48	46	57	44	47	49	60
Undergraduates known to use illegal drugs should be suspended or dismissed.	16	54	53	60	51	52	55	62
Drinking age should be 21 in all states.	NA	59	59	60	51	58	64	64

NA: Not asked.

Source: The Carnegie Foundation for the Advancement of Teaching, National Survey of Undergraduates, 1976 and 1984.

Proper conduct also means caring for one's health and being concerned about the well-being of others.

If state laws say alcohol use is illegal for those under twenty-one, colleges should make this fact clearly known to students and affirm that it will support the law rather than ignore it. Such a stand is not only a legal mandate for the college, it is in the interest of the students, too. They need models of courage, not equivocation. In a community of learning, as in any community, we need a sense of order to protect the requirements of all, while still respecting the dignity and rights of individuals.

The goal is not to have a list of unenforceable commandments. Rather, it is to assure that all parts of college life, academic and social, are governed by high standards. The search for values needs to have an open quality, of course. But an educated person, while always searching, is also guided by civility and integrity, by commitments and convictions.

The residence hall cannot stand apart from this challenge. We urge that college presidents become directly involved in the planning and oversight of residential life. The president should receive regular reports on both problems and creative programs inside the residence halls. He or she should meet with R.A.s, visit the residence halls, and make sure the staff is well trained for its heavy responsibilities.

Using residence halls as learning centers has been in practice for many years—at Michigan State, at the University of the Pacific, at Connecticut College, and many others.[29] At the University of Vermont, a Living-Learning Center—a college within a college—houses 580 students, who live and study together. The Center also has faculty apartments, classrooms, and a dining room. Students go on field trips and have special seminars, in addition to their regular course work. An Integrated Humanities Program, run by three faculty members, meets weekly or biweekly in the residence hall.[30]

At Princeton University, a major effort has been made within the last five years to extend the undergraduate program into residence halls and social lounges. To this end, Princeton created five undergraduate "colleges," whose freshmen and sophomores eat together in units of manageable size, enjoy play and study areas, plan social and academic events, have counseling and guidance services, profit from the presence of selected upperclassmen, invite university professors to meals, and have a distinguished professor as Master, with an office in the college.[31]

The important research of Arthur Chickering has shown that living in residence on campus improves prospects for retention, as well as social and intellectual growth. Resident students have more contact with faculty members, are more involved in student government, and show greater gain in artistic interests, liberalism, and interpersonal esteem than do commuters.[32] At the same time, residents are more likely to become more involved in drug and sexual activity.[33] Educational programs should be developed in the residence halls not only to foster a sense of community, but also to provide an enriching influence.

But not all students live in college housing. Some find private arrangements on their own, whereas others join private clubs, usually fraternities and sororities. The "Greeks" have been viewed as social havens, halfway between the restrictions of the dorm and the anonymity of the rented room. Only 3 percent of the undergraduates live in fraternity or sorority houses[34] and yet they often have a powerful influence on the campus while, paradoxically, creating a separate society that occasionally can result in social and economic and racial and religious barriers.

At one small college in our study, more than half the students are attached to its three fraternities and two sororities. At another, nearly 40 percent of the male students and nearly 50 percent of the women belong to the Greek societies. Admission is highly competitive. Freshman and sophomore women are said to take sorority rush so seriously that resident advisers are prepared to take those who don't receive a bid out to dinner in order to ease their despondency.[35]

At a midwestern state university's urban campus, fourteen groups, divided along racial lines, make up the Greek system: three white and four black sororities, and four white and three black fraternities. There is little interaction between the houses: Black and white groups have no common events, and even a white fraternity and white sorority will join forces only rarely for a party. Panhellenic Council members we talked to agreed that loneliness and alienation as freshmen or transfer students prompted them to join a sorority. One of them described her presorority life by saying, "After class, I'd get in my car and go to work or go home and see my high school friends."[36]

Others suggested that there were additional reasons beyond friendship for joining up. "The dean of education told me it would look good on my résumé," said one. Another suggested that belonging to a sorority or fraternity is academically beneficial because big sisters and brothers are willing to help with tutoring. And the Greek Life adviser admonished members to attend seriously to rush procedures, among other reasons, because "everything you learn here you'll use in the real world. Rush is basically selling yourself, and that's what you'll do when you go out to get a job." Finally, we were told that the national push to raise the drinking age to twenty-one has encouraged some students to join Greek-letter societies to have easier access to alcohol.[37]

At a liberal arts college that prides itself on "community," one student argued that the reason fraternities and sororities have grown in number from eight to fifteen in the past decade is that the college doesn't offer students enough to do on campus. "The biggest blotch this school has is its lack of social life. There are movies, but that's only two hours one night a week. The whole social life centers on frat parties. You find out what the frats are doing this weekend, and you do it."[38]

Occasionally, enlightened projects such as the March of Dimes walkathon and blood drives aid inter-Greek communication and promote campus cooperation. Through sorority and fraternity membership, students often feel a sense of belonging on an impersonal campus and members often feel responsibility for each other, helping them academically and socially as well. Overall, however, complaints about the divisive effect of the societies on student life persist. One student said to us that his old high school buddies had become "smug and standoffish" since they joined the frats.[39] The life of an independent can be hard.

Fraternities and sororities epitomize a paradox of student life. Some prejudices have been broken down, of course; but others fester. Fraternities and sororities will continue, but college administrators have a special obligation to draw them into the larger community on campus. Recent court rulings make it more difficult for administrators to escape responsibility for the actions of private clubs. An institution committed to liberal learning and human dignity cannot permit arrangements on campus that even indirectly perpetuate prejudice.

Williams College set an example in the 1960s when it abolished fraternities and moved to a residential house system. In 1983, a Commission on Campus Life at Colby College proposed to strengthen the spirit of community on campus. Residential life at Colby had consisted of a centrally operated dormitory system, supplemented by the fraternities. Dormitory life there, as elsewhere, was characterized by a certain rootlessness. Too often, the dorms were not part of a communal setting in which students could plan and share in joint activities, and it was the fraternities that offered an alternative to this anonymity on campus.[40]

The commission concluded that "our current system of anonymous dormitories and insular fraternities falls short of the residential life we would like for Colby. It fails to promote a community which can both reinforce students' sense of themselves and also welcome and incorporate diversity and individuality. It fails to grant all students both the responsibility and the satisfaction of collective control over their environment. We believe the time has come to reorganize the structure of residential life so as to approach the ideals of a collegial community."[41]

Colby regrouped its living units, including the former fraternity houses, into four distinct communities, which are called Residential Commons. Each common houses between three hundred and five hundred students, and varies in makeup from four dormitory units to eight. Each common also has: a dining room, adequate social space, at least one Faculty-in-Residence apartment, a group of eight to fifteen Faculty Affiliates, who commit themselves to working with student leaders to develop activities for the common, and new programming monies for social events as well as for speakers, forums, and the like.[42]

The commission concluded: "We are convinced that the Commons system proposed here will provide for all students the kind of residential experience that will most directly reinforce the College's educational mission and will lead to the kinds of growth—intellectual, social and personal—we seek to foster."[43] This is a goal that should guide the residential arrangements on every campus.

There is one final cause of concern: We found during our study a deep division between commuting and residential students. All too often students who commute are in the shadows. Most recreational, social, and cultural activities are geared to serve residential students. An observer at one college in our sample said, "Even more than race or class distinctions, commuter-resident distinctions are evident on this campus." A student newspaper exaggerated the differences only slightly in this caricature:

> Commuters talk about their kids. Dorm students talk about how much beer they drank the night before. Commuters dress as if they were going to the office. A dorm student's wardrobe consists of bluejeans, sweatpants and T-shirts. Commuter students have trouble finding a parking space every morning. Dorm students have trouble finding matching socks. When class is over, dorm students attend club meetings, act as campus hosts and hostesses, make posters for special events, play intramural sports and pursue a variety of other activities. Commuters go home. . . .[44]

One campus in our study has become so sharply divided between residential and commuter students that there is no evidence of activity that brings the two groups together. The vice-president said he is "disturbed" by the image of the institution as a commuter college. "For me that conjures up images of someone coming to campus, using the services here, and then leaving." The situation troubles the president, too, who told a meeting of student leaders: "We've got to get rid of the divided image we have." No solutions were forthcoming.[45]

Student leaders also puzzled over ways to get commuters, many of whom are older, more involved. "Most of the off-campus group couldn't care less about campus life," we were told. But we saw no evidence that efforts to reach them had been made. And on this campus there wasn't even a convenient place for commuters to assemble between classes.[46]

Bringing commuter students into the life of the college is an important and growing obligation. Arthur Chickering reports that students who live at home fall short of the kinds of learning and personal development typically desired by the institutions they attend.[47] But what can institutions do to make commuting students part of a larger community of learning, especially when they are often caught up in complicated schedules?

The most obvious step is to make certain that someone on campus is responsible for assisting nonresidential students. There should be an office where commuters can go to get help, file complaints, and learn about the special programs and services available to them. Beyond counseling, a whole range of possibilities is open. The National Clearinghouse for Commuter Programs, located in Washington, D.C., has identified thirty-seven specific activities for commuters, including information centers, off-campus housing referral, car-pooling assistance, shower facilities, lounges, and special bus service. Other services include child care, specialized meal plans, preferred parking, and overnight facilities.[48]

A college, concerned about community, cannot be unmindful of deep divisions on the campus. And it is in the residence hall arrangements, in the private clubs, and in the way commuters and part-time students are treated that some of the most fundamental values of the college are confronted—or avoided. Separateness in the name of individuality and personal preference may be another name for ignorance and prejudice.

In the context of student living, the challenge of creating an enthusiastic community of learning must be carefully considered. Are living arrangements simply a convenience or do they contribute to collegiate goals? Are commuters simply tolerated because they help pay the bills or are they full partners on the campus? Can a college with dormitory students, commuter students, and fraternity and sorority students find ways to make connections more vital than the separate parts?

13

SERVICE: GETTING INVOLVED

A professor in his early forties, when asked about the difference between his college generation and the present one, told our interviewer: "I'm blue jeans and they're suits and ties. We joke that many of the students dress better than the professors. I ask them why they're in college, and they say, 'To get a job.' All they think about is money, money, money. They don't have any social responsibility. That bothers me. There's all this emphasis on having careers."[1]

Today's students have been labeled the "me generation," concerned only about themselves and their future. But we found signs that undergraduates have hopes and aspirations that reach beyond personal ambition. Students are torn by ambiguous feelings—idealism on the one hand, and, on the other, the temptation to pursue narrow career interests that would leave them politically and socially disengaged. They are struggling to establish themselves, searching for identity and meaning.

Undergraduates may be uncertain about where to apply their good intentions, but many want—and have begun—to escape a preoccupation with self. The social analyst Daniel Yankelovich suggests that idealism among the young lies "just below the surface. . . . It will break out. In what form, I don't know."[2] A similar observation comes from George Gallup, Jr.: "I think the youth population has been misnamed the self-centered generation. . . . We found among

18–29 year olds in a study in Dayton, Ohio . . . that fully one-third of persons there said they would like to go into the social services as a life's career. I think that's an incredible finding."[3]

We, too, found that a growing minority of today's students believe they can make a difference and they are reaching out to help others. In our national survey 52 percent of the students reported that their high schools provided an opportunity for community service. And about one half participated in some kind of service activity during their college years (Table 40).[4]

Table 40   Participation of College Students in Volunteer Activities

Activity	Percent Participating
Fund raising	47
Service activity	45
Church service project	41
Charity organization project	31
Election campaign	20
Elderly and retirees	19
Environmental project	17
Hospital service	12

Source: The Carnegie Foundation for the Advancement of Teaching, National Survey of Undergraduates, 1984.

We also discovered that the spirit of service is far from dead on our nation's campuses. Several major national coalitions recently have been formed to give the movement a more coherent form. Two of the newest are the Campus Outreach Opportunity League and the Overseas Development Network. These programs provide student volunteers the opportunity for service in self-help projects.[5] In another, more formal arrangement, seventy-five college and university presidents have established a national coalition—the Project for Public and Community Service. The group agreed that colleges emphasize careers too much and volunteerism too little.[6]

We believe that service constitutes a vital part of an undergraduate education. It offers opportunities that cannot be obtained in any other way. And such an experience may be one of the first truly meaningful acts in a young person's life. Catherine H. Milton, who promotes volunteer programs at Stanford University, said recently: "When you're worried about whether you're going to get an A or a B on an exam, it does something to you to be working with a disabled child who's struggling to learn just to eat."[7]

Service introduces students to new people and new ideas. It establishes connections between academic life and the larger society. A Harvard senior has for three years been a Big Sister to a nine-year-old in a Cambridge housing development. "At least once a week I go down to visit her," she says. "Without doubt this has become the most important relationship I've developed while at college."[8]

Yale's Dwight Hall, the university's center for community service, places more than 1,100 student volunteers in the New Haven community each year. Most students work in hospitals or public schools, but they are also involved with recent immigrants and juvenile offenders. About thirty Yale students form most of the staff of Columbus House, a shelter for homeless people.[9] Student-initiated projects have included an alcohol hotline, a community soup kitchen, the New Haven Halfway House, Marrakech (a residence for mildly retarded women), and the Connecticut Fund for the Environment.[10]

At Princeton University, members of the Student Volunteers Council tutor inner city youth; visit correctional institutions, psychiatric hospitals, and nursing homes; and act as Big Brothers and Big Sisters. The Princeton Education Center at Blairstown, New Jersey, offers outdoor experience to "discover the world of nature" for several hundred disadvantaged children from the surrounding region.[11]

Vanderbilt University's Center for Health Services involves students in a program that gives medical examinations in rural and poor communities in Kentucky, Tennessee, and West Virginia; conducts health fairs and classes; works with local leaders to solve environmental and health problems; and provides maternity and infant health care. The project serves as a proving ground for programs later adopted nationally—like the practice of reimbursing nurse practitioners in rural clinics under Medicare.[12]

Kent State University's Office of Service-Learning annually involves about 1,500 undergraduates in volunteer programs. Students operate the campus ambulance service, spending many hours in training for crisis intervention, cardiopulmonary resuscitation, first aid, and vehicle operation. Others volunteer to be peer instructors or to work during freshman orientation. The campus has an office for disabled students, which coordinates volunteers to help such students by taking notes and transcribing them. Director Roger Henry says students are involved in crisis intervention, health care, and child abuse; a recent development has been involvement with Child Find. Volunteers serve in the arts, public radio and television, and justice.[13]

Henry reports that "about 90 percent of student volunteers say service-learning experience was as valuable or more valuable to them than classroom work."[14] Tutoring, for example, was found to increase significantly the empathy, altruism, and self-esteem of the tutor in addition to increasing his or her academic averages.[15] Service also often has a positive impact on motivation, ability to choose a career, and smoothing the assumption of increasing responsibility.[16]

Above all, service is a way for students to become responsible, engaged adults. Richard Fabrico, when a senior at Iona College, headed a weekly Special Olympics Program for seventy-five retarded children. When interviewed he said: "I need this kind of extracurricular activity to balance my life. It's a way for me to give back a little of what I've been blessed with. I think there's a new trend in my generation—it's a loving generation."[17]

Service must be something more than "do-goodism." College-sponsored programs must be as carefully thought out and as rigorously evaluated as are the academic programs. If students are not given the opportunity for serious reflection on their experience, they may miss the paradoxes of "doing good." Andrew Carnegie once remarked that he had found it more difficult to give money away wisely than to make it in the first place. Students must ask themselves: How do you help someone without making them dependent on you? How do you give support to the homeless or the addicted if they don't want your help? How do you avoid the imperialism of service, the Empire's "white man's burden," with its smug superiority?

We recommend that college service projects be designed, where possible, to help the needy help themselves. Student participation in community activities is necessarily a short-term commitment and students must sometimes learn to be followers. At Yale's center for community service, for example, student volunteers provide staff support to the New Haven residents who, in turn, direct the programs.[18]

We also realize the truth of that old saying: Charity begins at home. There are many tasks right on campus that need volunteers as well. At Warren Wilson College in North Carolina and Berea College in Kentucky, everyone does campus chores. At Warren Wilson, even the college president takes his turn.

This call for service returns us once again to the central theme of this report. The tradition of community, of placing one's life in larger context, is surely advanced as time is given to others. "In a lot of ways, college is an isolating experience," said a volunteer organizer. "These programs give students a sense that they live in the world, in a community."[19]

A report of the Potomac Institute notes: "To make a healthy transition to adulthood, to work out an identity that includes a sense of citizenship, and to affirm positive social values, young people need to become actively involved in the lives of others and in the needs of society." The report concludes that formal education does not meet this need, and work, while helpful, does not necessarily add up to service and is not, at any rate, completely available to young people.[20] Service is the remedy we propose.

But it is not students alone who have a service obligation. For the faculty, there exists the triad of responsibilities: teaching, research, and service. Almost every college we visited recited these functions almost as a ritual. And yet, we found that service is often shortchanged in favor of the other two. Even when the obligation is acknowledged, service is often defined in narrow, uninspired ways. A university faculty member may, for example, provide "service" as department chair or by serving on a professional committee, duties that are assumed to be a part of one's institutional obligations.

We believe the quality of campus life would be enriched if faculty service became more than a catchword. We commend faculty who participate, for example, in the public life of the neighborhood or city where they live—who serve on school boards, who serve as consultants to health agencies, or who work with youth groups in the inner city. In this way, a commitment to service is evidence that teaching is not just a job but a vocation.

Further, if service is to become a vital part of the educational experience of every student, faculty must help lead the program. At Princeton, Steve Slaby, a professor of engineering, led a group of his students in an energy conservation project in a poor neighborhood. His team taught residents how to save on their fuel bills by weatherproofing and using solar energy. Students learned not only the practical application of the theory they had learned in the classroom but its environmental and human impact, too.[21]

We conclude that today's undergraduates urgently need to see the relationship between what they learn and how they live. Specifically, we recommend that every student complete a service project —involving volunteer work in the community or at the college— as an integral part of his or her undergraduate experience. The goal is to help students see that they are not only autonomous individuals but also members of a larger community to which they are accountable. We further urge colleges to offer deferred admission to students who devote a year to voluntary service before coming to the campus.

Colleges that are deeply committed to the ideal of service might consider a formal contract drawn up during the freshman year, a formal agreement in which the student pledges to complete a service-learning unit, working closely with a mentor. Further, if a seminar were established that linked the service contract to the student's major, it would provide a forum for reflection and evaluation. If students make written and oral presentations about their service experience, then the college would, we believe, be fully justified in granting academic credit for the project.

In the end, the goal of the undergraduate experience is not *only* to prepare the undergraduates for careers, but to enable them to live lives of dignity and purpose; not *only* to give knowledge to the student, but to channel knowledge to humane ends. "It is not learning," said Woodrow Wilson, "but the spirit of service that will give a college place in the public annals of the nation."[22]

PART

VI

PATTERNS

TO PURPOSES

14

EXTENDING THE CAMPUS

Going to college once meant finishing course work on one campus in four consecutive years. Only then did a student enter the world of work or go on to further education. Today, new patterns are emerging. The time spent earning the baccalaureate is being lengthened. The average age of students continues to edge up, and the location of learning has moved beyond the campus to the home, the workplace, and around the world. The campus is being extended.

Almost every one of our twenty-nine site visit colleges has evening divisions that serve older students. Several colleges hold classes at off-campus sites, and most of them have early-morning and late-evening courses.[1] There are also weekend programs. About half the students at the College of Notre Dame of Maryland pursue bachelor's degrees solely through the Weekend College, which combines classes on Friday evenings, Saturdays, and Sundays with independent study.[2]

Empire State College is a college without a campus. It operates out of forty locations and is part of the State University of New York. The college admits students anytime during the year and awards degrees whenever the work is completed. Few of its professors teach traditional courses, and students seldom meet with one another. But by the time they gather for commencement, undergraduates at Empire State have completed a rigorous course of study judged equivalent to that of a traditional college.[3]

At Empire State, independent study—not classroom instruction —is the way most students learn. Typically, a student gets a bachelor's degree by combining almost fifty hours of transcript credits earned at traditional institutions, about twenty-five credit hours awarded for prior learning out of the classroom, and about fifty-four credit hours obtained through independent study.[4]

Along with Empire State, Metropolitan State College in Minnesota is another institution offering a nontraditional pattern. This college has few classes during normal working hours, opting instead for sessions in the evenings and on weekends. Starting with a course called "Individualized Educational Planning," students piece together their own baccalaureate programs, completing about 20 percent of the work through independent study.[5]

Through its School of New Resources, the College of New Rochelle offers bachelor's degrees at several sites around New York City, including the headquarters of District Council 37 of the American Federation of State, County, and Municipal Employees. Attending all their classes in the union's offices in a fourteen-story building in lower Manhattan, workers enrolled as students help design their own courses. The solidly liberal arts curriculum concludes with an integrative senior seminar called "Ways of Knowing." Lorraine Altman, an administrator in the School of New Resources, says, "The program respects the experience of students. Further, it gives students a voice in their own learning—treating them like the adults they are and making their programs more personalized."[6]

One of the more controversial practices in nontraditional education is the awarding of college credit for learning experiences off the campus, those related to work or self-directed study. At nontraditional colleges, candidates for such credits are likely to be a union steward who takes responsibility in a shop; a person who masters the intricacies of playing the clarinet through self-instruction; or a reader who, for pleasure, pursues the works of Hemingway and the accompanying literary criticism.

Peter Meyer of Queens College relates how, in the 1960s, the founders of The Adult Collegiate Education program at his institution involved faculty in the assessment of the nonacademic learning of prospective students who claimed knowledge equivalent to that covered in courses. This was done, Meyer said, because they "believed that students returning to college should be given academic credit for what they had learned through life and work."[7]

Thomas A. Edison College in New Jersey gives credits, not courses. The college has no faculty. Students submit transcripts from other colleges, licenses and credentials they have attained, portfolios showing what they have learned beyond the campus, and the results of tests that measure knowledge. A faculty adviser from another accredited college helps evaluate what the student has submitted and determines what must be done to complete a degree. Usually, this means enrolling somewhere for courses. Every public and private college in New Jersey has Thomas Edison students, whose average age is thirty-nine.[8]

Colleges are also beginning to make connections for retirees with strong personal rather than career interests. The Elderhostel movement contributed enormously to this effort. But it was also motivated by an increased consciousness about older Americans and their needs. Occasionally, higher education institutions use residence halls to accommodate these older students, providing not only housing but also continuing education. Other colleges are asking: If we can go into labor halls, why can't we also go into nursing homes and retirement villages? Why should a person, after a lifetime of productive work, be allowed to vegetate intellectually simply because of the physical limitations of age?

Opening up the residence hall and mixing age groups has both an educational and social benefit. It is not particularly healthy, we believe, for students to spend four or more years in a youth ghetto, being socialized only by their peers, denied the experiences of older people. We suggest that colleges consider learning arrangements that bring adults onto the campus, and seek a community of learning that permits an exchange of ideas and experiences across the generations.

To encourage connections between regular students and senior citizens, Eckerd College in Florida enrolls one hundred retired people in a program called the Academy of Senior Professionals. The Academy conducts weekly seminars and organizes discussions on political and literary topics for its members. Recently, retirees with professional skills and a lifetime of experience have served as "discussion colleagues" in several undergraduate classes. Academy members have been particularly helpful in the freshman course "Western Heritage." "The interchange with older people greatly enriches the discussion," says Academy program director Leo Nussbaum, "and it often leads to personal friendships of young and old that go far beyond the classroom."[9]

Fordham University has a program called College at Sixty at its Lincoln Center campus in Manhattan. Fordham's program offers classes exclusively for older people, giving them a chance to gain self-confidence before going into classes with students of traditional college age. "It is a sort of bridge for them, letting them ease into college while they resuscitate skills that they probably have not used in years," said Cira T. Vernazza, director of College at Sixty. "It gives them breathing space and room to decide if they can or if they want to do it." Many students leave after they have taken a course or two; others end up earning Fordham degrees and marching in commencement ceremonies with younger classmates.[10]

A few colleges are actually starting retirement centers in proximity to the campus. Messiah College in Pennsylvania is now planning such a center, called Grantham Woods. This facility for older citizens will link comfortable retirement housing to the educational, recreational, and cultural activities at the college. Students, in turn, will work and volunteer for service in the retirement village.[11] Young and old will be enriched by the mixing of the generations, a goal that is socially and educationally sound in a culture where students all too often remain isolated from the older generations.

Another development related to the extension of the campus is the increased education that is occurring in industry and business.

The world of learning and the world of work are beginning to intersect. Already there are nearly twenty corporate colleges that offer their own accredited degrees. Corporate education now offers a range of courses—from remedial English, to short-term intensive training, to sophisticated high-tech degree programs. These courses are beginning to gain academic legitimacy, being viewed as equivalent to many college courses and appearing on college transcripts. Records of this corporate course work can be sent to a National Registry at the American Council on Education, where credit is recorded and college transcripts are maintained for future use. Corporate courses also are given college credit as companies negotiate directly with a higher learning institution.[12]

In addition to these corporate classrooms, older patterns of cooperative education, where students earn college credit for compensated work in a business, governmental, or industrial setting related to certain fields of study—accounting, engineering, criminal justice, social work—are expanding greatly.

But pushing the boundaries of the campus to the workplace has risks. The corporation is concerned with productivity and profits. Students, therefore, are less likely in their course work to acquire the deeper insights and understandings that come from critical analysis and the examination of frameworks and ideas larger than the particular interests of a corporate sponsor. The goal of collegiate education, at its best, is to show how learning can give meaning to skills, place information in larger context, and discover the relationship of knowledge to life's dilemmas. While established colleges have much to learn from the corporate classroom, the danger is that, in a bid for survival, careerism will dominate the campus even more as colleges seek to imitate corporate education. If that happens, the college, having abandoned its own special mission, will find itself in a contest it cannot win.

In the end, colleges and corporations should build connections; but they must also protect their independence. The unique mission of the nation's colleges—to act as a moral force, to discover and transmit knowledge and larger meanings, to engage with integrity in the nation's service—must be preserved and strengthened. As we seek to understand and respect the emergence of corporate education, colleges need to clarify and reaffirm their own compelling and essential role.

While older students are extending their learning through a variety of flexible arrangements, traditional 18-to-22-year-olds are also breaking new paths. For many students, the time for completing the undergraduate degree is no longer four years, but five or six. At the University of Washington, for example, only 22 percent of its students get their degrees in four years.[13] At Harvard University, 25 percent of the undergraduates take leaves sometime before completing their degrees.[14]

Increasingly, traditional-aged undergraduates are taking "educational leaves" for purposes of work- or noncredit-related personal travel. Still others are seeking ways to participate in some form of internship—in a governmental agency in their state capitals or in Washington, D.C., or in social service and community advocacy agencies, enrolling in a summer term at another college, or taking a junior year abroad. We talked with one young woman enrolled at an elite liberal arts college who, during the summer, had taken a course at a West Coast university, and, during her junior year, had an internship semester in Washington. These experiences were, she said, the most valuable parts of her baccalaureate program.[15] We heard other students also speak glowingly of networks of learning beyond the campus.

One of the most urgent challenges, we believe, is to extend the campus beyond the borders of our nation and make connections to the wider world community. In the 1950s, after World War II, there was an eagerness, born of innocence perhaps, for the American college to concern itself with "international education," to reach out to other countries for development, for scholarship, and for study. Since that decade of involvement, colleges have been more cautious and less connected. In 1983, fewer than 1 percent of the 5.7

million students enrolled in baccalaureate programs in the United States participated in college-sponsored study overseas (Table 41).

Table 41 Number of United States Students Enrolled in College-Sponsored Study Abroad Programs in Selected Countries

	1980–81	1981–82	1982–83	Percent Change 1981–1983
Europe:				
United Kingdom	6,221	5,713	5,460	−12
France	4,235	4,158	4,201	−1
Italy	1,909	1,865	2,250	18
Germany	2,024	2,192	2,347	16
Spain	1,894	2,163	2,299	21
Asia:				
Israel	1,250	1,446	1,341	7
Japan	243	317	276	14
India	44	66	86	96
China	64	119	80	25
Taiwan	54	45	42	−22
Latin America:				
Mexico	1,034	594	1,121	8
Argentina	250	NA	NA	NA
Colombia	159	109	132	−17
Costa Rica	149	202	128	−14
Virgin Islands	74	100	NA	NA
Brazil	NA	40	46	NA
Peru	NA	23	45	NA
Africa:				
Egypt	84	94	80	−5
Sierra Leone	13	14	17	31
Liberia	8	4	12	50
Kenya	20	12	15	−25
Senegal	3	4	4	33
North America:				
Canada	31	142	34	10
Oceania:				
New Zealand	7	9	NA	NA
Australia	45	53	60	33
Polynesia	NA	15	13	NA

NA: Not applicable.

Source: Institute of International Education, New York, New York, Open Doors, 1984.

While only a relative handful of students actually study abroad, we found in our survey of undergraduates that 10 percent say they either *have* spent a term abroad or *intend* to do so (Table 42). All

**Table 42   Students Who Have Studied or Who
Intend to Study Abroad by Institutional
Classification**

	Percent
All Institutions	10
Liberal arts colleges	17
Research universities	11
Doctorate-granting universities	8
Comprehensive colleges	8

Source: The Carnegie Foundation for the Advancement of
Teaching, Undergraduate Survey, 1984.

indications are that the intentions don't materialize for very many.

Students at liberal arts colleges are more likely to study abroad than students from other types of institutions. Undergraduates at comprehensive colleges and doctorate-granting institutions have the lowest rate of participation (Table 42). On a related matter, we found that 34 percent of all college students we surveyed feel their college should require undergraduates to take more courses in a foreign language.[16]

Today's students stand at "the hinge of history." The late Barbara Ward, an eloquent economist and writer, fashioned that phrase fifteen years ago, and it is more than mere sentiment to suggest that there is a growing imperative for the undergraduate experience to introduce students to traditions and cultures other than their own.

For ten years, the State University of New York has had an exchange program with Moscow State University students.[17] Brown University offers an undergraduate exchange program with countries in Eastern Europe. Arrangements with the German Democratic Republic (East Germany) enable a few students from Brown to study each year for a semester or summer at the Wilhelm Pieck University in Rostock on the Baltic coast. Since its inception in 1979, this program has served over one hundred Brown University students.[18]

The University of Pittsburgh runs a Semester at Sea. The classroom has moved aboard a seafaring vessel that makes port calls to various countries. Students learn the history, culture, and politics of other nations while en route, and they are given time to explore and deepen their understanding of each country while the ship is docked in port. Depending on the expedition, students can visit Greece, Mexico, Italy, and other sites of historical interest.[19]

The University of Virginia's department of Spanish, Italian, and Portuguese languages runs a spring semester program in Valencia, Spain. There, students live with Spanish families as well as receive instruction in Spanish related to aspects of literature, culture, and civilization.[20]

Duke University provides an annual program of study in the People's Republic of China at both Nanjing University and Beijing Teachers College. Language training in Beijing is followed by a semester of study at Nanjing in literature, anthropology, and history.[21] Fairleigh Dickinson recently acquired a campus in England, when it bought Wroxton College.[22] The American International Schools Program of the State University of New York at Brockport provides a semester program in elementary and secondary school student teaching in West Germany, Portugal, and Brazil.[23]

Goshen College in Indiana put an international studies requirement into its curriculum in 1968, and over 80 percent of all Goshen students have an overseas experience. Most go to countries in Central America and the Caribbean to study with faculty members from the college who themselves have overseas assignments. Sessions are also available in China, West Germany, Korea, and Poland. During an intense preparation period, students have language instruction and hear lectures on the history and culture of the host country.[24]

As the campus reaches overseas, students have the opportunity to be part of several communities at once. Is it possible that in the twenty-first century the undergraduate who enrolls in an American college will view the world as the campus?

Several years ago, the International Council on Monuments and Sites released a list of 165 cultural and natural locations in countries around the world that represented the progress of humanity throughout the ages. On the list are such places as the ancient walls in Jerusalem; Brazil's historic towns of Ouro Preto and Olinda; Bulgaria's rock-hewn churches of Ivanovo, the ancient city of Nessebar, and the Thracian tomb of Kazanlak; Pakistan's ruins at Mohenjodaro and Takht-i-Bahi and the fort and Shalimar Gardens at Lahore; and Tanzania's Selous Game Reserve and Serengeti National Park.[25] One can imagine the day when these basic sites are viewed as an international network of learning—the campus of the world—with each location serving as a center for collegiate study, with students from all around the world moving in and out.

The trend is clear. In just a generation, assumptions about time and location of learning that historically have guided undergraduate education have been turned on end. Undergraduate education is beginning to break loose from traditional classroom encounters and even from the notion that all learning must be completed under the formal guidance of a teacher. The nation's colleges are discovering that the campus is as much a state of mind as a place. It exists, or at least *can* exist, wherever the student happens to be.

We are encouraged by the ways colleges have begun to embrace nontraditional students, those who are older and attend part time. These students have, in a very short time, woven themselves deeply into the fabric of higher education. We do not claim that the diverse patterns we observed for meeting the needs of nontraditional students will become the predominant patterns for collegiate education, nor do we argue that they should become the norm. Still, with more older people in the nation and more who need further education, colleges, to be of service, increasingly should push out the boundaries of learning. All colleges, we believe, should offer flexible study arrangements to those students whose life circumstances call for nontraditional procedures. Today's undergraduates, and generations of students to come, deserve no less.

We are also supportive of the increasing interest in encouraging more traditional students to find ways of doing some of their collegiate work in extended settings, to enlarge their perspective on the world. These students should be encouraged to look beyond the campus, stopping out and taking a semester off to work, to carry out projects on their own, to serve in internship settings, to travel and study overseas. Young students should learn that college is not just a place, but a way of life.

To extend the campus means that students and faculty members enlarge their sense of community to other people and places, indeed to the world at large. Students are not simply studying in new locations, with older persons or plant workers or citizens of another country; they must realize that they are coming into contact with substantial cultural differences and being affected by political, social, and religious values that are cherished by these people with whom they live and work. Through such experiences the student is enriched.

Even as we applaud the extended campus and the new patterns which are emerging, we are aware of the inevitable educational and social tensions. Throughout this report we have talked of building a community of learning. We have underscored the value of informal encounters between faculty and students and interaction among students. From this perspective one is forced to ask: What is lost when independent study deprives an undergraduate of contact with fellow learners? From where is a student who spends only an occasional weekend on campus going to draw the intellectual sustenance that comes from a more constant association with the symbols and ceremonies in which the full-time resident undergraduate becomes steeped? And how do students remain positively connected when they are engaged in an internship or overseas study, or doing a large share of their work in a corporate classroom?

There is still much to be discovered about how to preserve and transmit the deeper meaning of higher education to students for whom the college could easily become little more than a credit-issuing agency. The challenge is to be creative, not only in extending the campus but also in sustaining important values and traditions.

Once again a balance must be struck. It is precisely because we believe that an undergraduate education should be more than a mere accumulation of academic credits that we voice these concerns. We have stressed in this report that it is through group projects in the classroom that community can be built. But surely, part of what enriches the undergraduate experience also comes from the campus library, and the intellectual and social life that fills the campus environment. And it certainly comes from informal conversations about ideas and events that are part of the daily lives of so many students. Institutions need to find more ways of ensuring that such experiences are not completely absent from the collegiate life of nontraditional students.

Many colleges now have a January term, a period of short-term residence, as was once offered by Goddard College in Vermont, in connection with its nonresidential program.[26] This helps to make independent students a part of the college community. Nontraditional students should also have their own celebrations and traditions—convocations, orientation, and commencement, for example —so they too become citizens of a community of learning.

It is a challenge, perhaps even a threat as well, to a learning community to open up the campus. However, the college cannot live apart from the world. Our graduates must be prepared to participate in our give-and-take, vibrant, often contentious democracy. While extending the campus imposes breaks in continuity and challenges the college's aspirations as a community, it also opens up the possibility of students' being better prepared to be engaged in life. A more dynamic, flexible college experience can provide for today's students the skills and perspective they will need to live confidently in tomorrow's more interconnected world.

15

GOVERNING THE COLLEGE

During Woodrow Wilson's first term as President of the United States, this former university president is reported to have jokingly commented that, after Princeton, Washington politics was easy.

Tradition has it that a campus is a collegial place where people share ideas and work together. In reality, the formal decision-making mechanisms on most campuses are not working very well. Although faculty members feel a deep sense of loyalty to their professions, they are less committed to the institutions where they work. We also found that, almost without exception, the role of students in campus decision-making is not taken seriously in higher education.

At a well-established private college in our study the faculty had grown accustomed to setting, independently, the academic agenda. Departments operated like private fiefdoms, choosing faculty, deciding which course should be added or subtracted. Last year a new dean arrived. By mid-year, he had asked each department to submit a five-year plan for review and approval. The dean also proposed dropping the double major, increasing the liberal arts core by ten hours, and not allowing any student to take more than forty hours in his or her major area.[1]

When we arrived on campus we found faculty greatly upset that these proposals had been so abruptly introduced. "They weren't even discussed informally at a faculty assembly," we were told. A professor of chemistry complained: "The faculty feels excluded at this college. We have a governance structure, but the academic dean is assuming a lot of autonomy. There's a stifling process under way. It's as if no participation by the faculty is wanted. There's a time bomb ticking here."[2]

From the colonial era to the mid-nineteenth century, America's colleges were small, with uncomplicated organizations, and, by today's standards, easily managed. In 1859, The University of Michigan was among the largest institutions in the nation, yet it had only twenty faculty members.[3] The historian Laurence Veysey wrote that "early in the nineteenth century it had been possible to speak of the officers of an entire college—its president, its faculty, and its trustees—as being of one and the same mind."[4]

Theoretically, trustees were at the center of institutional authority. In practice, the mind of an early American college was preeminently the mind of its president. Selected for an unlimited term by the board of trustees, the president ordinarily served as its executive agent. At the same time, he was the principal teacher of the college. Because many college tutors were recent graduates on their way to a different occupation, "only the president could stand before the governing body as a mature man of learning."[5]

As universities became larger and more complex, confusion about decision-making increased and relationships between faculty and administration became more obscure. Most significant, faculty gained a larger influence in governance, even as their loyalty to the institution weakened. Our data show that today, whereas 26 percent of faculty feel their *college* is "very important" to them, 76 percent rate their *academic discipline* as "very important" (Table 43). The chair of the faculty senate at a large research university said that "on this campus I think a faculty member's sense of his community is a national community and not a university one. I have more in common with people in my field at UCLA, Berkeley, and other

Table 43 Faculty Attitudes Toward the College as Community: 1984

| | | | | Percent Agreeing, by Institution Type | | | |
	All Institutions	Public	Private	Research University	Doctorate-Granting Institution	Comprehensive College	Liberal Arts College
My college is "very important" to me.	26	23	37	21	22	28	44
My department is "very important" to me.	40	40	41	38	37	43	40
My academic discipline is "very important" to me.	76	77	74	79	71	78	70

Source: The Carnegie Foundation for the Advancement of Teaching, National Survey of Faculty, 1984.

places, than I do with the guy whose field is not that different from mine, who's next door to my office. My 'community' is maintained by WATS line, mail, the conferences I go to, and the journals I read."[6]

Although professors overwhelmingly say they feel good about their colleges, and seem to feel comfortable with their departments, about two thirds rate their administrators only "fair" or "poor." And about the same percentage describe the administrators at their institution as being "somewhat" or "very" autocratic. Over half also believe that when faculty become administrators they "lose sight of what it means to be a teacher or to do research" (Table 44).

Faculty increasingly see presidents as "managers." And we found that on many campuses an adversarial relationship has developed, with the allocation of scarce resources often generating tension. Such tensions, often persistent and occasionally destructive, divide the college, weakening faculty loyalty and threatening prospects for a vital community. At one large urban campus in the Northeast, the faculty council president complained: "Here everything is formalized but artificial." One faculty member put it still more bluntly: "On this campus collegiality is dead."[7]

At some of our twenty-nine site visit institutions, faculty have organized for collective bargaining. Nationwide, about 230 four-year colleges and universities, involving fewer than one third of the nation's four-year-college faculty, are represented in collective bargaining units.[8] Sixty-one percent of the faculty members we surveyed think collective bargaining brings higher salaries and improves benefits. And about half the faculty say there are circumstances in which a strike would be a legitimate action by the faculty (Table 45).

However, we also found that on matters of collective bargaining members of the faculty have become more conservative when compared with those surveyed in 1975. Fewer of today's faculty feel that collective bargaining *has* a place in higher education. They also are less inclined to believe that collective bargaining brings higher sala-

Table 44 Faculty Attitudes Toward Institutional Authority: 1975 and 1984

	All Institutions		1984: By Type of Institution					
	1975	1984	Public	Private	Research University	Doctorate-Granting University	Comprehensive College	Liberal Arts College
My department is "somewhat" or "very" autocratic.	29	31	33	24	38	31	29	19
This institution is "somewhat" or "very" autocratic.	60	67	69	59	66	68	72	49
I have ample opportunities to influence policies in my department.*	64	59	56	69	54	57	60	76
I have ample opportunities to influence policies at my institution.*	16	12	10	20	9	10	12	25
The administration here is "fair" or "poor."	64	67	69	57	62	68	72	55
Faculty members who become administrators soon lose sight of what it means to be a teacher or to do research.	NA	53	54	51	49	54	57	53

*"A great deal" and "quite a bit" of opportunity.

NA: Question not asked in 1975.

Source: The Carnegie Foundation for the Advancement of Teaching, National Surveys of Faculty, 1975 and 1984.

Table 45   Faculty Attitudes Toward Collective Bargaining: 1975 and 1984 (by percent agreeing)

	All Institutions 1975	All Institutions 1984	Public	Private	Research University	1984: By Type of Institution Doctorate-Granting University	Comprehensive College	Liberal Arts College
Collective bargaining by faculty members has *no* place in a college or university.	30	39	39	39	49	43	32	35
Collective bargaining is likely to bring higher salaries and improved benefits.	76	61	60	64	54	60	65	65
There are circumstances in which a strike can be a legitimate means of collective action by faculty.	61	51	51	52	43	50	57	53

Source: The Carnegie Foundation for the Advancement of Teaching, National Surveys of Faculty, 1975 and 1984.

ries, or that strikes are justified. Further, our data reveal a difference among the various types of higher learning institutions. On all counts, faculty at liberal arts and comprehensive colleges are more supportive of collective bargaining than are their counterparts at research and doctorate-granting institutions (Table 45).

At one West Coast university where the faculty had organized, the dean told our observer: "Some people have said this is the most organized faculty in America. I say it's the most organized group in the universe." He said his hands are tied by an agreement that defines how many hours each instructor will teach each year, regardless of his or her abilities and interests. But union activists insist that the agreement has tripled some faculty salaries into the $40,000 range in less than ten years, and has given teachers added dignity by forcing the administration to deal with them as equals.[9]

Even the president at this institution gave a kind of grudging approval to the idea of unionization. "If conditions at a university deteriorate to a certain point, then I think collective bargaining can help." But, as an afterthought, he added: "In the best of all possible worlds I would sweep the union from the campus. Let me be honest. I think collective bargaining is antithetical to the ideals and traditions of teaching. But collective bargaining clearly defines the issues between the parties. It may not be a system made in heaven, but it can be made to work."

The union movement on this campus did not spring full blown out of the imagination of its pioneers. Rather, it was an outgrowth of frustration over financial problems, low faculty salaries, and a teacher perception that the administration was not listening to wishes of the 250 or so full-time and part-time faculty. Today, at this university, the spirit of collegiality is lost.[10]

The organization of a faculty union, which is viewed on some campuses as the only means of providing adequate salaries and fair practices, is a dramatic move away from the traditional view of governance in American higher education. Communication and decision-making are more formalized. The spirit of community can be weakened. However, such impact may be lessened if faculty members are, themselves, in charge of negotiations, and if faculty senates and similar bodies continue to be used to deal with the full range of educational and administrative matters that fall within their traditional area of concern.

The larger issue, we believe, is how to strengthen traditional governance arrangements on the campus. Our study revealed that whereas 86 percent of the faculty say they "usually" participate in departmental meetings, only 18 percent are "usually" involved in faculty senate meetings and only 25 percent in campus-wide committee meetings. Again it is necessary to disaggregate the data. We found that faculty at liberal arts colleges, for example, are much more likely to be involved in campus governance—attend faculty-senate meetings, take an active role in general and committee meetings—than are their colleagues in the more complex universities (Table 46).

Governance, on most campuses we visited, was an ineffective Rube Goldberg-like arrangement. But several colleges in our study were trying to find a better way. At one institution, academic council meetings used to be composed of department and division heads only. Recently, key staff members have been included. At another college, faculty members recently have been placed on all administrative committees. The president believes the college is better off. "To have a viable institution and to have a well-respected decision-making process you've got to have more people involved. It is a little bit of a burden, but I think in time it's going to be routine."[11]

But not everyone is pleased. One professor, who has never been invited to an academic committee meeting, considers all the talk about cooperation and communication a sham: "Faculty at state schools like this are considered employees. There's no distinction between us and clerks or what have you. We're all part of the family. We don't have an administration-faculty relationship, we have an employer-employee distinction."

Part of the problem might be a breakdown between division

Table 46 Faculty Participation in Campus Governance, 1984 (percent responding)

	All Institutions	By Type of Institution						
		Public	Private	Research University	Doctorate-Granting University	Comprehensive College	Liberal Arts College
I participate in departmental faculty meetings.							
usually	86	86	87	85	86	86	91
sometimes/rarely	11	11	9	11	10	10	7
never	3	3	4	4	4	4	2
I participate in faculty senate meetings.							
usually	18	12	36	9	13	17	55
sometimes/rarely	38	39	36	39	38	41	28
never	44	49	28	52	49	42	17
I participate in campus-wide faculty committee meetings.							
usually	25	21	38	12	20	29	55
sometimes/rarely	44	46	35	46	48	45	27
never	31	33	27	42	32	26	18
I participate in administrative advisory committee meetings.							
usually	16	15	20	16	15	15	25
sometimes/rarely	37	37	34	37	37	37	33
never	47	48	46	47	48	48	42

Source: The Carnegie Foundation for the Advancement of Teaching, National Survey of Faculty, 1984.

chairs or deans and the rest of the faculty. Says a professor of education: "The division heads are not communicating. They feel a need to control things, and they're threatened if people don't conform. They need to be tolerant of different points of view. . . . The relationship could be better. I think people in a leadership position, given their automatic advantage, hold responsibility to overcome discomfort that's unavoidable because of their being administrators."

"You've got your teachers here, your administrators there. You can't please either of them," reports one exasperated chair who feels caught in an awkward middle ground. For the sake of better communication, the president wants people to feel free to say whatever they want at the monthly full-faculty meetings. The administration, he says, "is willing to risk embarrassment for the sake of airing all important issues and viewpoints." But embarrassment of the administration is not the question. Although many complaints are voiced in private, no one speaks out strongly at faculty meetings; indeed, few attend.[12]

As trust is eroded, the shared vision is reduced. And the undergraduate college becomes the victim, without strong advocates and an administrative structure of its own. The college becomes less able to define common goals, or shape the integrated core, or to enrich the major. Ultimately undergraduates are harmed educationally by this climate of confusion. They cannot be expected to feel loyalty to a college where they are not seriously consulted in matters that affect their lives.

Indeed, we found that student involvement in campus governance is almost nonexistent. The student senate at a Midwest public university we visited controls a large budget, mainly derived from student fees. These funds support a wide range of activities, including cultural events, speakers, and clubs. The senate serves as a forum for student issues of all kinds. And yet, most students on the campus do not know that their government has a $1 million budget, that its funding decisions can mean life or death for student organizations.

The feeling is that it's a "sand-box operation" dominated by a few campus politicians.[13]

On this campus, the Greek system, for years, controlled the student senate. Turnout for elections was low—usually about 10 percent among undergraduates. There was intense politicking and infighting for leadership among the few, but the students outside saw few results. "Candidates ran on issues like campus lighting and parking," one student recalls, "and they didn't even do anything about those." The senate was viewed as "a plaything for the fraternities." Last year, to everyone's surprise, the presidency and vice-presidency were captured by two self-styled anarchists running on what they called the "Costume Party" ticket. Their platform promised to eliminate the use of Robert's Rules of Order at senate meetings.[14]

Student government should be an important community-building institution, but on most campuses it is not taken seriously either by administrators or faculty. At one college a faculty member told us, "The joke among the faculty is 'What is the Mickey Mouse–issue student government going to fuss about this year?'" Most students ignore the whole effort. Their mood was captured by one who said, "Students don't know or care about 'campus issues.'" Asked to identify the "real issues," the woman replied: "Having enough money to go to college. Having a job when you get here. Having a job when you get out."[15]

We found that students do get stirred up occasionally over increases in tuition and fees, or moves to restrain residence hall visitation rules. In contrast, they simply do not seem to see a connection between student government and the academic objectives of the college. Except for honor students, the young people we interviewed rarely spoke about poor teaching, good and bad courses, or onerous requirements, or thought that students could or should do much about them. Student newspapers report on social life, but have virtually nothing to say about education. The closest they come is to protest when a well-liked professor is not tenured.

In our national survey, we asked students about the role they feel they *should* play in college decisions. We learned that most undergraduates want a limited, informal role in matters related to faculty promotion and student admissions. They see themselves playing a far more formal role in student discipline and residence hall regulation. Undergraduates also think they should have a say in faculty appointment and promotion decisions. About the same percentage think students have a part to play in deciding the content of courses. Significantly, today's students are less inclined to seek participation in regulating student behavior than were their counterparts in the 1970s (Table 47).

Student passivity is disturbing. Even more disturbing is the fact that most colleges in our study make too little effort to involve students in governance on the campus. We understand that students are only "passing through," as one administrator put it;[16] and yet, for several years they are members of a community that profoundly affects their lives. We feel that undergraduates should be encouraged not only to understand how decisions are made at the college where they are enrolled, but also they should be asked, indeed expected, to participate as campus citizens as well. If habits of good citizenship are not cultivated when students are in college—if they are kept at arm's length—it can hardly be surprising that later these same people remain detached from civic life.

If the college is to be an effective community, effective governance is essential. At every college and university, forums are needed to address common educational questions and to consider campus-wide matters that cannot be handled in any other way. Without such arrangements, the college drifts. Students, faculty, and administration will carry on their work in isolated pockets. Larger purposes are blurred, and the unity of the enterprise, so essential to the undergraduate experience, is lost.

We urge faculty vigorously to support a representative, campus-wide faculty senate capable of handling all matters relating to the institution's academic core. And we encourage leadership of these

Table 47   Student Opinion on Roles They Should Play in College Decisions (by percent favoring selected forms of participation, 1976 and 1984)

	Control		Voting on Campus Committees		Formal Consultation		Informal Consultation		Little or No Role	
	1976	1984	1976	1984	1976	1984	1976	1984	1976	1984
Faculty appointment and promotion	2	3	29	23	24	22	27	28	18	24
Admission Policy	2	2	23	18	25	24	25	27	24	29
Bachelor requirements	2	3	24	17	32	30	23	27	18	22
Content of courses	4	4	30	22	36	35	23	27	8	12
Student discipline	18	10	50	40	20	27	8	15	4	7
Residence hall regulations	27	15	50	47	14	23	6	10	3	5

Source: The Carnegie Foundation for the Advancement of Teaching, National Surveys of Undergraduates, 1976 and 1984.

bodies to provide for ongoing campus-wide discussions. To achieve these goals, released time for a faculty director for the senate and adequate staff support will be required.

We further recommend that student government receive strong backing on the campus and that undergraduates be more fully consulted in the full range of campus life. They should be on all standing campus committees that affect the educational and social aspects of the institution.

We especially urge that administrators work with the faculty senate, student government, and those who provide support services to the campus to create a special forum—an all-college council, perhaps—to discuss in more formal fashion campus-wide concerns such as those identified in this report—recruitment, orientation and advising, the quality of campus life, student assessment, and the rest.

We also conclude that the governing board constitutes the keystone in the governance structure of higher education. The paradox is that, despite the authority of governing boards, their role remains ambiguous. On some campuses, trustees operate in the shadows of the institution. They come to campus once or twice a year, remain marginally involved, and appear only ceremonially at homecoming and commencement. On other campuses, trustees meet more frequently, but tend to get bogged down in details.

A larger vision is required. In addition to the traditional functions of setting policy, selecting presidents, and approving budgets and key personnel appointments, trustees should participate in shaping institutional priorities, involving themselves especially in reviewing the quality of the undergraduate experience.

Finally, at an effective college there is an effective leader. Warren Bryan Martin, in his timely book *A College of Character*, comments on the connection between governance and presidential leadership: "Much has been said about changes in the style of presidential leadership, from charismatic to bureaucratic, from ideational to managerial, from seat-of-the-pants to the computer-style professional. Less has been said about what has been lost in the new leadership. We are beginning to sense the limits to life bolted to bureaucratic fixtures."[17]

Clark Kerr and others have argued persuasively that the modern president has leverage on the formulation of policy because of the respect and visibility of the office. The president controls certain discretionary funds that can work as "pump primers" for innovative projects and has access to foundations, corporate offices, and other sources of support. Mainly, the president has, or should have, however, the power of persuasion; appeals to a larger vision are limited only by the ingenuity of the leader.

There are aspects of leadership that cannot be reduced to formulas but remain unquestionably important. Martin also has observed that "the president need not be a lawyer: legal expertise is available to the college. The president need not be a businessperson: management skills and advanced technology will serve the office. The president's distinction should be a mind that integrates. . . . He or she thinks inclusively, transcends the categories, brings ideas together."[18]

Thus, presidents make a difference. It's a difference that has more to do with vision than with mandates. The loyalty people feel toward an institution—and their willingness to help to make it work—depends on the clarity with which goals have been defined, directions clarified, consequential tasks assigned, and accomplishments rewarded. It is here that the role of the president is the most enduring.

At a private college in the Northeast with 1,600 students, we found a determined effort to build an authentic academic community. It is a place that is neither rigid nor sentimental. There's the feeling that "we can solve our problems, we can work together as an academic community and have an effect on our environment." As one faculty member described the spirit of the institution, "There is general agreement here that we are all colleagues, regardless of the title."[19]

In the end, good governance is to be measured not by the formality of the structures but by the integrity of the participants, by the willingness of individuals to bond together in support of larger purposes. Wayne Booth of the University of Chicago wrote on one occasion that, all too often, our efforts to speak and listen to each other seem to be a vicious spiral, moving downward. "But we have all experienced," he said, "moments when the spiral moved upward, when one party's efforts to listen and speak just a little bit better produced a similar response, making it possible to try a bit harder —and on up the spiral to moments of genuine understanding."[20] Booth added: "When we are working together at our best, we repudiate . . . the warfare of fixed positions; instead we try out our reasons on each other, to see where we might come out. We practice a rhetoric of inquiry."[21]

The undergraduate college, more than any other division of higher education, must be guided by a sense of common purpose; it must be sustained and nurtured by purposes and procedures that cut across the separate departments and divisions. In governance, there must be a voice for all, and integrity is the key.

16

MEASURING THE OUTCOME

$\mathbb{A}$merican undergraduates are forever being measured. They go to class, take notes, write papers, have pop quizzes, report orally, and receive interim marks and final grades in every course. One sophomore complained: "We have quizzes every single week. We can hardly learn because we're always taking tests."[1]

Colleges and universities are evaluated too. At the colleges we visited, federal and state governments monitor the programs they fund. Six regional accrediting bodies blanket the nation, measuring the overall health of the institutions. One hundred and fifty-four professional accrediting bodies look at specialized programs on these campuses—ranging from agriculture to nursing education. And many of the states we visited have what are called coordinating bodies that try to keep collegiate programs well balanced. From this perspective, higher education in America is more than adequately assessed.

Still, there is growing concern that the pieces of a college education do not add up to a coherent whole. Reports about the poor quality of those in teacher preparation programs, nursing students who fail to pass state licensing exams, remedial education, graduates who can't read instructions—these and other "failures" have sparked what some describe as a "crisis in confidence" in higher education. Chester Finn, Assistant Secretary of Education of the United States, writes: "We have essentially no means of gauging how well American higher education as a whole is doing with respect to student learning."[2]

Is it enough for college students to be evaluated in each class, receive grades, and then, when enough credits have been earned, be handed a diploma? Or should the college seek to measure student progress against larger goals that reflect the overall purposes of the institution? Are there, in short, outcomes greater than the sum of the separate parts? The governors from the fifty states, at their annual meeting in Hilton Head, North Carolina, in August 1986, declared that they "wanted to hold institutions accountable for the performance of their students." A worthy goal, perhaps, but how is this to be most appropriately accomplished?

For the first two hundred years of its history, the American college had confidence in the kind of performance it demanded. Most of the small number of graduates were destined for the clergy, law, medicine, or public life—professions that required skill, even artistry, in public speaking. A student in the early American college, following in the tradition of British education, had to prove himself or herself not only in classroom recitations but also in a public final oral examination to demonstrate to the *whole academic community* intellectual and verbal skills worthy of an educated person.

At Amherst College in Massachusetts, for example, it was said that "Everybody was obliged to talk on his feet, unless he stammered or was physically incapable of standing upright."[3] The examinations were conducted by outside committees composed of "Literary Gentlemen of Good Standing." Even for young women at Mount Holyoke, to whom the professions of law and the ministry were closed, public oral examinations were the rule. One student wrote to a friend in 1846: "Just to think of reciting History topics, and explaining principles in Olmstead, before the Faculty and students of Amherst College, to say nothing of being pumped on Geology before the man that *wrote the book. . . .*"[4]

The almost universal practice of asking outside examiners to question students rested on the notion that, beyond the scrutiny of each teacher, it was the responsibility of a third party—a scholar removed from the process of instruction—to certify that graduates truly were equipped to enter the world of educated men and women. And, through declamation, the student demonstrated to peers and mentors what had been learned.

As the nineteenth-century curriculum expanded, the vision of a common outcome blurred. Further, with the growth of enrollment, there just were not enough qualified "outsiders" to assess seniors in their final "discourse," and as the student body became more diverse, the idea of college-wide evaluation yielded to the authority of individual professors, who both taught and tested their own students. Indeed, if we compare the patterns of teaching and the patterns of faculty authority before and after the Civil War, we find little change in teaching *practices* but a transformation in the professor's classroom *authority*. In this post–Civil War period, faculty set the standards for their courses and examined their own students to see if such standards had been met. The professor was both academic judge and jury, and the model was the nineteenth-century German university professor, who had complete independence in the lecture hall. No outsider was presumed to have the competence—possibly even the courage—to question his authority.

There remained, however, nagging questions. In 1869 Charles Eliot, himself a graduate of a German university, outlined in his inaugural address a system of electives that would free students to study subjects of their choice. He also called for a return to the external *examining* body, distinct from the *teaching* body, to evaluate the student before the college granted a degree. Then Eliot zeroed in: "When the teacher examines his class, there is no effective examination of the teacher."[5] After all, the external examination was a check not only on the student but on the professor, too. And without outside critique how could one be confident of the quality of faculty performance or, for that matter, of the validity of the degree itself?

In later years, Eliot lamented that the general examination was the only recommendation in his inaugural address that had not been carried out. Perhaps it was because his two key ideas—a more *open* approach to the curriculum and a more *closed* approach to evaluation —were, to some degree, at odds. With no common curriculum, how could there be a common examination by which the college's collective performance might be judged?[6]

The spread of electives was accompanied by a distinctive system of recording academic progress. From the 1880s on, each course was assigned a standard of value known as a *credit,* or unit of instruction, based on "seat time" in the classroom. Any approved two- or three-credit course was counted equally toward a degree, no matter the content or how well or poorly it was taught. Progress toward the degree was marked incrementally by the satisfactory completion of the separate units.

By the twentieth century, the self-contained course had become the centerpiece of collegiate education. In it reigned the faculty member who would teach, examine, and certify his students. A professor's classroom authority—both in teaching and testing—was unquestioned. In its 1915 General Declaration of Principles, the American Association of University Professors went so far as to compare such authority to that of a federal judge. "University teachers should be understood to be, with respect to the conclusions reached and expressed by them, no more subject to the control of the trustees, than are judges subject to the control of the President, with respect to their decisions. . . ."[6]

A. Lawrence Lowell, upon becoming president of Harvard early in this century, revived the call for general examinations, which, by that time, had "disappeared altogether."[7] In seeking to establish college-wide standards, Lowell was able to persuade the history, economics, and government departments at Harvard to require a final examination of all their students. Unless students in these fields could demonstrate mastery of the subject *as a whole,* they were to be considered ineligible for a degree, regardless of class record.

By the 1930s, general examinations again were fashionable, if not universally embraced. The American Council on Education, in a national survey of universities and colleges, found an upsurge in their use. Between 1925 and 1935, the number of colleges requiring some sort of general examination more than tripled, from 71 to 242. Only 19 of the same institutions had had such a requirement before World War I.[8]

Yet, this trend was short-lived. New students were coming to the campuses and the curriculum was becoming so broad that the idea of a single measure for all undergraduates seemed impractical, even impossible perhaps. Faculty members in each class continued to be sole arbiters in determining what had been learned. And today we are so accustomed to the wedding of the teaching and certifying (that is, credit-granting) functions that even the mention of separating them seems exotic.

Still, we have never fully resolved Eliot's dilemma: The call for better ways to measure the impact of a college education can once again be heard. How do you hold students and faculty to some recognized authoritative standard of excellence? The idea has appeal to politicians who worry about taxes, to educators who care about the effectiveness of their work, and to students and parents who want their growing educational investment to pay off.

A recent survey of college and university administrators revealed that 91 percent supported the idea of linking new assessment procedures to the improvement of instruction. They also agreed that measuring student outcomes would be an appropriate way to evaluate the overall effectiveness of the institution (Table 48).

Table 48   Administrators' Views on Assessment

	Percent Agreeing
Tie assessment to improvement of institution.	91
Tie assessment to institutional effectiveness.	88
College leaders fear misuse by external agencies.	67
States should require evidence of effectiveness.	43

Source: American Council on Education National Survey, Higher Education Panel Report #73, August 1986.

Grady Bogue, chancellor of Louisiana State University, captured the spirit of the moment when he said: "To know as much about our students on exit as we know about them on entry hardly seems an extraordinary expectation. . . . How can we possibly give any meaningful leadership to program and service improvement without data on what our graduates know and think?"[9]

It's hard to argue with this common-sense position, but have American colleges agreed upon objectives by which the progress of all students might be measured? If there are no transcendent purposes, if there is no vision that goes beyond the individual student and a final accumulation of 128 credits, then progress is best measured incrementally, perhaps, through the separate classes. If, however, there are commonalities appropriate for all, if there are expectations that grow out of, and yet transcend, the separate courses, then assessment can serve a larger purpose.

In this report we say that the first requirement for the undergraduate college is to help students achieve proficiency in written and oral language. We suggest that, to succeed academically, all students must be able to express effectively feelings and ideas. This concern for the effective use of English grows out of our belief that as undergraduates develop language skills they hone the quality of their thinking and become intellectually and socially empowered.

Evaluating language proficiency strikes us as an important objective. But the standards established and means used are absolutely crucial. Higher education is faced today with the embarrassing charge that there are even college graduates who cannot adequately read, write, and compute, and in the debate about college outcomes there is talk of giving all students a test in "basic skills." At least two states, Georgia and Florida, now require students to pass such examinations to advance to the junior level.

Reading, writing, and computation are essential. But if college graduates do not have an adequate vocabulary, cannot spell, or are unable to do basic arithmetic, the solution lies in better schools, better admissions procedures, and better remediation. Colleges should screen for such deficiencies on *entrance* and work hard to improve basic skills at the beginning of the college experience, when something can be done. It stretches the imagination to consider the assessment of basic skills, currently defined as minimal competence, as the measure of a college education.

The language skills we seek in college must be of a higher order. They have to do with the capacity to think critically, draw inferences, and convey, through effective written and oral communication, subtle shades of meaning. The assessment of these intellectual and linguistic qualities should occur in every class and throughout the whole of the undergraduate experience. In the end, the student's proficiency in language may also be evaluated through a senior essay and oral presentation that is carefully critiqued.

The second academic component is general education. During our study we found in many states growing interest in measuring the general knowledge outcomes of the baccalaureate experience. Still, there are problems. Educators seem more confident of the *idea* of general education than of the *knowledge* it should contain. In the midst of this confusion there is a danger that colleges will impose a general education examination on their students without first defining the goals or content to be covered.

Some colleges, for example, are using nationally normed examinations to measure the "general knowledge" of their students, even though purposes remain vague. One such test is the American College Testing (ACT) Freshman College Entrance Examination that covers English, social sciences, natural sciences, and mathematics. The "Achievement Tests" of the Educational Testing Service, which cover humanities, science, and social science, are also used frequently. Neither examination was designed for colleges to use this way.

Another general knowledge test that has gained national recognition is the College Outcomes Measures Project at ACT. This test battery examines facts and skills related to three areas: social institutions, science and technology, and the arts. In each of these areas, the tests measure the student's ability to communicate, solve problems, and clarify values. The content, however, often has little relationship to specific knowledge taught in college.

The third academic component of the undergraduate experience is the major, and there is increased interest in assessing the competence of the student in his or her special field of study. In the early 1970s, Northeast Missouri State University adopted a program often referred to as "value-added" assessment. In addition to basic skills and general education tests, seniors at Northeast Missouri are required to take a comprehensive exam in their major fields of study. Nationally normed tests are used. For example, a student majoring in accounting may sit for the examination by the American Institute of Certified Public Accountants. The business administration senior may be tested with the Undergraduate Assessment Program Business Test, whereas seniors in education might take the National Teacher Examination. Those entering nursing can complete the state licensure board examination, whereas seniors in political science, psychology, or other academic subjects may take the Graduate Record Examination in their respective fields.

Thus there are standardized tests available that seek to measure achievement in both general and special education. But for the most part, the tests are, we believe, restricted. Students are asked to recall facts, and interpret knowledge, perhaps, by drawing appropriate generalizations from the material presented. These are important intellectual skills, but the student still is working within a narrow structure that measures a limited range of outcomes.

Further, the current pattern of assessment may further fragment the baccalaureate degree as the evaluation of general and specialized education remains divided. Larger, more essential goals are overlooked, and colleges run the risk of measuring that which matters least. Such a testing strategy fails to offer students a larger, more integrated view of the baccalaureate degree.

But is this the end of the discussion?

We return to the conviction that college-wide assessment should extend and enrich classroom evaluation, not replace it. The evaluation conducted in class should measure the degree to which the student has achieved understanding in the separate courses.

In contrast, college-wide evaluation should focus on the overall purposes of the undergraduate experience. Through such examinations, students should be reminded that the truly educated person makes connections across the disciplines and ultimately relates what he or she has learned effectively to life.

But how is this larger vision to be accomplished? We suggest that the undergraduate college reintroduce a modern, more creative version of the old-fashioned senior declamation.

Specifically, we recommend that students be asked to write a senior thesis that would relate the major to historical, social, or ethical concerns. We further suggest that they participate in a senior seminar with no more than twenty other students, where students would present their reports orally and critique the papers of fellow students. Thus, through written and oral communication, each student will demonstrate, at the end of the undergraduate experience, a capacity to think clearly and to organize and communicate ideas in an effective, integrative way.

Finally, we suggest that every college and university conduct a Senior Colloquium Series in which a handful of graduating students would be invited to present their final papers to the college community. These public lectures, followed by discussion, would make it clear to all students that the outcomes of a college education are to be measured by the capacity to integrate knowledge and apply what they have learned.

At The School of Interdisciplinary Studies at Miami University in Ohio, all students enroll in a senior workshop. They meet weekly in small seminars and develop a written senior project to share their progress with each other and with faculty advisers. In the spring of their senior year, all undergraduates present orally their senior projects, and faculty and students from throughout the university take part in this event.[10]

A university brochure describes typical student experiences as follows: Patti Mulholland completed a program focusing on European culture and the role of Europe in international affairs. She took courses in foreign language, geography, history, political science, and international economics, and studied at Miami's European Center in Luxembourg. Her senior project examined the efforts of one nation to solve a national problem through international cooperation. Patti is currently enrolled in a master's program at the London School of Economics.

Jeffrey Payne combined zoology and chemistry in his major. Especially interested in scientific research methods, he completed a senior project that studied habitat evaluation and winter survival of white-footed mice, and did an additional study of food preferences of foxes and gray squirrels. Jeff is now attending veterinary school at Ohio State University.

Mary Rogers combined music and women's studies in her program. She earned both a degree in interdisciplinary studies and a Bachelor of Fine Arts degree in music. For her senior project she wrote, produced, and performed a one-act opera about contemporary women in America. Mary is currently working on a subscription campaign for the Cincinnati Symphony Orchestra.[11]

A further point needs to be made. We found in the catalogs of our site visit colleges, as well as in others we reviewed, references to students "becoming mature," "developing their personal skills," and "acquiring humane values." Statements also included references to traits such as honesty, objectivity, tolerance, and self-understanding. These characteristics—which go beyond the intellectual impact —are perhaps among the most important college outcomes, and yet it is difficult, certainly in the short run, to determine whether these goals have been accomplished.

Here again, there are tests of one kind or another available to the college. And surveys may be useful in learning how students, as a group, are influenced by the culture of the institution. But current personal development instruments often do not get close to subtle changes in individual students. Robert Pace at the University of California in Los Angeles warns persuasively that many of these instruments are not appropriate for use in an evaluation of higher education, "partly because what they measure is not clearly related to educational objectives, partly because some personality traits are rather deeply embedded by the time a student reaches college age, and spending a few years in college is unlikely to change them in any highly visible way."[12]

Further, Martin Trow observes: "Most of the indicators of change in our research on the effects of higher education leave us dissatisfied: They are not adequate measures of things we are really interested in, such as the growth and refinement of a student's sensibilities, the development of independence of mind, personal integrity, and moral autonomy. We know that these qualities are extremely difficult to study systematically: we don't know how to measure them; their appearance in action is often delayed until long after the college years; they are the products of a person's whole life experience, so that it is difficult to disentangle the independent effects of the college experience on them."[13]

Still, the caution is well taken. There is one aspect of the nonacademic student life that might be considered in assessment—the extent to which the undergraduate has engaged in extracurricular activities and fulfilled the service requirement we propose. Colleges might ask students to prepare a portfolio, recording the activities in which they have participated as campus citizens—student government, clubs, cultural events, and most importantly, voluntary service. This portfolio could address the student's progress in meeting social and cultural objectives.

Education is for life, and, to gain additional perspective, colleges also may wish to interview graduates to find out about the pattern of further education and careers, and survey alumni too. Do they vote, volunteer for service programs, and participate in community affairs?

We come to the final question: Who benefits from evaluation?

Measuring the outcome of a college education, in the end, is an assessment of the institution. And only as we gain greater clarity about the mission of the college—about the purposes that the functions are to serve—will we have the standards against which to measure our procedures. Only as college leaders clarify goals will they have the confidence to proceed with any form of evaluation.

In the current climate, there is great danger that politicians, not educators, will shape the process as funding formulas are linked to narrow yardsticks of assessment. The integrity of higher education requires that public agencies not get involved and begin even indirectly to control the education process. State-imposed "outcome measures" should be resisted. Such efforts often measure that which matters least and fail to consider the most essential traditions of higher education.

Thus, educators must continue to search for ways to evaluate their work. They must seek constructive and credible means for public accountability related closely to their purposes. If they fail to take more seriously their responsibility for evaluation, do not become, for example, far more articulate about goals, do not become much more knowledgeable about their students and their growth, nor become more thoughtful about the coherence of their academic programs, major decisions will be taken out of their hands. Those who know most about what goes on in the university and who have the capacity to see the larger picture will be bypassed.

In the end, excellence in education will be achieved not simply through better testing but through better teaching. If we look down the road, it is unimaginable that the American college, in the foreseeable future, will *not* have courses and will *not* rely primarily on the classroom teacher to both instruct and test. It is hard to imagine that such evaluation—course by course—will not remain the primary means of quality control. Talk about external measures is simply a diversion if it assumes that quality is to be achieved by bypassing the professors and their classrooms.

In measuring outcomes, the task then is to strike a balance between the progress of each student—as measured by the courses completed and the grades assigned, and the credits earned—and the overall impact of the undergraduate experience, not just in academic matters but in commitment to community as well. And through evaluation the expectations of the undergraduate experience should not be diminished, but enhanced.

PART

VII

GRADUATION
AND BEYOND

17

TO WORK AND
FURTHER LEARNING

"I'm pretty much in the dark about how I'd like to spend the rest of my life," a student in his senior year told our interviewer. "Maybe a few years of working will help me figure out my goals and let me learn more about what I want to do with my life. After a few years of work, I may continue my education. Of course, there is the chance I won't find a job I want after I graduate and then I'd just go right on to law school."[1]

Students, regardless of their major, are preparing for productive work. As with engineering and business and computer science, those who major in English or biology or history and who may go on to further education will, it is assumed, someday become productively employed. Colleges expect their graduates to move on to careers and it is a great embarrassment for a department when its majors cannot "get placed."

Thirty-five percent of the college students we surveyed said they worried "quite a lot" or "a great deal" about job prospects after college. Another 46 percent were "somewhat anxious" about the kind of job they could expect following graduation (Table 49). Students have cause to worry. From now until 1990 it is estimated that there will be only twelve to thirteen million positions requiring a college degree and fifteen million college graduates chasing after them.[2] However, such projections should be viewed cautiously, since they do not take into consideration the dramatic changes that

Table 49   College Student Apprehension About Job Prospects

| | Total | | Percent Agreeing by Type of Institution, 1984 | | | | | |
	1976	1984	Public	Private	Res.	Doc.	Comp.	LA
How much do you worry about job prospects after leaving college?								
A great deal	13	13	13	13	12	10	14	15
Quite a lot	21	22	22	20	20	25	22	20
Somewhat	42	45	46	45	49	42	45	45
Not at all	24	20	19	22	19	23	19	20

Source: The Carnegie Foundation for the Advancement of Teaching, Surveys of Undergraduates, 1976 and 1984.

continually take place in the employment structure, especially in a predominately service economy.

Many factors contribute to a person's success in life. Still, there is solid evidence to suggest that a college education is beneficial. It opens doors and, to some degree, affects income, too. Today, a male who did not go beyond high school will earn, on average, $861,000 by the time he retires at age sixty-four. But a male college graduate will earn, on average, $1,190,000 (40 percent more). It is estimated that a female high school graduate today will earn $381,000 in her lifetime; a female college graduate will make one third more, $523,000.[3] Moreover, the income gap between the college graduate and the nongraduate is widening.

The benefits are distributed unevenly, however. Both the college attended and the field of study are important. The most sought-after graduates next hiring season will be those who majored in electrical and mechanical engineering, computer science, and accounting.[4] In 1983, at the University of Illinois, over 90 percent of the engineering majors had confirmed employment plans at graduation time.[5] That was also true for business majors. In contrast, only 19 percent of those in the humanities, 30 percent of life science majors, and 30 percent of those majoring in social science and psychology had acquired jobs before they graduated.[6]

Not only do business and engineering majors receive more job offers, their salaries are more attractive too. In July 1986, business majors were offered average monthly salaries of between $1,603 and $1,903 and engineering majors received average monthly salary offers from $1,883 to $2,750, depending on the field of specialization. In contrast, humanities majors averaged only $1,608, economics majors averaged $1,867, and other social science majors were offered no more than $1,665 on average.[7]

If there is worry about jobs among graduates, there is double worry for those majoring in the liberal arts. More than half of these graduates step from the commencement line to the unemployment line (Table 50). It is not that they never get jobs, it's just that liberal arts majors typically have not been able to secure employment before they graduate. Often, while marking time, they take a blue-collar or pink-collar job for which they may be overqualified. This has prompted some observers to question the value of a liberal education.

Long-term prospects are much brighter. The University of Illinois conducted a follow-up survey to see how successful its graduates have been at finding jobs. The study revealed that although liberal arts graduates may have a tougher time immediately after graduation, they close the gap over time (Table 50). Further, liberal arts alumni tend to be satisfied with their education.[8] This was typical of the comments received: "College didn't fit me for any certain career, but it taught me how to learn."[9] When degree satisfaction was compared *among* liberal arts majors, those specializing

Table 50 Percent of College Graduates Employed

	At Graduation	After 1 month	After 2 months	After 3 months	After 9 months
Engineers	83	89	91	94	98
Education	24	47	63	82	97
Liberal Arts*	38	55	64	74	94

*Figures are mid-points data presented in source.

Source: Barnard, Clayton L., and David S. Bechtel, "Influences and Considerations: Issues Guiding Placement and Recruiting Today," *Journal of College Placement,* Winter 1983, vol. 44, no. 2, p. 35.

in science and math were the most satisfied with their education, followed by those in the humanities. Social science majors indicated the least satisfaction.[10]

Most significant, perhaps, eight out of ten liberal arts alumni say they would advise a high school graduate to select a liberal arts major[11] and 85 percent said that, if given the choice, they would take a liberal arts major again. The vast majority of the alumni felt their undergraduate study prepared them well for later life. Further, five years after receiving their bachelor's degrees, 87 percent of those who majored in the liberal arts were satisfied with their careers.[12] We conclude that students should arrange their academic program with the confidence that a well-educated person, regardless of his or her major, will find a place to serve with effectiveness and satisfaction.

It is also our position that, just as colleges have an obligation to guide students through higher education, they also should be conscientious in helping them get placed. How do colleges assist students as they make the transition from the campus to the world of work? One small liberal arts college, Westmar in Iowa, has "guaranteed" jobs for its graduates. If a student has maintained a grade-point average of 2.5 (C+) or above, completed a course in job-seeking skills, taken part in a job internship, and has annually reviewed his career plans with an adviser, the college agrees to refund $2,000 if the graduate is still unemployed six months after graduation. This school, which has five hundred students, has a 95-percent success rate in placement.[13]

More typically, colleges give guidance, not guarantees. The placement office at the University of North Carolina, Chapel Hill, served 10,355 students last year. It holds forty job workshops and other training programs each semester. As many as one hundred students a day come in, well dressed, to sit quietly, waiting for a half-hour-long interview with a recruiter. The director of the office remarked, "Our students are very serious about the job search, right down to wearing their best suits. They are interested in making money, being successful, and finding a job with a Fortune 500 company."[14]

Every college in our study has a placement office. But these offices varied greatly in quality and impact. Fewer than 30 percent of the students responding to our survey said they had used the placement office.[15] We found that many placement offices were modest in size and underfunded. Placement directors, on average, earn only about $20,000 a year and have limited staff support. Their annual budgets range from $750 to $75,000.[16]

We have argued in this report for the enriched major and suggested that collegiate education, for all students, should be considered useful. Therefore we urge that placement activities be given a much higher status on the campus. Specifically, we recommend that college placement offices be headed by professionals who are knowledgeable about job opportunities and have the support needed to assist students in their search for employment. A special priority should be given to students in the liberal arts, who are the least likely to be tapped by current recruiters.

Further, we suggest that in their surveys of alumni, colleges periodically inquire into the work patterns of their graduates, asking whether their college experience was a satisfactory preparation for vocation. The results should be used by the various academic departments in the evaluation and reshaping of the programs, to enrich the liberal arts programs, not supplant them.

Some students, upon getting their diplomas, head directly to graduate or professional school, rather than to work. But in recent years, the percentage of those choosing this option has been going down. About fifteen years ago, half of all college seniors planned to get a master's degree, and 28 percent expected to get a doctorate or professional degree.[17] Fewer than 10 percent said they had *no* plans for further education.[18] Today, the percentage of students rejecting graduate education has increased; about one out of every five college seniors now say they do not plan to go to graduate school.[19] This decline in interest reflects, at least in part, the current sharp reduction in opportunities for college and university teaching.

But how do the graduates sort themselves out? Who goes on to further study, and why? Our research revealed that neither the sex nor the age of the student makes a difference.[20] We also found no significant relationship between the amount of money a student has borrowed as an undergraduate and his or her plans to continue advanced education. However, those with vocational majors—education, engineering, health, and business—are less certain about going to graduate or professional school than those who majored in the liberal arts and sciences.[21]

The students at elite liberal arts colleges are just as likely as those attending research universities to go on to further education. Indeed, a recent study has shown that these liberal arts colleges rank at or near the top in the training of scientists who have gone on to earn Ph.D.s (Table 51).

Table 51   Production of Ph.D.s Among All Baccalaureates at Selected Types of Higher Learning Institutions

Institutional Group	Number of Baccalaureates*	Number of Ph.D.s**	Doctoral Productivity Ratio*** Per Capita
The 48 Liberal Arts Colleges	14,372	35,424	8.22%
The Ivy League Universities	11,841	27,846	7.84%
The NAS Top-Rated 20 Universities	41,186	85,486	6.92%
The Big 10 Universities	34,973	44,776	4.27%

Definitions:

*Mean aggregate number of baccalaureate degrees conferred (all fields) per year, 1946 to 1976.

**Total numbers of doctoral degrees granted between 1951 and 1980 (30 yrs.) to individuals having earned undergraduate degrees from the various institutional groups.

***Ratio of mean annual Ph.D. production over the period to mean annual total baccalaureate production (expressed in percentage terms).

Note: The proportion of all recent baccalaureates graduated from the 48 liberal arts colleges going on to earn the Ph.D. exceeds that of three sets of major universities.

Source: Davis-Van Atta, David, Sam C. Carrier, and Frank Frankford, *Educating America's Scientists: The Role of the Research College* (Oberlin, OH: Oberlin College, May 1985), p. 29.

What accounts for the high productivity at selective liberal arts colleges? The first point is that these colleges have a tradition of attracting gifted students who have high aspirations. These institutions also have a high proportion (one quarter) of their teaching staff in the basic sciences, and slightly over half the science faculty are tenured.[22] The science faculty at these colleges is active in research, and a large percentage of their students work closely with faculty mentors and often complete a research project on their own. But the greatest reason for Ph.D. productivity in the most selective liberal arts colleges in the nation is the quality of student-faculty interaction.

While the number of students going on to graduate education was declining, professional schools in the United States were being flooded with applicants. Many of the best undergraduates, who, in prior years, might have considered academic careers, turned to law and medicine and business. During the late 1960s and early 1970s, some campuses became little more than preprofessional training centers. Undergraduates were subjected to competitive pressures. Business majors, for example, vied for grades that would get them into the most prestigious M.B.A. programs. They bypassed electives that would broaden their liberal arts background in order to take marketing, finance, and accounting courses that would enhance their credentials. To improve their chances for good grades, pre-med majors were known to sabotage each other's experiments in chemistry laboratories. Students in political science, expecting to compete for entrance to law school, tore pages from reserved books on assigned reading lists so others would not have access to information.

During the 1960s new law schools were spreading almost like McDonald's franchises. Applications soared and enrollment just about doubled. There was an enrollment gain of another 50 percent in the 1970s.[23] Graduate business schools shared a similar pattern, with the M.B.A. degrees conferred in 1984 soaring to thirteen times their number in 1960.[24] Students coming out of the most elite graduate schools of business had starting salaries of $55,000 to $60,000. The health-related fields—most especially medicine, dentistry, and veterinary science—also became intensely competitive as students fought for coveted spots in the prestigious schools.

By the mid-1980s, change was in the wind again. Professional schools lost their gloss. Undergraduates became less confident that the investment of time and money in such institutions would pay off. Applications for dental schools, for example, declined from a high of 15,000 in 1975 to 5,100 in 1986.[25] Even medical schools lost appeal (Table 52). This is not to suggest that medical school applicants have necessarily deteriorated in quality. There is still a great deal of self-selection going on, and in 1985 the grade-point average of all applicants not accepted to medical school was 3.1. Those accepted had an average of 3.5.[26]

During campus visits we were reminded time and time again just how much graduate and professional schools influence undergraduate education, just as colleges, inevitably, shape the schools. This gives rise to early specialization and often leaves little room for the general education sequence. A few institutions, in order to give more space and autonomy to collegiate education, have created a separate faculty for each level.

Perhaps, as the post-baccalaureate pressure recedes, the undergraduate college may be able to move out of the shadow of professional and graduate schools and reaffirm a mission and a climate of its own. Jaroslav Pelikan, Sterling Professor of History and former Dean of the Graduate School at Yale, in a provocative essay argues

Table 52 Medical School Applicants, Acceptees, and Matriculants, 1974–84

Year	Applicants	Acceptees	Matriculants
1974	42,624	15,066	NA
1975	42,303	15,365	NA
1976	42,155	15,774	15,277
1977	40,557	15,977	15,511
1978	36,636	16,527	16,038
1979	36,141	16,886	16,307
1980	36,100	17,146	16,590
1981	36,727	17,286	16,660
1982	35,730	17,294	16,567
1983	35,300	17,209	16,480
1984	35,944	17,194	16,395

NA: Not applicable.

Source: The Association of American Medical Colleges, Office of Minority Affairs, *Minority Students in Medical Education: Facts and Figures, II* (Washington, D.C.: March 1985), pp. 4, 8.

that graduate schools must coordinate their emphasis on general education with undergraduate colleges, and that the liberal arts major should not be seen solely as the groundwork for post-baccalaureate education. Here is Pelikan's position: "The case for the conventional major . . . ought to rest principally on its importance as a summation and a climax for undergraduate study rather than, as it often does now, on the foundation it supposedly lays for graduate study."[27]

If the undergraduate college is once again to take command of its own destiny, we urge that graduate school deans consult with key administrators in undergraduate programs to improve the curriculum linkage between the separate levels. Above all, we strongly recommend that graduate and professional schools reduce the requirements they impose on the undergraduate college. The college should be free to plan, with integrity, a program of its own.

As colleges are essential to the education that follows and precedes it, so minority students are essential to the diversity and quality of all sectors, too. During the past two decades, the enrollment of blacks and Hispanics in graduate and professional schools followed the pattern of other students. Starting in the 1960s, applications grew as new social priorities led to aggressive recruiting of minorities. Recently, however, a decline in professional school enrollments among blacks has been evident in almost all fields (Table 53).

Table 53　Number of Minority Students Earning Ph.D.s in Selected Fields, 1983

Engineering	40
Physical science	59
Computing science	4
Biological science	24
Social science	166

Source:　Blackwell, James E., "Increasing Access and Retention of Minority Students in Graduate and Professional Schools," prepared for the invitational conference on Educational Standards, Testing and Access sponsored by the Educational Testing Service, New York, N.Y., October 27, 1984, pp. 13, 14.

We are deeply troubled by this pattern. Bringing these young people into the mainstream of American life requires a renewed commitment to equal opportunity. And any attack on the problem will surely benefit from efforts that begin as early as junior high school, when students are acquiring attitudes and choosing courses that influence their participation in higher education. Between 1975 and 1980, the Danforth Graduate Fellowship Program lifted the percentage of minority fellowship winners from 6 to 8 percent of each year's class to 25 to 27 percent.[28] This astonishing change was achieved not by diluting standards but by sustained and intensive recruitment of minority candidates for these awards. Promising undergraduate students were identified early, in the freshman year, and were encouraged and supported in their study. By the time they were seniors, these students were fully competitive and ultimately successful.

We urge a renewed effort by undergraduate colleges to identify minority students who are candidates for graduate and professional schools, and recommend that colleges work closely with schools and that the effort begin by bringing more minority students into college. We also recommend that an increase in financial aid funds—graduate fellowships and loans—be made available to enable minority group students to enroll in, and complete, further education.

As we move toward the year 2000, almost everyone will need some form of post–high school education if he or she is to remain personally empowered, economically productive, and civically prepared. The twin mandates—quality and equality—remain the unfinished agenda for higher education.

There is one additional point to be underscored.

Most college graduates—both minority and non-minority—will not seek advanced degrees. They should, however, both as workers and members of their community go on learning long after college days are over. If the college is the institution of the book and a place that cherishes ideas, criticism, and creativity, the graduate of the college will continue to read and think, study, and reflect throughout life. Without continued learning, graduates will lose both their intellectual vitality and their capacity effectively to serve.

If the undergraduate college has succeeded, students, after they are handed their diplomas, will be well equipped to put their work in context and move with success from one intellectual challenge to another. More than that, they should be able to see their jobs in larger perspective. Only then can they be truly creative and fulfilled as individuals.

18

FROM COMPETENCE
TO COMMITMENT

John Gardner urged a group of students at a Stanford conference to consider what their lives would be like after graduation. He warned:

> I have to tell you candidly that an education at any of the great universities, followed by a graduate degree, followed by a plunge into the world of young professionals moves you steadily further from the bedrock of everyday American experience. If you're lucky you will escape the root ailments of the young urban professional —an overvaluing of intellect as against character, of getting there first as against growing in mind and spirit, of food for the ego as against food for the hunger of the heart.[1]

Today's students have ambiguous feelings about their role in the world. They are devoting their energies to what seems most real to them: the pursuit of security, the accumulation of material goods. They are struggling to establish themselves, but the young people with whom we spoke also admitted to confusion: Where should they put their faith in this uncertain age? Undergraduates are searching for identity and meaning and, like the rest of us, they are torn by idealism of service on the one hand, and on the other, the temptation to retreat into a world that never rises above self-interests.

In the end, the quality of the undergraduate experience is to be measured by the willingness of graduates to be socially and civically engaged. Reinhold Niebuhr once wrote, "Man cannot behold except he be committed. He cannot find himself without finding a center beyond himself."[2] The idealism of the undergraduate experience must reflect itself in loyalties that transcend self. Is it too much to expect that, even in this hard-edged, competitive age, a college graduate will live with integrity, civility—even compassion? Is it appropriate to hope that the lessons learned in a liberal education will reveal themselves in the humaneness of the graduate's relationship with others?

Clearly, the college graduate has civic obligations to fulfill. There is urgent need in American teaching to help close the dangerous and growing gap between public policy and public understanding. The information required to think constructively about the agenda of government seems increasingly beyond our grasp. It is no longer possible, many argue, to resolve complex public issues through citizen participation. How, they ask, can nonspecialists debate policy choices of consequence when they do not even know the language?

Should the use of nuclear energy be expanded or cut back? Can an adequate supply of water be assured? How can the arms race be brought under control? What is a safe level of atmospheric pollution? Even the semi-metaphysical questions of when a human life begins and ends have become items on the political agenda.

Citizens have tried with similar bafflement to follow the debate over Star Wars, with its highly technical jargon of deterrence and counter-deterrence. Even what once seemed to be reasonably local matters—zoning regulations, school desegregation, drainage problems, public transportation issues, licensing requests from competing cable television companies—call for specialists, who debate technicalities and frequently confuse rather than clarify the issues. And yet, the very complexity of public life requires more, not less, information; more, not less, participation.

For those who care about government "by the people," the decline in public understanding cannot go unchallenged. In a world where human survival is at stake, ignorance is not an acceptable alternative. The full control of policy by specialists with limited perspective is not tolerable. Unless we find better ways to educate ourselves, as citizens, unless hard questions are asked and satisfactory answers are offered, we run the risk of making critical decisions, not on the basis of what we know, but on the basis of blind faith in one or another set of professed experts.

What we need today are groups of well-informed, caring individuals who band together in the spirit of community to learn from one another, to participate, as citizens, in the democratic process.

We need concerned people who are participants in inquiry, who know how to ask the right questions, who understand the process by which public policy is shaped, and are prepared to make informed, discriminating judgments on questions that affect the future. Obviously, no one institution in society can single-handedly provide the leadership we require. But we are convinced that the undergraduate college, perhaps more than any other institution, is obliged to provide the enlightened leadership our nation urgently requires if government by the people is to endure.

To fulfill this urgent obligation, the perspective needed is not only national, but global. Today's students must be informed about people and cultures other than their own. Since man has orbited into space, it has become dramatically apparent that we are all custodians of a single planet. In the past half century, our planet has become vastly more crowded, more interdependent, and more unstable. If students do not see beyond themselves and better understand their place in our complex world, their capacity to live responsibly will be dangerously diminished.

The world may not yet be a village, but surely our sense of neighborhood must expand. When drought ravages the Sahara, when war in Indochina creates refugees, neither our compassion nor our analytic intelligence can be bounded by a dotted line on a political map. We are beginning to understand that hunger and human rights affect alliances as decisively as weapons and treaties. Dwarfing all other concerns, the mushroom cloud hangs ominously over our world consciousness. These realities and the obligations they impose must be understood by every student.

But during our study we found on campus a disturbing lack of knowledge and even at times a climate of indifference about our world. Refugees flow from one country to another, but too few students can point to these great migrations on a map or talk about the famines, wars, or poverty that caused them. Philosophers, statesmen, inventors, and artists from around the world enrich our lives, but such individuals and their contributions are largely unknown or unremembered.

After visiting dozens of colleges and speaking with hundreds of faculty members and students, we are forced to conclude that a dangerous parochialism pervades many higher learning institutions. While some students have a global perspective, the vast majority, although vaguely concerned, are inadequately informed about the interdependent world in which they live. They lack historical understanding and have little knowledge of significant social trends that will consequently shape their lives.

American young people remain shockingly ignorant about their own heritage and about the heritage of other nations. Students cannot identify world leaders or the capitals of other countries at a time when the destinies of all nations are interlocked. The undergraduate experience must help students see beyond the boundaries of our own narrow interests.

University of Notre Dame campus minister William Toohey wrote recently, "The trouble with many colleges is that they indulge the nesting instinct by building protected little communities inside their great walls."[3]

The site visitor at one college in our study described the place as "a lost island." A day after India's prime minister was assassinated, a professor commented: "Students here don't keep up with world events. If you go around and ask about Indira Gandhi, I'll bet my eyeteeth that thirty percent of them won't recognize the name."[4] The world has shrunk, and yet the curriculum barely reflects this global view.

In a recent address, Henry Steele Commager, John Woodruff Simpson Lecturer at Amherst College, spoke of the eighteenth century as an era that was, perhaps, more enlightened than our own. It was, he said:

> An age when the United States, speaking through Franklin, and France, through Jacques Necker, could decree immunity for Captain Cook and his men during time of war because "they were common friends of mankind"; when Rousseau could pay tribute to "those great cosmopolitan minds that make light of the barriers designed to sunder nation from nation and who embrace all mankind within the scope of their benevolence." It was an age when Washington hailed Lafayette "a citizen of the great republic of humanity at large," and Tom Paine designated himself a citizen of the world.[5]

One point emerges with stark clarity from all we have said: Our world has undergone immense transformations. It has become a more crowded, more interconnected, more unstable place. A new generation of Americans must be educated for life in this increasingly complex world. If the undergraduate college cannot help students see beyond themselves and better understand the interdependent nature of our world, each new generation will remain ignorant, and its capacity to live confidently and responsibly will be dangerously diminished.

Jacob Bronowski, in a vivid description of his 1945 visit to Nagasaki harbor, raised deeply unsettling questions about education's response to humanity's most profound concerns. The visit was, he said, a "universal moment," one in which modern man's knowledge was transformed into horror. At that instant of confrontation, he later wrote, "each of us in his own way learned that his imagination had been dwarfed."[6]

Hiroshima and Nagasaki—not to mention Dachau, Buchenwald, and Auschwitz—have the odd effect of forcing us to inquire once again into deeply troubling questions about the ends of a college education. The destruction Bronowski witnessed was a technological achievement built on trained intelligence, and we cannot help wondering what discipline of mind, what knowledge more adequately comprehended, what values more effectively conveyed, could have an equally powerful impact not for destruction, but for human betterment?

Throughout our study we were impressed that what today's college is teaching most successfully is competence—competence in meeting schedules, in gathering information, in responding well on tests, in mastering the details of a special field. Today the capacity to deal successfully with discrete problems is highly prized. And when we asked students about their education, they, almost without exception, spoke about the credits they had earned or the courses they still needed to complete.

But technical skill, of whatever kind, leaves open essential questions: Education for what purpose? Competence to what end? At a time in life when values should be shaped and personal priorities sharply probed, what a tragedy it would be if the most deeply felt issues, the most haunting questions, the most creative moments were pushed to the fringes of our institutional life. What a monumental mistake it would be if students, during the undergraduate years, remained trapped within the organizational grooves and narrow routines to which the academic world sometimes seems excessively devoted.

Students come to campus at a time of high expectancy. And yet, all too often they become enmeshed in routines that are deadening and distracting. As we talked with teachers and students, we often had the uncomfortable feeling that the most vital issues of life—the nature of society, the roots of social injustice, indeed the very prospects for human survival—are the ones with which the undergraduate college is least equipped to deal.

The outcomes of collegiate education should be measured by the student's performance in the classroom as he or she becomes proficient in the use of knowledge, acquires a solid basic education, and becomes competent in a specific field. Further, the impact of the undergraduate experience is to be assessed by the performance of the graduate in the workplace and further education.

But in the end, students must be inspired by a larger vision, using the knowledge they have acquired to discover patterns, form values, and advance the common good. The undergraduate experience at its best will move the student from competence to commitment.

A recent college graduate wrote about the commitments of young people and their future. She asks: "What kind of nation will we be if we cannot even commit ourselves to other people, much less to a set of abstract values? . . . What kinds of politicians will we elect if self-interest is our highest value, humanity an 'inoperative' commodity?"[7]

When all is said and done, the college should encourage each student to develop the capacity to judge wisely in matters of life and conduct. Time must be taken for exploring ambiguities and reflecting on the imponderables of life—in classrooms, in the rathskellers, and in bull sessions late at night. The goal is not to indoctrinate students, but to set them free in the world of ideas and provide a climate in which ethical and moral choices can be thoughtfully examined, and convictions formed.

This imperative does not replace the need for rigorous study in the disciplines, but neither must specialization become an excuse to suspend judgment or diminish the search for purposeful life objectives.

We are keenly aware of the limited impact people and their institutions seem to make these days on the events of our time. But our abiding hope is that, with determination and effort, the undergraduate college can make a difference in the intellectual and personal lives of its graduates, in the social and civic responsibilities they are willing to assume, and ultimately in their world perspective. These intangibles, which reveal themselves in ways that are very real, are the characteristics by which, ultimately, the quality of the undergraduate experience must be measured.

EPILOGUE:
A GUIDE TO A GOOD COLLEGE

From Sophocles' *Antigone* to Arthur Miller's *Death of a Salesman*, Western society expresses its most profound tensions when it affirms that men and women are not means, but ends, and yet, that the individual must, at times, be guided by community. Balancing these two values—sometimes complementary, sometimes conflicting—is the tightrope of history upon which our society walks. By leaning too much in one direction, anarchy will result; leaning too much into the other, the outcome is totalitarianism.

The tension between individuality and community has been the central theme of our study. The college is committed, on the one hand, to serve the needs of individual students, celebrating human diversity in its many forms, encouraging creativity and independence, and helping students become economically and socially empowered. A college of quality is also guided by community concerns. It has goals that are greater than the sum of the separate parts and reminds students, in formal and informal ways, that there is an intellectual and social community to which they are inextricably connected.

Is it possible for the modern campus, with all of its separations and divisions, to find points of common interest? In the prologue, we emphasized that the college is weakened by separations and divisions. The four-year undergraduate college, the institution at the center of higher education in America, is, we found, defined in so many ways and living so many lives that its identity and distinctiveness seem to have been clouded.

There is no single model of "the good college." Missions and circumstances vary greatly from one campus to another. But there are, we believe, characteristics widely enough shared to support the suggestions made in the body of our report.

We now refer back to many of these recommendations, stating them in the form of questions to be asked of individual institutions. While the standards suggested may be high, they are, we believe, within reach and, when taken together, provide for students and their parents a guide to a good college.

The quality of the undergraduate college is measured first by the extent of its cooperation with the schools, by its willingness to smooth the transition between school and higher education. The way students are recruited helps to shape college expectations, and a good college conducts its recruitment and selection so as to serve the best interests of the student.

Does the college present itself honestly in its promotional materials and recruitment methods? Are the criteria used in selecting students clearly described? Does the college make available to prospective students the percentage of last year's applicants who were admitted and report the percentage of admitted students who actually enrolled? If test scores are required for admission, does the college actually use the results and also make available not just the *average* scores, but also the number of students admitted *by quartile*, so that the range of student aptitudes can be taken into account? Also, does the college provide its regional accrediting association with regular reports on attrition and retention?

Prospective students should not hesitate to ask questions about any aspect of the transition from school to college. Representatives of a good college will not resist sharply focused questions. After all, in choosing a college, one of life's major decisions is being made. A lot of time, money, and effort will be involved. The shape and quality of the student's life may rest on the outcome.

When all is said and done, the procedures colleges use in the selection of their students cannot be divorced from institutional goals, nor can they be separated from the social context in which colleges carry on their work. Colleges and universities have an urgent obligation to maintain diversity on campus, and we ask: Does the college strongly reaffirm, as a central objective, its commitment to educational opportunity for historically bypassed students? Are black and Hispanic students well represented on the campus?

A quality college is guided by a clear and vital mission. The institution cannot be all things to all people. Choices must be made and priorities assigned. And there is, we believe, in the tradition of the undergraduate college, sufficient common ground on which shared goals can be established and a vital academic program built.

An essential test is this: Does the college have clearly stated goals that relate directly to the undergraduate experience? Do these objectives recognize the need to serve individual students while also giving significant attention to community concerns? Do students know about college purposes and what use is being made of them, both in academic planning and in campus life?

Most students come to college with high hopes. The transition is a major rite of passage. First impressions are often lasting impressions. The first weeks on campus will probably have a significant influence on the entire undergraduate experience. This is a time when prospects for community are diminished or enhanced and yet, undergraduates are often largely uninformed about the values and traditions of higher learning.

Here are key questions: Is the freshman year viewed as something special? Does the college offer a well-planned orientation program, perhaps with a new-student convocation, and a course that features the academic as well as the social and personal aspects of campus life? Is the orientation program actively supported by the faculty? Does the president give as much attention to incoming students as he or she does to alumni?

Because students need guidance, a college of quality has a year-round program of academic advising and personal counseling, structured to serve all undergraduates, including part-time and commuting students. But is the faculty available to freshmen to talk about their disciplines, and do faculty give guidance to young students as they consider choices for careers? A college worthy of commendation works as hard at holding students as it does at getting them to the campus in the first place. What has been the retention rate at the college during the past five years? Is it more than 50 percent? Does the college have a program to help identify students who are having trouble and give them guidance?

One of the great barriers to success in college and later life is deficiency in language. While the mastery of a second or even third language is vitally important, the reality is that students will not be prepared for American life if they cannot communicate effectively in English.

In identifying the academic goals of a college we must ask: Does the institution give priority to language? Is the reading and writing capability of each student carefully assessed at the time he or she enrolls? And are those who are not well prepared in written and spoken English placed in an intensive, noncredit course that meets daily during the first academic term?

Further, does the college offer for all students, not just those in need of remediation, a freshman-year language course where both written and oral communication are stressed? And, are these skills emphasized in every class? Does the college have a program of collaboration with surrounding schools that strengthens language teaching? Language is the skill central to all others. And proficiency in the written and spoken word is the first prerequisite for a college-level education.

The special challenge confronting the undergraduate college is to shape a common learning curriculum that will express the claims of community. Students must have freedom to follow their own interests, develop their own aptitudes, and pursue their own goals.

But truly educated persons must also gain perspective, see themselves in relation to other people and times, understand how their own origins and interests are tied to the origins and interests of others.

The specific questions are these: Does the college have a coherent general education sequence—an integrated core—something more than a loosely connected distribution arrangement? Does this core program provide not only for an integration of the separate academic disciplines but also for their application and relationship to life?

The integrated core we have in mind would be spread throughout the entire baccalaureate experience—from the freshman to the senior years—and be pursued not only through courses, but through informal seminars and all-college convocations.

Further, at a good college, the academic major will broaden rather than restrict the perspective of the student. We ask: Does the major not only allow the student to explore a subject in depth, but also to put such study in perspective? Does it present, in effect, an *enriched* major?

An enriched major, as we have defined it in our study, will respond successfully to three essential questions: What is the history and tradition of the field to be examined? What are the social and economic implications to be pursued? What are the ethical and moral issues within the specialty that need to be confronted? Rather than divide the undergraduate experience into separate camps—general versus specialized education—the curriculum at a college of quality will bring the two together.

A coherent curriculum is only the beginning. Good faculty are essential to a good college. Members of the faculty determine the quality of the undergraduate experience. And the investment in teaching is a key ingredient in the building of a successful institution.

Questions about the faculty include these: At research institutions, is good teaching valued as well as research, and is it an important criterion for tenure and promotion? Is superior teaching rewarded through recognized status and salary incentives? Do other institutions have a flexible policy, recognizing that some faculty are great teachers, others great researchers, and still others offer a blend of both? Are *all* professors, even those who are not publishing researchers, encouraged to be *scholars,* remaining on top of their discipline?

There are other matters to be examined: Does the college support faculty renewal and professional growth in such practical ways as making leaves available and providing funds for teachers to improve their pedagogical practices? Is teaching evaluated by students, and does the college offer, to faculty, a program to improve their teaching?

Part-time teachers are beneficial economically and can enrich the campus. There are, however, central questions to consider. What is the impact of part-time faculty on the spirit of community on campus? Does the college restrict the use of part-time teachers? And is their employment educationally justified?

The satisfaction of seeing students develop intellectually while participating in the building of an institution of higher learning should offer faculty members a sense of satisfaction as great as seeing their names in print in a professional journal or hearing the applause of fellow scholars at a professional meeting.

The undergraduate experience, at its best, also means encouraging students to be active rather than passive learners. In measuring the quality of a college one should ask if the institution has a climate that encourages independent, self-directed study. Is priority given to the required lower-division classes? Is teaching more than lecturing? Do general education courses have small discussion sessions in which students work together on group assignments? Are undergraduate courses taught by the most respected and most gifted teachers on campus? Because much learning occurs outside the classroom, it is important to know how accessible faculty are to their students, through office hours, to be sure, but also elsewhere on the campus—for some, at athletic or cultural events; for others, in the student center, for example, over a Coke or coffee.

Other important questions to be pressed are these: Is good teaching encouraged through student evaluation? Does the college help faculty learn how to reach more effectively as well as to measure the progress of their students, not only separately but through group projects, too?

When all is said and done, the central qualities that make for successful teaching are the ones that can be simply stated: command of the material to be taught, a contagious enthusiasm for the play of ideas, optimism about the potential of one's students, and—not least —sensitivity, integrity, and warmth as a human being. At a good college this combination is present in the classroom.

A quality undergraduate college also is a place that gives high priority to independent study, to learning resources outside the classroom. The library is often called the "heart" of the institution, and yet we often found it to be underfunded and underused.

One must ask: Is the library more than a study hall? Are students encouraged to spend at least as much time with library resources as they spend in classes? Do students, in their use of the library, seek out original sources and contemporary writings? Does the college ensure that a minimum of 5 percent of the total operating budget is provided for library support? And does the library's acquisition policy resist domination by narrow scholarly interests, serving also undergraduate education? Are those who direct the library also considered teachers?

Today another teaching tool—the microcomputer—offers great potential for learning on the campus. Does the college have a comprehensive plan for computer use before it purchases the hardware? Are campus terminals linked to wider networks? And does the college connect technology, the library, and the classroom, letting each resource do what it does best and encouraging students to engage in creative, independent learning?

Students spend most of the undergraduate years outside the

classroom, and what they do during this time profoundly shapes the form and quality of their experience. From lecture series and concerts to sports and student organizations, students learn important lessons.

The college that deserves support is one that sees academic and nonacademic functions as related. Because college is intended to prepare students for life, the lessons of the classroom should be applied first in the college community itself.

Therefore, in measuring the quality of the college one should ask: Are there well-supported campus-wide activities—lectures, symposia, debates, concerts, and the like—that encourage community, sustain college traditions, and stimulate both social and intellectual interaction? Are these events well attended by both faculty and students? Are college athletics kept in proper balance, with the college ensuring that its educational purposes are never sacrificed? Does the college actively promote a broad intramural program for all students?

There are health matters to be considered, too: Are students at the college educated about the importance of nutrition and exercise and encouraged to participate in a regular program of physical activity? Does the college cafeteria provide a healthful diet? Do college administrators back local and state laws regarding the use of drugs and alcoholic beverages? Does the college sponsor programs to help deal with these problems? In short, does the college have standards not just in academic matters but in nonacademic matters, too—expectations that help to define the college as a community?

Residential living can be one of the most chaotic parts of campus life, and yet it has the potential of being one of the most rewarding. It is appropriate to ask: Are residence halls not only a place for sleeping and parties but for education, with seminars, colloquia, and informal learning? Does the college president receive regular reports on both problems and programs inside the residence halls? And does he or she occasionally visit the hall to meet with students as well as with resident assistants? It is our position that, at a good college, students discover that all parts of college life are measured by high standards, and that educated people are guided in their behavior by civility and decency.

In evaluating campus life, careful attention also must be paid to the growing number of nonresident students: Are commuters simply tolerated or are they full-fledged members of the community? Does the college meet the needs of such students by providing them first-rate educational, social, and recreational services?

If co-curricular life can be linked to classrooms, if the college sponsors convocations and celebrations, and if there are opportunities for sharp intellectual exchanges and reflection—then a college is united, not by routine requirements and procedures, but by a concern for consequential issues, by respect for lively debate, and the clarifying of convictions. At such a place, the total campus, not just the classroom, is viewed as a place for learning.

Today's students have been labeled the "me generation," concerned only about private ends. But we found that this generation of undergraduates has hopes and aspirations that reach beyond themselves. Still, undergraduates are torn by ambiguous feelings— idealism on the one hand, and on the other, the temptation to pursue private interests that would leave them politically and socially disengaged. Like people everywhere, they are searching for identity and meaning.

A good college affirms that service to others is a central part of education. The questions we pose are these: Are students encouraged to participate in voluntary service? Does the college offer the option of deferring admission to students who devote a year to service before coming to campus? Are the service projects drawn into the larger educational purposes, helping students to see that they are not only autonomous individuals but also members of an intentional community? And does the faculty set an example and give leadership to service?

The vision of service is also reflected in the quality of campus governance. A good college has effective decision-making arrangements. The distance between faculty and administrators is reduced and students become active participants as well. College and community citizenship is affirmed. We ask: Are the faculty senate and student government respected, well-supported organizations? Does the college work to keep open the lines of communication that cut across student, faculty, and administration structures? Is there an all-college forum to address common educational questions and consider campus-wide matters? Do trustees participate in shaping priorities for the college? Finally, in affirming the central role of the college president, we pose this question: Does the president offer the college an inspired vision?

In the end, governance is to be measured not by the formality of the structure but by the integrity of the participants, by the willingness of individuals to work together in support of shared objectives.

Throughout our study, we were regularly reminded that new educational patterns are emerging. New types of students are enrolling, and the location of learning has moved beyond the campus—to the home, the workplace, and around the world. A college of consequence avoids isolation and develops programs that meet new patterns.

The tests are these: Are traditional students encouraged to look beyond the campus, either through a semester of work or internship? And does the college have foreign study that offers careful introductions to another culture? Do nontraditional students participate in campus life in ways that help them overcome their isolation and become part of a community of learning? An effective college designs creative ways to both extend and encourage diversity on the campus.

A quality undergraduate college is concerned about outcomes. It asks questions about student development that go beyond the evaluation. But a good college, in its college-wide assessment, will avoid measuring that which matters least. We speak here of the need of students to think clearly, to be well informed, to be able to integrate their knowledge, and to apply what they have learned. We have suggested that each student might participate in a senior seminar in which he or she presents a thesis orally and critiques the papers of fellow students. Does the college encourage such a project, which would relate some aspect of the student's major to historical, social, and ethical concerns?

The impact of college extends beyond graduation, and a quality college will provide placement guidance to its students and follow their careers. Students at such a college will be well equipped to put their work in context and also be adequately prepared to move from one intellectual challenge to another. The graduate will continue to read and think, study and reflect throughout life. The undergraduate experience also has prepared students to see beyond the boundaries of their own narrow interests and discover connections that are global.

In judging the quality of a college these questions should be posed: Do graduates understand the dignity of work and, at the same time, are they prepared to venture beyond technical skills in their education? Do students see the connection between what they learn and how they live, looking for the deeper significance, for the moral dilemmas and the ethical responses? The college succeeds as its graduates are inspired by a larger vision, using the knowledge they have acquired to form values and advance the common good.

This brings us, again, to the heart of our report. Throughout this book we have talked about the two great traditions of individuality and community in higher education. Colleges, we have said, should help students become independent, self-reliant human beings, yet also they should give priority to community. In implementing these two priorities, a balance must be struck.

But here we insert an important word of caution. To draw the line too sharply between these two traditions may, in fact, mask a more fundamental truth: To serve private priorities while neglecting social obligations is, ultimately, to undermine self-interest. And it is more than mere sentiment to suggest that altruism richly benefits the self as well.

In *Habits of the Heart*, Robert Bellah and his associates say, "Perhaps the notion that private and public lives are at odds is incorrect. Perhaps they are so deeply involved with each other that the impoverishment of one entails the impoverishment of the other. Parker Palmer is probably right when he says that 'in a healthy society the private and the public are not mutually exclusive, not in competition with each other. They are, instead, two halves of a whole, two poles of a paradox. They work together dialectically, helping to create and nurture one another.' "[1]

This point, properly understood, brings us to our vision of the undergraduate experience. It warns against making too great a distinction between careerism and the liberal arts, between self-benefit and service. We more comfortably embrace the notion that the aim of the undergraduate experience is not only to prepare the young for productive careers, but also to enable them to live lives of dignity and purpose; not only to generate new knowledge, but to channel that knowledge to humane ends; not merely to study government, but to help shape a citizenry that can promote the public good.

The undergraduate college in America has never been a static institution. For 350 years, it has shaped its program in response to the changing social and economic context. As we look to a world whose contours remain obscure, we conclude the time has come to reaffirm the undergraduate experience and, in so doing, help students move from competence to commitment and be of service to their neighborhoods, the nation, and the world.

APPENDIX A: OBSERVERS FOR THE CARNEGIE FOUNDATION COLLEGE STUDY

Ms. Madeleine Adamson
Baltimore, Maryland

Mr. Seth Borgos
Washington, D.C.

Mr. Bosah Ebo
Iowa City, Iowa

Ms. Laurie A. Evans
Takoma Park, Maryland

Ms. Debra L. Fabiszak
Towson, Maryland

Ms. Denise Graveline
Flemington, New Jersey

Mr. Alex Heard
Washington, D.C.

Ms. Bonnie L. Hufford
Athens, Ohio

Ms. Susan R. Kincaid
Athens, Ohio

Mr. David William McElwain
Colby, Kansas

Ms. Elizabeth A. Owens
Minneapolis, Minnesota

Mr. Paul Parsons
Manhattan, Kansas

Mr. Bill Shaw
Noblesville, Indiana

Mr. David L. Stewart
Fairport Harbor, Ohio

Ms. Susan Walton
Washington, D.C.

Mr. Robin Witt
Sacramento, California

NOTES

PROLOGUE: A House Divided

1. The Carnegie Foundation for the Advancement of Teaching, *A Classification of Institutions of Higher Education* (Princeton, New Jersey: Carnegie Foundation for the Advancement of Teaching, forthcoming).
2. U. S. Department of Education, National Center for Education Statistics, *The Condition of Education: 1985* (Washington, D.C.: U. S. Government Printing Office, 1985), p. 94.
3. Quoted in Russell Thomas, *The Search for a Common Learning: General Education 1800–1960* (New York: McGraw-Hill, 1962), p. 73.
4. The Carnegie Foundation for the Advancement of Teaching, College Visits, 1984–85.
5. Sheldon Rothblatt, " 'Standing Antagonisms': The Relationship of Undergraduate to Graduate Education," in Leslie Koepplin and David Wilson (eds.), *The Future of State Universities* (Elizabeth, New Jersey: Rutgers University Press, 1986), p. 59.

1. Where College Dreams Begin

1. The Carnegie Foundation for the Advancement of Teaching, Survey of the Transition from High School to College, 1984–85.
2. Staff communication with Fred Moreno, College Entrance Examination Board, July 15, 1986.
3. The Carnegie Foundation for the Advancement of Teaching, Survey of the Transition from High School to College, 1984–85.
4. Ibid.
5. Ibid.
6. Ibid.
7. Ibid.
8. Ibid.
9. Ibid.

10. The Carnegie Foundation for the Advancement of Teaching, College Visits, 1984–85.

11. Ibid.

12. The Carnegie Foundation for the Advancement of Teaching, Survey of the Transition from High School to College, 1984–85.

13. Ibid.

14. The Carnegie Foundation for the Advancement of Teaching, Staff Interviews, 1984–85.

15. Diane J. Harrison, "Review of College Guides," unpublished paper, Carleton College, October 1984.

16. The Carnegie Foundation for the Advancement of Teaching, Survey of the Transition from High School to College, 1984–85.

17. Ibid.

18. Ibid.

19. Ibid.

20. Ibid.

21. Ibid.

22. U.S. Department of Commerce, Bureau of the Census, *Statistical Abstract of the United States, 1986* (Washington, D.C.: Government Printing Office, 1985), p. 450; U.S. Department of Labor, Bureau of Labor Statistics, Listing of Consumer Price Indices, 1949 to 1985, unpublished; and Cathy Henderson, "Forecasting College Costs Through 1988–89," *American Council on Education Policy Brief,* January 1986, p. 4.

23. Henderson, "Forecasting College Costs Through 1988–89," p. 4.

24. The Carnegie Foundation for the Advancement of Teaching, National Survey of Undergraduates, 1984.

25. The Carnegie Foundation for the Advancement of Teaching, Staff Interviews, 1984–85.

26. American Association of Collegiate Registrars and Admissions Officers, American Council on Education, College Entrance Examination Board, National Association of College Admissions Counselors, and National Association of Secondary School Principals, *Self-Regulation Initiatives: Guidelines for Colleges and Universities, No. 2* (Washington, D.C.: American Council on Education, October 1979).

2. Making the Match

1. The Carnegie Foundation for the Advancement of Teaching, Survey of the Transition from High School to College, 1984–85.

2. Edward B. Fiske, *Selective Guide to Colleges* (New York: New York Times Books, 1982).

3. Staff calculation based on College Board data.

4. The Carnegie Foundation for the Advancement of Teaching, College Visits, 1984–85.

5. Arthur Levine, *Handbook on Undergraduate Curriculum* (San Francisco: Jossey-Bass, 1978), p. 540.

6. Ernest L. Boyer and Martin Kaplan, *Educating for Survival* (Washington, D.C.: Change Magazine Press, 1977), p. 21.
7. Verne A. Stadtman (ed.), *The Centennial Record of the University of California* (Berkeley: University of California Printing Department, 1967), p. 20; and staff communication with Bancroft Library archivist, University of California, Berkeley, June 1986.
8. "Requisites for Admission," *Antioch College Catalogue, 1858–59*, p. 13.
9. *Catalogue of the Officers and Students of the College of New Jersey 1850–51* (Princeton, New Jersey: John J. Robinson, 1851), p. 20.
10. Claude M. Fuess, *The College Board: Its First 50 Years* (New York: Columbia University Press, 1950), pp. 6–7.
11. Ibid., p. 7.
12. Fred Hechinger and Grace Hechinger, *Growing Up in America* (New York: McGraw-Hill, 1975), p. 321.
13. Ibid.
14. Fuess, *The College Board*, p. 40.
15. Ibid., p. 42.
16. Gene I. Maeroff, *School and College: Partnerships in Education* (Princeton, New Jersey: The Carnegie Foundation for the Advancement of Teaching, 1983), p. 9.
17. Scott D. Thomson, *College Admissions: New Requirements by the State Universities* (Reston, Virginia: National Association of Secondary School Principals, 1982), pp. 4–7.
18. Ohio Advisory Commission on Articulation Between Secondary Education and Ohio Colleges, *Final Report* (Columbus, Ohio: Ohio Board of Regents and the State Board of Education, April 1981).
19. Ibid.
20. The College Board, *Academic Preparation for College: What Students Need to Know and Be Able to Do* (New York: College Entrance Examination Board, 1983).
21. Staff communication with Fred Moreno, College Entrance Examination Board, July 15, 1986.
22. Staff communication with Gerry Johnston, the American College Testing Program, July 15, 1986.
23. The Carnegie Foundation for the Advancement of Teaching, Staff Interviews, 1984–85.
24. The Carnegie Foundation for the Advancement of Teaching, Survey of the Transition from High School to College, 1984–85.
25. Alexander Astin, *Achieving Educational Excellence* (San Francisco: Jossey-Bass, 1985), p. 93.
26. The Carnegie Foundation for the Advancement of Teaching, Survey of the Transition from High School to College, 1984–85.
27. "Dallas Schools Win $1-Million Grant to Raise Test Scores," *Education Week*, January 8, 1986, p. 3.
28. The Carnegie Foundation for the Advancement of Teaching, Survey of the Transition from High School to College, 1984–85.

29. Princeton University, *Admissions Information 1985–86*, p. 32.
30. The Carnegie Foundation for the Advancement of Teaching, Staff Interviews, 1984.
31. The Carnegie Foundation for the Advancement of Teaching, College Visits, 1984–85.
32. Warren W. Willingham, *Success in College* (New York: College Entrance Examination Board, 1985), p. 8.
33. Cliff Wing and Michael Wallach, *College Admissions and the Psychology of Talent* (New York: Holt, Rinehart and Winston, 1971).
34. John Holland and James Richards, *Academic and Non-Academic Accomplishment: Correlated or Uncorrelated?*, Research Report No. 2, American College Testing Program, April 1965. See also Leo Munday and J. C. Davis, *Varieties of Accomplishment After College: Perspectives on the Meaning of Academic Talent*, Research Report No. 62, ACT, March 1974.
35. Staff communication with Leon Bouvier, Population Reference Bureau, July 9, 1986; staff communication with Information Services, Census Bureau, November 5, 1985; and unpublished data from the *Current Population Survey*.
36. Carnegie Commission on Higher Education, *Quality and Equality: New Levels of Federal Responsibility for Higher Education* (Hightstown, New Jersey: McGraw-Hill, 1968), p. 1.

3. Orientation: Affirming the Traditions

1. Harvard University, *Statutes and Laws of the University in Cambridge, Massachusetts* (Cambridge, Massachusetts: University Press–Hilliar and Metcalf, 1826), p. 4.
2. Mirra Komarovsky, *Women in College: Shaping New Feminine Identities* (New York: Basic Books, 1985), p. 18.
3. The Carnegie Foundation for the Advancement of Teaching, College Visits, 1984–85.
4. Ibid.
5. Ibid.
6. Ibid.
7. Ibid.
8. Ibid.
9. Ibid.
10. V. Tinto, "Dropouts from Higher Education: A Theoretical Synthesis of Recent Research," *Review of Recent Research*, Winter 1975, pp. 89–125.
11. Ernest T. Pascarella and associates, "Orientation to College and Freshmen Year Persistence/Withdrawal Decisions," *The Journal of Higher Education*, March/April 1986, pp. 155–75.
12. The Carnegie Foundation for the Advancement of Teaching, College Visits, 1984–85.
13. Thomas J. Grites, "Noteworthy Academic Advising Programs," in Roger B. Winston, Jr., and associates, *Developmental Academic Advising: Addressing Students' Educational, Career, and Personal Needs* (San Francisco: Jossey-Bass,

14. Cecilia A. Ottinger, *1984–85 Fact Book on Higher Education* (New York: American Council on Education, 1984), p. 80.
15. The Carnegie Foundation for the Advancement of Teaching, College Visits, 1984–85.
16. Gerald Gurin and associates, *Part-Time Students and Their Ambivalent Hosts,* working paper prepared for The Carnegie Foundation for the Advancement of Teaching, April 1985, pp. 76, 79.
17. The Carnegie Foundation for the Advancement of Teaching, College Visits, 1984–85.
18. Ibid.
19. Ibid.
20. Ibid.
21. Grites, "Noteworthy Academic Advising Programs," pp. 470–72.
22. Staff communication with Donna Boen, assistant director of news bureau, Miami University, September 3, 1986.

4. Two Essential Goals

1. James Bryant Conant, *The Child, the Parent and the State* (Cambridge, Massachusetts: Harvard University Press, 1959), p. 1.
2. Charles Frankel, "A Promise of Lifelong Discomfort," *Swarthmore College Bulletin,* November 1978, p. 1.
3. Gerald Grant and David Riesman, *The Perpetual Dream: Reform and Experiment in the American College* (Chicago: University of Chicago Press, 1978), p. 377.
4. The Carnegie Foundation for the Advancement of Teaching, College Visits, 1984–85.
5. Ibid.
6. Ibid.
7. Ibid.
8. Ibid.
9. Ibid.
10. Frederick Rudolph, *The American College and University: A History* (New York: Alfred A. Knopf, 1962), p. 13.
11. Andrew Hacker, "The Decline of Higher Learning," *The New York Review of Books,* February 13, 1986, p. 5.
12. Lawrence A. Cremin, *American Education: The Colonial Experience 1607–1783* (New York: Harper & Row, 1970), p. 214.
13. John S. Brubacher and Willis Rudy, *Higher Education in Transition: A History of American Colleges and Universities 1636–1976* (New York: Harper & Row, 1976), p. 13.
14. Cremin, *American Education,* pp. 321, 326.
15. Quoted in Lawrence A. Cremin, *American Education: The National Experience 1783–1876* (New York: Harper & Row, 1980), p. 116.
16. Rudolph, *The American College and University: A History,* pp. 48–49.
17. Ibid., p. 229.
18. Faculty of Yale University, "Yale Report of 1828," in Richard Hofstadter and

Wilson Smith, *American Higher Education: A Documentary History,* vol. 1 (Chicago: University of Chicago Press, 1961), p. 283.

19. Ibid., pp. 281, 283.
20. Rudolph, *The American College and University: A History,* p. 231.
21. Fred M. Hechinger and Grace Hechinger, *Growing Up in America* (New York: McGraw-Hill, 1975), p. 291.
22. Rudolph, *The American College and University: A History,* p. 238.
23. Quoted in Laurence R. Veysey, *The Emergence of the American University* (Chicago: University of Chicago Press, 1965), p. 63.
24. Rudolph, *The American College and University: A History,* p. 65.
25. Charles William Eliot, *A Turning Point in Higher Education: The Inaugural Address of Charles William Eliot as President of Harvard College, October 19, 1869* (Cambridge, Massachusetts: Harvard University Press, 1969); reprinted in Arthur Levine, *Handbook on Undergraduate Curriculum* (San Francisco: Jossey-Bass, 1978), p. 562.
26. Frederick Rudolph, *Curriculum: A History of the American Undergraduate Course of Study Since 1636* (San Francisco: Jossey-Bass, 1977), p. 194.
27. Quoted in John Hajnal, *The Student Trap: A Critique of University and Sixth-Form Curricula* (Middlesex, England: Penguin Books, 1972), p. 104.
28. Quoted in Veysey, *The Emergence of the American University,* pp. 13–14.
29. Brubacher and Rudy, *Higher Education in Transition,* p. 115.
30. Ibid., p. 272.
31. *Columbia University Catalog, 1919–1920.*
32. Ernest L. Boyer and Arthur Levine, *A Quest for Common Learning: The Aims of General Education* (Princeton, New Jersey: The Carnegie Foundation for the Advancement of Teaching, 1981), p. 10.
33. Ibid., p. 10.
34. Ibid., p. 14.
35. Staff communication with Christina Dodds, Wesleyan University archives, July 3, 1986.
36. Harvard Committee, *General Education in a Free Society* (Cambridge, Massachusetts: Harvard University Press, 1945), p. xiii.
37. Ibid., p. 32.
38. Quoted in Karen J. Winkler, "Scholars Diagnose 'Cancerous' Individualism in the Character of American Citizens," *Chronicle of Higher Education,* April 24, 1985, p. 7.
39. Alexis de Tocqueville, *Democracy in America,* J. P. Mayer (ed.), (Garden City, New York: Doubleday, 1969), pp. 508, 510.

5. Language: The First Requirement

1. The Carnegie Foundation for the Advancement of Teaching, College Visits, 1984–85.
2. Quoted in Richard Hofstadter and Wilson Smith (eds.), *American Higher Education: A Documentary History,* vol. 1 (Chicago: University of Chicago Press, 1961), pp. 254–55.

3. National Institute of Education, *Involvement in Learning: Realizing the Potential of American Higher Education* (Washington, D.C.: National Institute of Education, 1984), p. 48.

4. Alexander W. Astin, *Achieving Educational Excellence* (San Francisco: Jossey-Bass, 1985), p. 212.

5. Helen S. Astin, "Providing Incentives for Teaching Underprepared Students," *Educational Record*, Winter 1985, p. 26.

6. John E. Roueche, George A. Baker, and Suanne D. Roueche, *College Responses to Low Achieving Students: A National Study* (Orlando, Florida: Harcourt Brace Jovanovich, 1984), pp. 29–31.

7. Marie Jean Lederman, Susan Remmer Ryzewic, and Michael Ribaudo, *Assessment and Improvement of the Academic Skills of Entering Freshmen: A National Survey* (New York: City University of New York, Office of Academic Affairs, September 1983), p. 1.

8. The Carnegie Foundation for the Advancement of Teaching, College Visits, 1984–85.

9. Derek Bok, "Toward Education of Quality," *Harvard Magazine*, May/June 1986, p. 63.

10. Staff communication with Jim Gray, National Writing Project, January 1984.

11. "In Box," *Chronicle of Higher Education*, October 3, 1984, p. 17.

12. Jilian Mincer, "Learning from a Jury of Their Peers," *The New York Times Winter Education Supplement*, January 6, 1985, p. 32.

13. James L. Kinneavy, "Writing Across the Curriculum," *ADE Bulletin*, Winter 1983, p. 18.

14. Gene Maeroff, *School and College: Partnerships in Education* (Princeton, New Jersey: Carnegie Foundation for the Advancement of Teaching, 1983), p. 39.

15. Ibid., p. 40.

16. Staff communication with Deborah Keller-Cohen, director, English Composition Board, The University of Michigan, March 10, 1986.

17. The Carnegie Foundation for the Advancement of Teaching, College Visits, 1984–85.

18. E. D. Hirsch, Jr., "Cultural Literacy," *The American Scholar*, Spring 1983.

19. Ibid., p. 165.

6. General Education: The Integrated Core

1. The Carnegie Foundation for the Advancement of Teaching, College Visits, 1984–85.

2. Ibid.

3. Ibid.

4. Ibid.

5. Andrew Hacker, "The Decline of Higher Learning," *The New York Review of Books*, February 13, 1986, p. 11.

6. The Carnegie Foundation for the Advancement of Teaching, Survey of General Education, 1985.

7. The Carnegie Foundation for the Advancement of Teaching, College Visits, 1984–85.

8. Ibid.

9. Ibid.

10. Ibid.

11. Ibid.

12. Ibid.

13. Ibid.

14. Ibid.

15. Michael Polanyi, *The Tacit Dimension* (Garden City, New York: Doubleday, 1967), p. 72.

16. Frank H. T. Rhodes, "The Selling of the Liberal Arts," *Phi Kappa Phi National Forum*, Summer 1985, p. 5.

17. Clifford Geertz, "Balanced Genres: The Refiguration of Social Thought," *The American Scholar*, Spring 1980, pp. 165–66.

18. Ann Hulbert, "Curriculum Commotion," *The New Republic*, May 6, 1985, p. 28.

19. Staff communication with Cornell University Professor Linda Waugh, June 20, 1986.

20. *Brown University Course Announcement 1985–86*, p. 65; and staff communication with Brown University Professor Robert Meskill, June 27, 1986.

21. *Northeastern University Course Description and Curriculum Guide 1984–85*, p. 97.

22. *Bulletin of Wake Forest University, 1984–85*, p. 106; and staff communication with Wake Forest University Professor Cyclone Covey, July 10, 1986.

23. "Three Crises in Western Culture: Civilization on Trial," *Forum for Liberal Education*, October 1985, p. 14.

24. "Saint Anselm College: Values-Oriented Education for the Twenty-First Century," *Forum for Liberal Education*, October 1985, pp. 4–5.

25. *University of Chicago, The College: Courses and Programs of Study, 1984–85*, p. 435.

26. Staff communication with Hampshire College Professor David Smith, January 10, 1986.

27. *Skidmore College Bulletin 1985–86*, p. 91.

28. Harvard University, *Courses of Instruction, 1986–87*.

29. Carleton College, *General Information and Courses Recommended for New Students*, May 1985, pp. 10–11.

30. Staff communication with Professor Terrence Flower, College of St. Catherine, June 27, 1986.

31. Robert Kanigel, "Technology as a Liberal Art: Scenes from the Classroom," *Change*, March/April 1986, p. 27.

32. Staff communication with Carole Brown, Assistant Dean of the College of Liberal Arts, Hamline University, July 7, 1986.

33. Staff communication with Associate Professor David A. Kideckel, Central Connecticut State University, July 8, 1986.

34. *Princeton University Undergraduate Announcement, 1985–86*, p. 263.

35. Staff communication with Randolph-Macon College Professor Joseph Beatty, August 20, 1986.
36. Staff communication with Richard Elias, coordinator of "After Hiroshima: Life and Death in the Nuclear Age," Ohio Wesleyan University, August 15, 1986.
37. Staff communication with Jeff Thomas, Office of International Education and Off-Campus Programs, Eckerd College, September 5, 1986.
38. Charles Frankel, "A Promise of Lifelong Discontent," *Swarthmore College Bulletin*, November 1978, p. 2.

7. Specialization: The Enriched Major

1. The Carnegie Foundation for the Advancement of Teaching, National Survey of Undergraduates, 1984.
2. The Carnegie Foundation for the Advancement of Teaching, College Visits, 1984–85.
3. Ibid.
4. Ibid.
5. Quoted in Daniel Rosenheim, "The New Demand for Liberal Arts Grads," *San Francisco Chronicle*, August 25, 1986, p. 24.
6. Russel W. Rumberger and Henry M. Levin, *Computers in Small Business* (Washington, D.C.: Institute for Enterprise Advancement, forthcoming).
7. Victor R. Lindquist, *The Northwestern Endicott Report: Trends in the Employment of College and University Graduates in Business and Industry, 1986* (Evanston, Illinois: Northwestern University, 1985), p. 5.
8. The Carnegie Foundation for the Advancement of Teaching, College Visits, 1984–85.
9. Ibid.
10. Ibid.
11. Ibid.
12. Frederick Rudolph, *Curriculum: A History of the American Undergraduate Course of Study Since 1636* (San Francisco: Jossey-Bass, 1977), p. 178.
13. The Carnegie Foundation for the Advancement of Teaching, College Visits, 1984–85.
14. Samuel Eliot Morison, *The Founding of Harvard College* (Cambridge, Massachusetts: Harvard University Press, 1935), p. 7.
15. Arthur Levine, *Handbook on Undergraduate Curriculum* (San Francisco: Jossey-Bass, 1978), pp. 496–98.
16. C. P. Snow, *The Masters* (New York: Charles Scribner, 1951), pp. 363–64.
17. Speech by Thomas F. Green, based upon his book *Work, Leisure, and the American Schools* (New York: Random House, 1968).
18. Alfred North Whitehead, *The Aims of Education and Other Essays* (New York: Free Press, 1967), p. 32.
19. I am grateful to Arthur Chickering for his helpful insights on this point.
20. Norman Cousins, "How to Make People Smaller Than They Are," *Saturday Review*, December 1978, p. 15.

21. Whitehead, *The Aims of Education and Other Essays,* p. 48.
22. The Carnegie Foundation for the Advancement of Teaching, College Visits, 1984–85.
23. Ibid.
24. Ibid.
25. Staff communication with Executive Vice-President John A. Curry, Northeastern University, September 30, 1986.
26. Stanford University, *Stanford University: Courses and Degrees, 1985–86,* pp. 440–42.
27. *Worcester Polytechnic Institute Undergraduate Catalog,* 1984–85, p. 6.
28. Eric Ashby, *Technology and the Academics: An Essay on Universities and the Scientific Revolution* (New York: St. Martin's Press, 1966, © 1958), pp. 84–85.

8. Faculty: Mentors and Scholars

1. The Carnegie Foundation for the Advancement of Teaching, College Visits, 1984–85.
2. Ibid.
3. Ibid.
4. James Morgan Hart, "James Morgan Hart Compares the German University and the American College During the 1860s," in Richard Hofstadter and Wilson Smith (eds.), *American Higher Education: A Documentary History,* vol. 2 (Chicago: University of Chicago Press, 1961), p. 578.
5. Robert H. Edwards, "Faculty Development," speech delivered at Ursinus College, November 3, 1984, p. 4.
6. The Carnegie Foundation for the Advancement of Teaching, College Visits, 1984–85.
7. Burton P. Clark, *Different Worlds: Academic Life in America* (Princeton, New Jersey: The Carnegie Foundation for the Advancement of Teaching, forthcoming).
8. The Carnegie Foundation for the Advancement of Teaching, College Visits, 1984–85.
9. Norman Hackerman, "Science Is Universal: The Practitioners Are Not," *Science,* August 10, 1984, p. 577.
10. Christopher Jencks and David Riesman, *The Academic Revolution* (Garden City, New York: Doubleday, 1968), pp. 531–32.
11. The Carnegie Foundation for the Advancement of Teaching, College Visits, 1984–85.
12. Ibid.
13. Howard R. Bowen and Jack H. Schuster, *American Professors: A National Resource Imperiled* (New York: Oxford University Press, 1986).
14. Staff communication with Helen Nelson, Office of the President, Carleton College, September 8, 1986.
15. Staff communication with John Archabal, The Bush Foundation, June 9, 1986.
16. Staff communication with John Schilb, Associated Colleges of the Midwest, June 24, 1986.

17. "National Exchange Network Increases Faculty Mobility," *Higher Education and National Affairs*, July 15, 1985, p. 6.
18. Staff communication with Boston University, July 1986.
19. The Carnegie Foundation for the Advancement of Teaching, National Survey of Faculty, 1984.
20. The Carnegie Foundation for the Advancement of Teaching, College Visits, 1984.
21. Ibid.
22. Kenneth E. Eble, "The Aims of College Teaching," speech delivered at the Leadership Development Seminar, Central State University, Edmond, Oklahoma, September 24, 1985; reprinted in the *1985–86 Annual Report of the Oklahoma Network of Continuing Higher Education*, p. 9.

9. Creativity in the Classroom

1. The Carnegie Foundation for the Advancement of Teaching, College Visits, 1984–85.
2. Ibid.
3. Ibid.
4. Ibid.
5. Quoted in Elaine Yaffe, "What Are Today's Students Really Like?" *Colorado College Bulletin*, February 1985, p. 7.
6. The Carnegie Foundation for the Advancement of Teaching, College Visits, 1984–85.
7. Ibid.
8. Ibid.
9. Ibid.
10. Ibid.
11. Ibid.
12. Ibid.
13. Arthur Levine, *Handbook on Undergraduate Curriculum* (San Francisco: Jossey-Bass, 1978), p. 171.
14. Ibid., p. 173.
15. Ibid., p. 173.
16. Andrew Hacker, "The Decline of Higher Learning," *New York Review of Books*, February 13, 1986, p. 7.
17. See the excellent discussion in Roberta M. Hall and Bernice R. Sandler, *The Classroom Climate: A Chilly One for Women?* (Washington, D.C.: Association of American Colleges, February 1982), pp. 7–8.
18. Mortimer J. Adler, *The Paideia Proposal: An Educational Manifesto* (New York: Macmillan, 1982), p. 23.
19. Quoted in William McCleery, *Conversations on the Character of Princeton* (Princeton, New Jersey: Princeton University Press, 1986), p. 106.
20. The Carnegie Foundation for the Advancement of Teaching, College Visits, 1984–85.
21. Ibid.

22. Ibid.
23. Ibid.
24. Ibid.
25. Ibid.
26. Ibid.
27. Ibid.
28. Ibid.
29. Ibid.
30. Ibid.
31. Ibid.
32. Staff communication with Dean of Faculty Carol Thompson, and Assistant to the Dean of the College Chris McKinley; Princeton University, July 31, 1986.
33. The Carnegie Foundation for the Advancement of Teaching, College Visits, 1984–85.
34. Hacker, "The Decline of Higher Learning," pp. 8–9.
35. Staff communication with William Jackson, associate director, Office of Instructional Development, University of Georgia, July 31, 1986.
36. Harvard University, "Harvard-Danforth Center for Teaching and Learning," brochure, no date, pp. 1–9.
37. Staff communication with Pat Terando, Northwestern University Center for the Teaching Profession, August 6, 1986.
38. Staff communication with Michele Fisher, director, Center for Teaching and Learning, Stanford University, August 4, 1986.
39. The Carnegie Foundation for the Advancement of Teaching, College Visits, 1984–85.
40. Ibid.
41. National Institute of Education, *Involvement in Learning: Realizing the Potential of American Higher Education* (Washington, D.C.: National Institute of Education, 1984), p. 45.

10. Resources: Printed Page and Printouts

1. The Carnegie Foundation for the Advancement of Teaching, College Visits, 1984–85.
2. Evan Ira Farber, "College Libraries and the University-Library Syndrome," in Evan Ira Farber and Ruth Walling (eds.), *The Academic Library: Essays in Honor of Guy R. Lyle* (Metuchen, New Jersey: Scarecrow Press, 1974), p. 17.
3. The Carnegie Foundation for the Advancement of Teaching, College Visits, 1984–85.
4. Ibid.
5. B. Harvie Branscomb, *Teaching with Books: A Study of College Libraries* (Chicago: Association of American Colleges and American Library Association, 1940), reprint (Hamden, Connecticut: Shoe String Press, 1964), pp. 5, 7, 52.
6. The Carnegie Foundation for the Advancement of Teaching, College Visits, 1984–85.
7. Ray L. Carpenter, "College Libraries: A Comparative Analysis in Terms of the ACRL Standards," *College and Research Libraries,* January 1981, p. 7.

8. U.S. Department of Education, National Center for Education Statistics, *Digest of Education Statistics, 1983–84* (Washington, D.C.: Government Printing Office, 1984), p. 203.

9. The Carnegie Foundation for the Advancement of Teaching, College Visits, 1984–85.

10. U.S. Department of Education, National Center for Education Statistics, *Digest of Education Statistics, 1983–84*, p. 148.

11. The Carnegie Foundation for the Advancement of Teaching, College Visits, 1984–85.

12. National Assessment of Educational Progress, *Reading, Thinking, and Writing* (Boulder, Colorado: Education Commission of the States, 1980), p. 7.

13. William G. Bowen, "The Princeton Library," *Princeton Alumni Weekly*, April 23, 1986, p. 8.

14. Evan Ira Farber, *The Library in Undergraduate Education*, working paper prepared for The Carnegie Foundation for the Advancement of Teaching, March 1985, p. 45.

15. Andrew Postman, "High-Tech Libraries: The Demise of the Old Oaken Drawer," *The Washington Post*, April 20, 1986, p. 3.

16. "Reference Works and Popular Nonfiction Dominate 'Top 40' Library Books," *Chronicle of Higher Education*, February 20, 1985, p. 10.

17. The Carnegie Commission on Higher Education, *The Fourth Revolution: Instructional Technology in Higher Education* (New York: McGraw-Hill, 1972), p. 25.

18. The Carnegie Foundation for the Advancement of Teaching, National Survey of Undergraduates, 1975.

19. The Carnegie Foundation for the Advancement of Teaching, National Survey of Undergraduates, 1984.

20. Steven W. Gilbert and Kenneth C. Green, "New Computing in Higher Education," *Change*, May/June 1986, p. 33.

21. Judith Axler Turner, "A Personal Computer for Every Freshman: Even Faculty Skeptics Are Now Enthusiasts," *Chronicle of Higher Education*, February 20, 1985, p. 14.

22. Ibid., pp. 1, 15.

23. Marc S. Tucker (ed.), *Computers on Campus: Working Papers*, Current Issues in Higher Education, no. 2 (Washington, D.C.: American Association for Higher Education, 1983–84), p. 2.

24. M. Mitchell Waldrop, "Personal Computers on Campus," *Science*, April 26, 1985, p. 438.

25. The Carnegie Foundation for the Advancement of Teaching, College Visits, 1984–85.

26. Ibid.

27. Steven Muller, "The Post-Gutenberg University," *Colleges Enter the Information Society*, Current Issues in Higher Education (Washington, D.C.: American Association for Higher Education, 1983–84), p. 32.

28. Staff communication with Professor Harry Holland, Yardley University, December 1984.

29. Ibid.

30. Waldrop, "Personal Computers on Campus," p. 441.
31. Turner, "A Personal Computer for Every Freshman," p. 14.
32. Ibid.
33. Derek Bok, "Looking into Education's High-tech Future," *Harvard Magazine*, May/June 1985, p. 38.
34. Eric Ashby, quoted in David P. Gardner, "The Charge of the Byte Brigade: Educators Lead the Fourth Revolution," *Educational Record*, Winter 1986, p. 15.

11. Life Outside the Classroom

1. Fred M. Hechinger and Grace Hechinger, *Growing Up in America* (New York: McGraw-Hill, 1975), p. 352.
2. Ibid., p. 355.
3. Ibid., p. 359.
4. Ibid., p. 358.
5. Newell Yost Osborne, *A Select School: The History of Mount Union College and an Account of a Unique Educational Experience, Scio College* (Mount Union, Ohio: Mount Union College, 1967), p. 151.
6. Frederick Rudolph, *The American College and University: A History* (New York: Alfred A. Knopf, 1962), p. 348.
7. The Carnegie Foundation for the Advancement of Teaching, College Visits, 1984–85.
8. Ibid.
9. Ibid.
10. Howard J. Savage, *American College Athletics* (New York: The Carnegie Foundation for the Advancement of Teaching, 1929), pp. 307–308.
11. The Carnegie Foundation for the Advancement of Teaching, College Visits, 1984–85.
12. David Starr Jordan, "The Future of Football," *Collier's Weekly*, December 9, 1905, p. 19.
13. Savage, *American College Athletics*, p. 307.
14. The Carnegie Foundation for the Advancement of Teaching, College Visits, 1984–85.
15. Ibid.
16. Ibid.
17. Staff communication with Haverford College Food Service Manager Peter Lyster, December 4, 1985.
18. The Carnegie Foundation for the Advancement of Teaching, College Visits, 1984–85.
19. Ibid.
20. Felicia Halpert, "Who Is Behind the Right-Wing Press on Campus?" *Ms.*, October 1984, p. 79.
21. Thomas J. Meyer, "Conservative Students Plan Drive Against Investments in Russia," *Chronicle of Higher Education*, June 26, 1985, p. 26.
22. Kim Hirsh, "No-Nuke Network," *Ms.*, October 1984, p. 87.

23. See Alexander W. Astin, "Involvement: The Cornerstone of Excellence," *Change*, July/August 1985, pp. 35–39.
24. The Carnegie Foundation for the Advancement of Teaching, College Visits, 1984–85.
25. Ibid.
26. Carl Schorske, "Community Experience and Cultural Creativity: Basel and Vienna," unpublished paper submitted to Library of Congress Council of Scholars conference "Creativity," Washington, D.C., October 1981.

12. A Home Away from Home

1. Staff communication with Pat Prischman, housing office, University of Wisconsin–Milwaukee, August 12, 1986.
2. Staff communication with Marn Dunder, housing office, University of Oregon, August 12, 1986.
3. Staff communication with Dawn Ellingson, housing office, University of North Dakota, August 12, 1986.
4. Elizabeth Greene, "Many Campuses Report Shortage of Dorm Rooms," *Chronicle of Higher Education*, September 5, 1984, vol. 29, no. 2, p. 1.
5. The Carnegie Foundation for the Advancement of Teaching, College Visits, 1984–85.
6. Alexander W. Astin and associates, *The American Freshman: National Norms for Fall 1985* (Los Angeles: Cooperative Institutional Research Program, Graduate Program on Education, University of California, 1985), p. 57.
7. Barbara Keller, "A Legal Perspective of the Parietal Rule," unpublished paper, 1975, ERIC Document # ED191393.
8. The Carnegie Foundation for the Advancement of Teaching, College Visits, 1984–85.
9. Ibid.
10. Ibid.
11. Ibid.
12. Ibid.
13. Ibid.
14. Ibid.
15. Ibid.
16. Ibid.
17. Kenneth C. Green and Alexander W. Astin, "The Mood on Campus: More Conservative or Just More Materialistic?" *Educational Record*, Winter 1985, p. 47.
18. Zoe Ingalls, "Higher Education's Drinking Problem," *Chronicle of Higher Education*, July 21, 1982.
19. The Carnegie Foundation for the Advancement of Teaching, College Visits, 1984–85.
20. Thomas J. Meyer, "1 in 3 College Students Tries Cocaine, Study Finds; Bennett Urges Presidents to Crack Down on Drugs," *Chronicle of Higher Education*, July 16, 1986, p. 1.

21. The Carnegie Foundation for the Advancement of Teaching, College Visits, 1984–85.
22. Ibid.
23. Ibid.
24. Ibid.
25. Ibid.
26. Ibid.
27. John Millett, "Management, Governance, and Leadership," speech delivered at the Leadership Development Seminar, Central State University, Edmond, Oklahoma, September 12, 1985; reprinted in the *1985–86 Annual Report of the Oklahoma Network of Continuing Higher Education,* pp. 5–6.
28. Edward Shils and Michael Young, "The Meaning of the Coronation," *Sociological Review,* December 1953, p. 66; quoted in Lloyd J. Averill, *Learning to Be Human: A Vision for the Liberal Arts* (Port Washington, New York: Associated Faculty Press, 1983), p. 131.
29. Staff communications with Michigan State, University of the Pacific, and Connecticut College, August 26, 1986.
30. Staff communication with John Sama, director, Living-Learning Center, University of Vermont, November 21, 1985.
31. Princeton University, *A Princeton Profile 1983–84,* university brochure, September 1983, p. 8.
32. Arthur W. Chickering, *Commuting Versus Resident Students: Overcoming the Educational Inequities of Living Off Campus* (San Francisco: Jossey-Bass, 1974), pp. 53–68.
33. Alexander Astin, *Achieving Educational Excellence* (San Francisco: Jossey-Bass, 1985), p. 148.
34. The Carnegie Foundation for the Advancement of Teaching, National Survey of Undergraduates, 1984.
35. The Carnegie Foundation for the Advancement of Teaching, College Visits, 1984–85.
36. Ibid.
37. Ibid.
38. Ibid.
39. Ibid.
40. Trustee Commission on Campus Life, *Report of the Trustee Commission on Campus Life* (Waterville, Maine: Colby College, December 1983).
41. Ibid.
42. Ibid.
43. Ibid.
44. The Carnegie Foundation for the Advancement of Teaching, College Visits, 1984–85.
45. Ibid.
46. Ibid.
47. Chickering, *Commuting Versus Resident Students,* pp. 84–85.
48. Penny Rue and Jeanne Ludt, "Organizing for Commuter Student Services," in Sylvia S. Stewart (ed.), *Commuter Students: Enhancing Their Educational*

Experiences, New Directions for Student Services, no. 24 (San Francisco: Jossey-Bass, 1983), p. 34.

13. Service: Getting Involved

1. The Carnegie Foundation for the Advancement of Teaching, College Visits, 1984–85.
2. Daniel Yankelovich, quoted in Sarah Stiansen, "Baby Boomers Set to Embrace Idealism—Researcher," *Trenton Times,* March 19, 1985, p. A1.
3. George Gallup, Jr., quoted in Michael W. Sherraden and Donald J. Eberly (eds.), *National Service: Social, Economic and Military Impacts* (New York: Pergamon Press, 1982), p. 18.
4. The Carnegie Foundation for the Advancement of Teaching, National Survey of Undergraduates, 1984.
5. Elizabeth Greene, "An Appalachian Summer: Student Interns and Seminarians Encounter Rural Poverty," *Chronicle of Higher Education,* August 13, 1986, p. 24.
6. Elizabeth Greene, "New College Presidents' Group to Promote Public and Community Service by Students," *Chronicle of Higher Education,* October 23, 1985, p. 27.
7. Thomas J. Meyer, "More Students Finding Time to Give the Needy a Hand," *Chronicle of Higher Education,* February 27, 1985, p. 20.
8. Rhoda M. Gilinsky, "When Helping Others Is a Part of Learning," *The New York Times,* January 6, 1985, p. 24.
9. Meyer, "More Students Finding Time to Give the Needy a Hand," pp. 20–21.
10. Henry B. Freeman, "Dwight Hall," *Synergist,* Spring 1980, p. 41.
11. Princeton University, "Campus Fund Drive" announcement, 1984.
12. Staff communication with Richard Couto, director, Vanderbilt University Center for Health Services, August 16, 1985.
13. Staff communication with Roger Henry, director, Kent State University Office for Service-Learning, August 15, 1985.
14. Ibid.
15. Abraham Yogev and Rachel Ronen, "Cross-Age Tutoring: Effects on Tutor's Attributes," *Journal of Educational Research,* May/June 1982, pp. 261–68.
16. Donald J. Eberly, "Youth Service Initiatives: A Promise for the Future," *NASSP Bulletin,* May 1985, p. 85.
17. Gilinsky, "When Helping Others Is a Part of Learning," p. 24.
18. Meyer, "More Students Finding Time to Give the Needy a Hand," pp. 20–21.
19. Ibid., p. 20.
20. The Potomac Institute, *Youth and the Needs of the Nation,* report of the Committee for the Study of National Service (Washington, D.C.: The Potomac Institute, January 1979), p. 87.
21. Staff communication with Professor Steve Slaby, Princeton University, September 5, 1986.
22. Quoted in "Woodrow Wilson on 'Princeton in the Nation's Service,' " in Richard Hofstadter and Wilson Smith (eds.), *American Higher Education: A*

Documentary History, vol. 2 (Chicago: University of Chicago Press, 1961), p. 694.

14. Extending the Campus

1. The Carnegie Foundation for the Advancement of Teaching, College Visits, 1984–85.
2. Staff communication with College of Notre Dame of Maryland, July 1986.
3. *Bulletin of Empire State College,* 1985, p. 2.
4. Ibid., p. 33.
5. Staff communication with Metropolitan State College, July 1986.
6. Staff communication with Lorraine Altman, School of New Resources, College of New Rochelle, July 1986.
7. Peter Meyer, *Awarding College Credit for Non-College Learning* (San Francisco: Jossey-Bass, 1975), pp. xviii–xvii.
8. Thomas A. Edison College, *Opening Doors,* brochure, no date, pp. 1, 2.
9. Staff communication with Director Leo Nussbaum, Academy of Senior Professionals, Eckerd College, April 2, 1986.
10. Staff communication with director of College at Sixty Program, Fordham University, September 1986.
11. James O. Banks, "Grantham Woods," brochure, Messiah College, 1986.
12. Ernest L. Boyer, "Forward," in Nell P. Eurich, *Corporate Classrooms: The Learning Business* (Princeton, New Jersey: The Carnegie Foundation for the Advancement of Teaching, 1985), p. x.
13. Staff communication with the University of Washington, August 1986.
14. Staff communication with Harvard University, August 1986.
15. The Carnegie Foundation for the Advancement of Teaching, College Visits, 1984–85.
16. The Carnegie Foundation for the Advancement of Teaching, National Survey of Undergraduates, 1984.
17. Staff communication with Alex Shane, director, Office of International Programs, State University of New York at Albany, October 2, 1986.
18. Duncan Smith, "Foreign Study in Eastern Europe," *Travel and Learning Abroad,* March/April 1985, p. 14.
19. Council on Learning, *Education for a Global Century: Handbook of Exemplary International Programs* (New Rochelle, New York: Change Magazine Press, 1981), p. 116.
20. "News and Notes," *Travel and Learning Abroad,* March/April 1985, p. 32.
21. Ibid., p. 36.
22. Ibid., p. 36.
23. Ibid., p. 37.
24. Council on Learning, *Education for a Global Century,* p. 34.
25. U.S. Committee/International Council on Monuments and Sites, *World Heritage List* (Washington, D.C.: January 1984).
26. Staff communication with Goddard College, July 1986.

15. Governing the College

1. The Carnegie Foundation for the Advancement of Teaching, College Visits, 1984–85.
2. Ibid.
3. Staff communication with Martin Burke, university archives, The University of Michigan, September 3, 1986.
4. Laurence Veysey, *The Emergence of the American University* (Chicago: University of Chicago Press, 1965), p. 57.
5. Frederick Rudolph, *The American College and University* (New York: Alfred A. Knopf, 1962), p. 165.
6. The Carnegie Foundation for the Advancement of Teaching, College Visits, 1984–85.
7. Ibid.
8. Staff communication with Greg Giebel, Academic Collective Bargaining Information Service, September 4, 1986.
9. The Carnegie Foundation for the Advancement of Teaching, College Visits, 1984–85.
10. Ibid.
11. Ibid.
12. Ibid.
13. Ibid.
14. Ibid.
15. Ibid.
16. Ibid.
17. Warren Bryan Martin, *A College of Character* (San Francisco: Jossey-Bass, 1982), p. 91.
18. Ibid., p. 92.
19. The Carnegie Foundation for the Advancement of Teaching, College Visits, 1984–85.
20. Wayne Booth, "Mere Rhetoric, Rhetoric, and the Search for Common Learning," in Ernest L. Boyer and associates, *Common Learning* (Washington, D.C.: Carnegie Foundation for the Advancement of Teaching, 1981), p. 54.
21. Ibid., p. 34.

16. Measuring the Outcome

1. The Carnegie Foundation for the Advancement of Teaching, College Visits, 1984–85.
2. Chester Finn, "Trying Higher Education: An Eight Count Indictment," *Change*, May/June 1984, p. 48.
3. Claude Moore Fuess, *Amherst: The Story of a New England College* (Boston: Little, Brown, 1935), p. 194.
4. Mary Lovett Smallwood, *An Historical Study of Examinations and Grading Systems in Early American Universities: A Critical Study of the Original Records*

of Harvard, William and Mary, Yale, Mount Holyoke, and Michigan from Their Founding to 1900 (Cambridge, Massachusetts: Harvard University Press, 1935), p. 36.

5. Charles William Eliot, "Inaugural Address as President of Harvard, 1869," in Richard Hofstadter and Wilson Smith (eds.), American Higher Education: A Documentary History, vol. 2 (Chicago: University of Chicago Press, 1961), p. 607.

6. Hofstadter and Smith, American Higher Education: A Documentary History, p. 866.

7. A. Lawrence Lowell, "Examination of Subjects Instead of by Courses," The Harvard Graduates' Magazine, June 1912, p. 584.

8. Edward Safford Jones, Comprehensive Examinations in American Colleges (New York: Macmillan, 1933), p. 251.

9. Grady Bogue, "Outcomes: An Issue of Caring and Daring," State Education Leader, Spring 1984, p. 10.

10. Staff communication with Associate Dean Carl Schilling, Miami University, September 5, 1986.

11. "A Look at Western College: The School of Interdisciplinary Studies," brochure, Miami University, no date, p. 16.

12. C. Robert Pace, "Perspectives and Problems in Student Outcomes Research," in Peter T. Ewell (ed.), Assessing Educational Outcomes, New Directions for Institutional Research, no. 47 (September 1985), pp. 10–11.

13. Martin Trow, "Higher Education and Moral Development," Proceedings of the 1974 Educational Testing Service Invitational Conference—Moral Development (Princeton, New Jersey: Educational Testing Service, 1974–75).

17. To Work and Further Learning

1. The Carnegie Foundation for the Advancement of Teaching, Staff Interviews, 1986.

2. Samuel M. Ehrenhalt, "What Lies Ahead for College Graduates?" American Demographics, September 1983, p. 33.

3. U.S. Department of Commerce, Bureau of the Census, "Lifetime Earnings Estimates for Men and Women in the United States: 1979," Current Population Reports, Series P-60, no. 139.

4. Recruiting '85, The College Placement Council, Inc., October 1984.

5. Clayton L. Barnard and David S. Bechtel, "Influences and Considerations: Issues Guiding Placement and Recruitment Today," Journal of College Placement, Winter 1983, p. 30.

6. Ibid., p. 31.

7. College Placement Council, Inc., "Salary Survey: A Study of 1985–86 Beginning Offers," Formal Report No. 3, July 1986, p. 2.

8. Robert Calvert, Jr., Career Patterns of Liberal Arts Graduates (Cranston, Rhode Island: The Carroll Press, 1969), p. 121.

9. Ibid., p. 122.

10. Ibid., p. 138.

11. Ibid., p. 46.

12. Ibid., p. 125.

13. Staff communication with Marcia van Diepen, Director of Career Planning and Placement, Westmar College, August 27, 1986.

14. Liz McMillen, "A Successful Campus Career-Planning Center Isn't Just an Employment Agency for Students," *Chronicle of Higher Education*, June 19, 1985, p. 24.

15. The Carnegie Foundation for the Advancement of Teaching, National Survey of Undergraduates, 1984.

16. The Carnegie Foundation for the Advancement of Teaching, College Visits, 1984–85.

17. Leonard L. Baird, *The Graduates: A Report on the Plans and Characteristics of College Seniors* (Princeton, New Jersey: Educational Testing Service, 1973), p. 17.

18. Ibid., p. 18.

19. The Carnegie Foundation for the Advancement of Teaching, National Survey of Undergraduates, 1984.

20. Ibid.

21. Ibid.

22. The Carnegie Foundation for the Advancement of Teaching, National Survey of Faculty, 1984.

23. American Bar Association, *A Review of Legal Education in the United States, Fall 1982: Law Schools and Bar Admission Requirements* (American Bar Association, 1983), p. 39.

24. Bill Reinhard, "Business Schools Lag Behind Changes in Modern Economy," *Higher Education Daily*, May 20, 1985, p. 1.

25. Staff communication with Eric Solomon, American Association of Dental Schools, August 4, 1986.

26. Staff communication with the Association of American Medical Colleges, November 10, 1986.

27. Jaroslav Pelikan, *Scholarship and Its Survival* (Princeton, New Jersey: The Carnegie Foundation for the Advancement of Teaching, 1983), pp. 33–34.

28. Staff communication with Gene Schwilck, The Danforth Foundation, September 8, 1986.

18. From Competence to Commitment

1. John W. Gardner, "You Can Make a Difference: Entrepreneurs in the Public Interest," speech transcript in Stanford University *Campus Report*, February 29, 1984, p. 16.

2. Reinhold Niebuhr, quoted in Frank H. T. Rhodes, "More Than Tinkering," speech delivered at the Leadership Development Seminar, Central State University, Edmond, Oklahoma, September 24, 1985; reprinted in the *1985–86 Annual Report of the Oklahoma Network of Continuing Higher Education*, p. 7.

3. William Toohey, *Life After Birth: Spirituality for College Students* (New York: Seabury Press, 1981), pp. 72–73.

4. The Carnegie Foundation for the Advancement of Teaching, College Visits, 1984–85.

5. Henry Steele Commager, "Science, Nationalism, and the Academy," *Academe*, November/December 1985, p. 10.

6. J. Bronowski, *Science and Human Values* (New York: Julian Messner, 1956), p. 10.

7. Ingrid Canright, "What Has Nuclear War Got to Do with Romance?" *Chronicle of Higher Education*, June 5, 1985, p. 72.

EPILOGUE: A Guide to a Good College

1. Parker J. Palmer, *The Company of Strangers: Christians and the Renewal of America's Public Life* (New York: Crossroad, 1981), p. 31; quoted in Robert N. Bellah and associates, *Habits of the Heart: Individualism and Commitment in American Life* (Berkeley: University of California Press, 1985), p. 163.

INDEX

9553

Tuition, 12–13, 21–22
"Two cultures," 105–15

Union College, 62, 178
University of California, 27–28, 79
University of Chicago, 65, 95–96, 99–100, 107
University of Georgia, 156
University of Illinois, 268–69
University of Maryland, 56
University of Michigan, 27, 80–81, 149, 201, 236
University of North Carolina [at Chapel Hill], 270
University of North Dakota, 196
University of Notre Dame, 281
University of Oregon, 196
University of the Pacific, 206
University of Pittsburgh, 230–31
University of South Carolina, 49
University of Southern Maine, 94–95
University of Texas (at Austin), 80
University of Vermont, 206
University of Virginia, 231
University of Washington, 228
University of Wisconsin:
  at Madison, 80
  at Milwaukee, 196

Vanderbilt University, 215–16
Vernazza, Cira T., 226
Veysey, Laurence, 236
Volunteerism. *See* Service

Wake Forest University, 94
Wallach, Michael, 38
Ward, Barbara, 230
Warfield, Ethelhard D., 29
Warren Wilson College, 217
Washington University (St. Louis), 194
Wellesley College, 97
Wellness programs, 186–87
Wesleyan University (Connecticut), 65
Westmar College, 270
Wichita State University (Kansas), 56
William and Mary, 61
Williams College, 209
Willingham, Warren, 37–38
Wing, Cliff, 38
Worcester Polytechnic Institute, 114
Writing programs, 79–81

Yale University, 26, 61, 62, 166, 215, 217
Yankelovich, Daniel 213
Young, Michael, 204
Young Conservative Foundation, Inc., 189